SO-CFX-948

ARE MEN
NECESSARY?

ALSO BY MAUREEN DOWD

Bushworld:
Enter at Your Own Risk

headline

ARE MEN NECESSARY?

· *When Sexes Collide* ·

MAUREEN DOWD

Copyright © 2005 Maureen Dowd

The right of Maureen Dowd to be identified as the Author of
the Work has been asserted by her in accordance with the
Copyright, Designs and Patents Act 1988.

First published in 2005 by G. P. Putnam's Sons,
a division of Penguin Group (USA) Inc

First published in Great Britain in 2006
by HEADLINE BOOK PUBLISHING

Apart from any use permitted under UK copyright law, this publication
may only be reproduced, stored, or transmitted, in any form, or by
any means, with prior permission in writing of the publichers or, in
the case of reprographic production, in accordance with the terms of
licences issued by the Copyright Licensing Agency.

Every effort has been made to trace and contact the copyright holders of all
materials in this book. The author and publisher will be glad to rectify any
omissions at the earliest opportunity.
The columns on which some of this book is based originally appeared in *The New
York Times*, and to the extent they are reprinted here, they are reprinted with
permission. Inquiries concerning permission to reprint any column or portion
thereof should be directed to The New York Times Company, News Services
Division, The Times Agency, Ninth Floor, 229 West 43rd Street, New York,
NY 10036 or rights@nytimes.com
Excerpt from WOMAN: AN INTIMATE BIOGRAPHY by Natalie Angier.
Copyright © 1999 by Natalie Angier. Excerpted by permission of
Houghton Mifflin Company. All rights reserved.
Dorothy Parker poem excerpted by permission of Penguin Group (USA) Inc.
All rights reserved.
Illustrations copyright © 2005 by Owen Smith. All rights reserved.

ISBN 0 7553 1550 2

Printed and bound in Great Britain by Mackays of Chatham plc, Chatham, Kent

Headline's policy is to use papers that are natural, renewable and recyclable
products and made from wood grown in sustainable forests. The logging
and manufacturing processes are expected to conform to the
environmental regulations of the country of origin.

Book design by Amanda Dewey

HEADLING BOOK PUBLISHING
A division of Hodder Headline
338 Euston Road
London NW1 3BH

www.headline.co.uk
www.hodderheadline.com

For men
Friends and more, past, present and future.
You know who you are.

Acknowledgments

I want, first, to thank my mom, *mo cuishle,* who taught me that true beauty is achieved by helping those less fortunate and who long ago advised me, when I was feeling blue or self-doubting about men, that the best thing to do was go out and buy a red lipstick or a red dress.

"It will be your red badge of courage," she said.

Peggy Dowd was a man's woman, a woman's woman and a mom of moms, a queen of vitality who died at a luminous ninety-seven just as I finished this book, after living through history that spanned the 1912 crash of the *Titanic* to the 2001 crash of the Twin Towers.

I'm beholden to three of the most remarkable women I've ever known; my sister, Peggy, and my nieces, Jennifer and Dana.

I'm indebted to the rest of my family: Michael, Martin, Kevin, Brendan, Patrick, Brian, Michael Francis, Tara, Ellen, Jone, Judy and Kathleen, whose love and sensitivity helped get me through the most painful two weeks of my life.

I also want to thank Hope Smith, Dr. Barry Simon, Msgr. Thomas Duffy and Jeff Rose for their ministrations to my mom.

I'm grateful to Arthur Gelb and Leon Wieseltier, the most necessary of men and the most scintillating. (And thanks, Leon, for an unforgettable week on the editing couch.)

It was swell of Julie and Janice Bosman to share the Bosman Principles. And just like all those other Hitchcock blondes, my lovely partner in crime, Julie, was cool and calm, never losing her footing in the *Vertigo* of my chaos.

I'm the luckiest girl in the world when it comes to infinitely creative and giving friends to help interpret the inscrutable Y mind, without whom this book would not have been possible: Carl Hulse, Bill Carter, Adam Nagourney, Aaron Sorkin, Adam Clymer, Frank Bruni, Nick Wade, Don Van Natta, Tom Friedman, Joe Lelyveld, Ray Hernandez, Evan Thomas, Michael Kinsley, Steve Weisman, David Geffen, Sean Daniel, Craig Bierko, Howard Schultz, Bill Schmidt, Bill Safire, Alec Baldwin, Gerry Rafshoon, Frank Rich, Todd Purdum, Phil Taubman, Rick Berke, Michael Beschloss, Campbell Robertson, Reihan Salam, Aaron Sterling, Paul Costello, Craig Ferguson, Bill Maher, and my mom's faves, Tim Russert, Mike Isikoff, Frank Clines, Marc Santora, Don Imus, Chris Matthews, James Carville and George Stephanopoulos.

And where would I be without my X file of magical babes

who could easily run the globe if men disappear? My friends Alessandra Stanley, Michi Kakutani, Jill Abramson, Jane Mayer, Dana Calvo, Rebecca Liss, Robin Toner, Gioia Diliberto, Dorothy Samuels, Rita Beamish, Barbara Gelb, Nora Ephron, Anna Quindlen, Sarah Lyall, Julia Baird, Lizette Alvarez, Betsy Kolbert, Zenia Mucha, Lynette Clemetson, Sally Quinn, Marie Sigismondi, Alex Kuczynski, Tina Alster, Eden Rafshoon, Barbara Howar and Pat Wexler.

I want to thank my generous bosses, Arthur Sulzberger Jr. and his sweet dad, Arthur Sr.; Bill Keller, Gail Collins and Andy Rosenthal; my friends on the tenth floor, Linda Lake, Marion Greene and Johanna Jainchill; and my pals at Putnam, my editor, Neil Nyren, and Marilyn Ducksworth and Tony Davis; and Esther Newberg at ICM. And attention must be paid to my excellent *Times* copy editors: Karen Freeman, Sue Kirby and Bob Rudinger.

And finally, thanks to the talented artist Owen Smith, for making my dream of a pulp noir paperback cover come blazing to lush life. The girl in the red dress will always be my red badge of courage.

• Contents •

Introduction 1

One • HOW TO SET YOUR BEAR TRAP IN THE
MINK DEPARTMENT OF BERGDORF'S 15

Two • WHY PANDORA'S BOX IS NO TENDER TRAP 77

Three • WHIPPING THE PANTS OFF THE WOMEN
WHO WEAR THEM 89

Four • WHY THE WELL-HUNG Y IS WILTING, EVEN AS THE X IS EXCELLING 135

Five • OF PUSSYCATS, BOOTY CALLS, ROAD BEEF AND SLUMP BUSTERS 167

Six • THE DRAG OF GOING STAG 191

Seven • WHENCE THE WINCE? 211

Eight • HOW GREEN IS MY VALLEY OF THE DOLLS 257

Nine • HOW HILLARY SMUSHED CUPCAKES AND FILLETED FEMINISM 269

· Introduction ·

don't understand men.

I don't even understand what I don't understand about men.

They're a most inscrutable bunch, really.

I had a moment of dazzling clarity when I was twenty-seven, a rush of confidence that I had cracked the code. But it was, alas, an illusion.

I think I overcomplicated their simplicity. Or oversimplified their simplicity. Are they as complicated as a pile of wood? Or as simple as a squid?

I was loath to accept the premise of Jerry Seinfeld, who claims that "men are really nothing more than extremely advanced dogs" who want the same thing from their women that they want from their underwear: "A little bit of support and a little bit of freedom."

I was more prone to go with the thesis of James Thurber and E. B. White in their seminal 1929 treatise, *Is Sex Necessary?*, that the American male was the least understood of all male animals, and that more attention needed to be paid to his complexity—"the importance of what he is thinking about and what he intends to do, or at least what he would like to do. . . .

"How often do you hear it said that the little whims and desires of a man should be cherished, or even listened to? You don't hear it said at all. What you do hear is that 'the way to a man's heart is through his stomach.' A thing like that hardens a man. He may eat his spinach and say nothing, but he is being hardened just the same."

Thurber and White don't date the start of the troubles between men and women to the snaky Eve.

They contend that things got bollixed up in the 1920s, when the female, "face-to-face with the male's simple desire to sit down and hold her" (aka "the attack of the male"), retaliated with irritating Diversion Subterfuges—such as Fudge Making and Indoor Games for groups—meant to fend off and put Man in his place.

"The American male's repugnance to charades, which is equaled, perhaps, by his repugnance to nothing at all, goes back to those years," the authors explained.

I know women are disorienting to men, too.

In his memoir about *The New Yorker*, *The Years with Ross,*

Thurber tells this story from the early '30s about the legendary editor's reaction to having a baby girl:

"One morning, I found Ross, worried and stoop-shouldered, pacing a corridor, jingling those pocket coins. He came right out with his current anxiety. 'Goddamn it, I can't think of any *man* that has a daughter. I think of men as having boys, and women as having girls.'

" 'I have a daughter,' I said, 'and I wanted a daughter.'

" 'That's not natural, is it?' he demanded. 'I never heard of a man that didn't want a son. Can you name any, well, you know, goddamn it—terribly masculine men with daughters?'

"The sun and moon of reassurance shone in his face when I came up with 'Jack Dempsey has two children, both girls.' His day was saved from the wreckage of despair, but he still had one final depressed word. 'Goddamn it, I hate the idea of going around with female hormones in me.' "

In the final analysis, Thurber and White decided matters went irretrievably awry during the Jazz Age when flappers began to imitate men, smoking, drinking, wanting to earn money ("not much, but some") and thinking they had "the right to be sexual." All these strained attempts at equality, they contend, destroyed the mystery of the sexual tango, or sexual Charleston, if you will.

This spurt of cocky independence faded, and over the decades women lapsed back into domesticity and deference, until their only avatars were perfect gingham moms such as Donna Reed, June Cleaver and Harriet Nelson.

Then came the Sexual Revolution. When I entered college,

in 1969, women were bursting out of their '50s chrysalis. The Jazz Age spirit flared in the Age of Aquarius. Women were once again imitating men and acting all independent: smoking, drinking, wanting to earn money (not as much, but some) and thinking the Pill gave them "the right to be sexual."

I didn't fit in with the brazen new world of hard-charging feminists. I was more of a fun-loving (if chaste) Carrie Bradshaw type, a breed that wouldn't come into vogue for several more decades.

I hated the dirty, unisex jeans and no-makeup look and drugs that zoned you out, and I couldn't understand the appeal of dances that didn't involve touching your partner.

In the universe of Eros, I longed for style and wit. I loved the Art Deco glamour of '30s movies. I wanted to dance the Continental like Fred and Ginger in white hotel suites; drink martinis like Myrna Loy and William Powell; live the life of a screwball heroine like Katharine Hepburn, wearing a gold lamé gown cut on the bias, cavorting with Cary Grant, strolling along Fifth Avenue with my pet leopard.

My mom would just shake her head and tell me that my idea of the '30s was wildly romanticized. "We were poor," she'd say. "We didn't dance around in white hotel suites."

I took the idealism and passion of the '60s for granted, simply assuming we were sailing toward perfect equality with men, a utopian world at home and at work.

I didn't listen to my mom when she advised me to get a suitcase with wheels before my first trip to Europe. I didn't listen to her before my first cocktail party, when she told me that men prefer homemade dinner rolls stuffed with turkey and ham to expensive catered goose pâté and exotic cheese wheels. "Simplicity pays," she said smugly, when all the guys swarmed around her sandwiches.

And I didn't listen to her when she cautioned me about the chimera of equality.

On my thirty-first birthday, she sent me a bankbook with a modest nest egg she had saved for me. "I always felt that the girls in a family should get a little more than the boys even though all are equally loved," she wrote in a letter. "They need a little cushion to fall back on. Women can stand on the Empire State Building and scream to the heavens that they are equal to men and liberated, but until they have the same anatomy, it's a lie. It's more of a man's world today than ever. Men can eat their cake in unlimited bakeries."

I thought she was just being Old World, like my favorite jade, Dorothy Parker, when she wrote:

By the time you're his,
Shivering and sighing,
And he vows his passion is
Infinite, undying—
Lady, make a note of this:
One of you is lying.

I thought the struggle for egalitarianism was a cinch, so I could leave it to my earnest sisters in black turtlenecks and Birkenstocks. I figured there was plenty of time for me to get serious later, that America would always be full of passionate and full-throated debate about the big stuff—social issues, sexual equality, civil rights—rather than tinny right-left food fights and shrieking conservative babes with blond hair, long legs and miniskirts going on TV to trash women and women's rights.

No Cassandra, I.

Little did I realize that the sexual revolution would have the unexpected consequence of intensifying the confusion between the sexes, leaving women in a tangle of dependence and independence as they entered the twenty-first century. The fewer the barriers, the more muddied the waters. It never occurred to me that the more women aped men, in everything from dress to orgasms, the more we would realize how inalienably different the sexes are.

Or, most curious of all, that women would move from playing with Barbie to denouncing Barbie to remaking themselves as Barbie.

Maybe we should have known that the story of women's progress would be more of a zigzag than a superhighway, that the triumph of feminism would last a nanosecond while the backlash lasted forty years.

And that all the triumphant moments of feminism—from the selection of Geraldine Ferraro to the Anita Hill hearings to the co-presidency of buy-one-get-one-free First Lady Hillary Rodham Clinton—would unleash negative reactions toward women.

Despite the best efforts of philosophers, politicians, historians, novelists, screenwriters, linguists, therapists, anthropologists and facilitators, men and women are still in a muddle in the boardroom, the Situation Room and the bedroom.

At the risk of raising the question Am I necessary?, I admit I have no answers. But for decades now I've loved asking the questions. This book is not a systematic inquiry of any kind, or a handy little volume of sterling solutions to the American woman's problems. I possess no special wisdom about redemption in matters of sex and love. I am not peddling a theory or a slogan or a policy. I'm always as baffled as the next woman.

As Dinah Brand, the hard-boiled, mercenary dame in Dashiell Hammett's 1929 novel *Red Harvest*, complained, "I used to think I knew men, but, by God! I don't. They're lunatics, all of them."

I certainly understand if some men prefer to think of themselves as individuals and opt to wriggle out of one broad's broad generalizations.

This book offers only the diligent notes—on the job and off—of a fascinated observer of our gender perplexities.

And what a spectacle gender in America is!

The entanglements between men and women come in three forms: tragedies, comedies and tragicomedies. Outrage regularly alternates with silliness. Illusions are often more interesting than realities. Causes and desires are regularly mixed up. Will there ever be peace? I doubt it. But there should always be laughter.

My mom, a soft touch who loved men, suggested that I change my title to *Why Men Are Necessary*. "Men *are* necessary for breeding and heavy lifting," she said wryly.

But, difficult as it is, we must face up to the tough questions. As a species, it's possible that men are ever so last century. Are they any longer necessary for procreation? Have they proven themselves emotionally incapable of governing the country because they are really the ones subject to hissy fits and hormonal imbalances? Is their pillaging and plundering, warmongering, empire-building Y chromosome melting faster than the Wicked Witch of the West? Is it time to dispense with all those oxygen-depleting men batting out opinions in newspapers, TV and blogs, and those computer-generated-looking male anchor clones on network news?

And what about women? Are we regressing? Or advancing along the winding scenic route in ways we hadn't predicted? I'm continually astonished, provoked and flummoxed by the odd and stunning trajectory men and women have traveled from the big bang of the Sexual Revolution to the big busts of the Plastic Revolution.

The free-love idea that sex could be casual and safe and unfraught was, in retrospect, chuckleheaded. As my friend Leon Wieseltier, the literary editor for *The New Republic*, observes: "Sex is a spiritual obligation. It makes up for the poverty of bourgeois experience. We're too late for the Spanish Civil War. We missed the landing at Omaha Beach. But still we need to know what we're capable of. So it is in the realm of private life that we have to risk ourselves, to disclose ourselves, to vindicate ourselves; and the more private, the more illuminating. Our theater of self-discovery is smaller. And in this lucky but shrunken theater, the bedroom looms very large. It is the front line, the foxhole.

"The bedroom is where people who live otherwise safe lives can learn how cowardly or courageous they are, what their deepest and most dangerous desires are, whether they can follow the unreason within them to what it, too, can teach. Tolstoy said that modern tragedy should be set in the bedroom."

If Gloria Steinem had had a crystal ball and flashed forward to a 2005 filled with catfights and women scheming to trap men, snag the coveted honorific "Mrs.," get cosmetic procedures to look like Playmate bombshells and dress, as Dave Chappelle says, like "whores," would the sister have even bothered to lead that bonfire of the bras?

I think not.

Whether or not American feminism will be defeated by American conservatism, it is incontrovertibly true that American feminism was trumped by American narcissism.

This is a season when the female beau ideal is not Gloria Steinem, a serious bunny, but Jessica Simpson, a simple bunny, and when Hollywood's remake of *The Stepford Wives* stumbled because it was no longer satire but documentary.

I had to live through disco, pointy polyester shirt collars, greed is good, me decade, yuppie consumerism and cigar bars—coming full circle from platform shoes and Diane von Furstenberg wrap dresses to platform shoes and Diane von Furstenberg wrap dresses—before I was hit with a pang of nostalgia for the opportunity I'd missed in college.

We would never again be so consumed with changing the world. The more time passed, the more Americans simply focused on changing themselves. We've become a nation of Frankensteins, and our monster is us. With everyone working so hard at altering their facades, we no longer have natural selection. We have unnatural selection.

Emma Woodhouse learned the hard way about the dangers

of makeovers. She tried to turn her simple friend, Harriet Smith, into a girl with airs and aspirations. Too late, Jane Austen's heroine realized that she had altered Harriet for the worse, from humble to vain. Literature is rife with cautionary tales about experiments in identity—from Dorian Gray to Jay Gatsby to Tom Ripley, whose murderous motto was: "Better a fake somebody than a real nobody."

But our contemporary carnival of makeovers does not concern itself with virtue, only vanity. We have grown superficial even about surfaces. The whole country seems to have embraced Oscar Wilde's teaching that "It is only the shallow who do not judge by appearance." The national obsession with appearance is a chronicle of social psychosis straight out of Philip K. Dick.

We had the Belle Epoque. Now we have the Botox Epoch, permeated by plastic emotions from antidepressants and plastic veneers from collagen, silicone, cosmetic surgery and Botox. This, freedom?

I came of age in interlocking male institutions: My dad was a police detective, I was in the Catholic Church and I had three brothers. The nation's capital we lived in was peppered with statues honoring men. When I first got into journalism, I covered sports, then politics, at a time when they were even more male-dominated arenas.

Along the way, I got into the habit of tweaking the oppressors. I imagined that women were forever destined to a life of dissidence.

Though the science is mainly of metaphorical interest to me—a fascinating biological parable—the new research into sex chromosomes suggests that all that antler crashing over the centuries has tuckered out the Y. Men are now the weaker sex, geneticists say, and could soon disappear altogether—taking March Madness and cold pizza in the morning with them.

Only another hundred thousand years—or ten million, if you believe the Y optimists—and the male chromosome could go the way of the dial-up connection.

So, dear readers of the soon-to-be-extinct male persuasion, you're on notice.

In the year 102,005, or 10,002,005 at the latest, we'll finally have our fair share of female network anchors, female priests, female columnists, female Supreme Court justices, corrupt female CEOs and philandering female presidents.

And we'll run the world.

In a manly way, of course.

One

HOW TO SET YOUR BEAR TRAP IN THE MINK DEPARTMENT OF BERGDORF'S

My mom, who considered men most necessary, gave me three essential books on the subject. The first, when I was thirteen, was *On Becoming a Woman*. The second, when I was twenty-one, was *365 Ways to Cook Hamburger and Other Ground Meats*. The third, when I was twenty-five, was Yvonne Antell's *How to Catch and Hold a Man*.

Because I received *How to Catch and Hold a Man* at a time when we were entering the Age of Equality, I put it aside as an anachronism. After all, sometime in the 1960s, flirting went out of fashion, as did ironing boards, makeup and the idea that men needed to be "trapped" or "landed."

The way to approach men, we reasoned, was forthrightly

and without games, artifice or frills. Unfortunately, history has shown this to be a misguided notion.

I knew it even before the 1996 publication of *The Rules*, a dating bible that encouraged women to return to prefeminist mind games by playing hard to get. ("Limit phone time to 10 minutes . . . Even if you are the head of your own company . . . when you're with a man you like, be quiet and mysterious, act ladylike, cross your legs and smile. . . . Wear black sheer panty-hose and hike up your skirt to entice the opposite sex!")

I knew this before fashion magazines became crowded with crinolines, bows, ruffles, leopard-skin scarves, '50s party dresses, frilly little aprons and other sartorial equivalents of flirting, and with articles like "The Return of Hard to Get." ("I think it behooves us to stop offering each other these pearls of feminism, to stop saying, 'So, why don't you call him?' " a writer lectured in *Mademoiselle*. "Some men must have the thrill of the chase.")

I knew things were changing because a succession of my single girlfriends had called, sounding sheepish, to ask if they could borrow my out-of-print copy of *How to Catch and Hold a Man*.

With a serious male shortage developing, a distasteful fact loomed in the late '80s: Women were going to have to start being nice to men again.

Decades after the feminist movement promised an idyllic world of sisterhood and equality with men, it was becoming increasingly apparent that many women would have to brush up on the venerable tricks of the trade. We had all but forgotten how to be charmingly insincere and claw each other's eyes out for men. As Oscar Wilde noted, "In matters of grave importance, style, not sincerity, is the vital thing."

Required reading included Zsa Zsa Gabor's groundbreaking work, *How to Catch a Man, How to Keep a Man, How to Get Rid of a Man* ("The best way to attack a man immediately is to have a magnificent bosom and a half-size brain and let both of them show") and the guide of the latter-day Zsa Zsa, Paris Hilton ("It's all about being hard to get. No one would want caviar if it was cheap").

It is possible to learn from the great flirts of literature.

There's Scarlett O'Hara: "I stayed up all night trying to make up my mind which of you two boys is handsomer."

And Becky Sharp: "Oh, you droll creature! As if I care a pin for you."

And Gwendolyn Fairfax: "What wonderfully blue eyes you have! I hope you will always look at me just like that, especially when there are other people present."

Or simply follow the advice Alfred Hitchcock gave Eva Marie Saint before she filmed her sultry train scenes in *North by Northwest*: "Speak in a low voice. Don't move your hands. And always look directly into Cary Grant's eyes."

Modern temptresses would need to return to basics: an absurdly charming little laugh, a pert toss of the head, an air of saucy triumph, dewy eyes and a full knowledge of music, drawing, elegant note writing and geography.

It would once more be considered captivating to lie on a chaise longue, pass a lacy handkerchief across the eyelids and complain of a case of springtime giddiness.

Many high-powered career women were secretly thrilled to

return to the era of artful minxes. No matter how low you murmur, it's hard to beguile when you are discussing the yuan-dollar relationship or the effect of OPEC on NASDAQ on IPEX.

Amiable mewings of the sort perfected by Marilyn Monroe—"That sounds creamy" and "You are so-o-o delicious"—were once again the perfect ripostes at cocktail parties.

As a public service, I will reveal the six key axioms in *How to Catch and Hold a Man* for women who would be wives:

- Do not make abrupt gestures of any kind.
- Men are fascinated by bright, shiny objects, by lots of curls, lots of hair (on the head), by bows, ribbons, ruffles and bright colors.
- If he has a girlfriend, try to become a good friend of hers.
- Sarcasm is dangerous. Avoid it altogether. It ruins the aura of softness, womanliness and kindness you should be attempting to create around yourself.
- Avoid saying a direct no and instead seek surroundings that make it difficult for him to approach you. Sit in a narrow armless chair or keep a lighted cigarette between you.
- Keep thinking of yourself as a soft, mysterious cat. In order to get "the feline look," you must "stand relaxed, bend your knees slightly, tuck in your behind, pull in your stomach, relax your shoulders. For standing, adopt the position above, put one foot forward and rest your weight on the back foot. If this gets tire-

some, put the other foot forward, always keeping your weight on the back foot."

Chapter Nine, "How to Use the Telephone," is critical: "Whenever you are about to answer the telephone, hold your breath, then release it very slowly as you answer. Smile as you speak. Speak in a fairly low voice, directly into, and close to, the receiver. Always sound delighted when a male calls (it will encourage him to call more often), and never argue with him or reproach him on the telephone. A good trick is to sound as sexy as possible since he's not around and you don't have to defend yourself. It will make him feel that under your apparent coolness lies a fiery little soul that he can bring out if he only uses the right technique, and he will spend much of his time trying to discover such a technique."

This revisionist approach to romance could be difficult at first for women who thought that having your own American Express card meant never having to feign interest.

But with enough practice, and enough leopard-skin scarves, any woman can act as feline as a cat. And avoid sarcasm— altogether.

• • •

Movies in the '40s and '50s were chockablock with cunning mantrap techniques.

In the 1953 *How to Marry a Millionaire*, Lauren Bacall, Marilyn Monroe and Betty Grable set their "bear trap" by hanging around Bergdorf's mink department. "All you need is just one big fat one," Miss Bacall purred.

In the 1954 *Three Coins in the Fountain,* Maggie McNamara's character catches an Italian prince by researching his tastes, from wine to opera to the piccolo, and pretending hers are the same.

In the 1959 *Ask Any Girl,* Shirley MacLaine snares Gig Young by stealing his little black book and imitating his favorite girlfriends. He likes one datemate's red hair. She dyes hers flame-colored. He likes another's perfume. She douses herself in it.

In the 1948 *Every Girl Should Be Married,* shopgirl Betsy Drake tries to lasso pediatrician Cary Grant with The Plan. She ferrets out his preferences with his barber, his trainer, his tobacconist, his masseur, his florist, his launderer, past girlfriends and his old college glee club book. Giving new meaning to the term social science research, she learns he likes clear turtle soup, steak with mushrooms, potatoes Lyonnaise, asparagus with Hollandaise sauce, martinis with small olives, 1933 Piper-Heidsieck champagne and banana cream pie.

"Why, if you don't use your imagination, you'll just wind up married to any-old-body," she tells her girlfriend, defending her strategizing: "You might as well tell a fish to look out for the hook."

Monica Lewinsky, who once posed for *Vanity Fair* in iconic '50s pinup poses à la Jane Russell and Marilyn Monroe, adapted those '50s seduction methods to bag her president. ("POTUS" actually flashed on her home caller ID.)

There's a fine—sometimes indistinguishable—line between trapping and stalking.

The White House intern followed the old-fashioned prescription that men (and fish) are attracted by bright, shiny objects. She stationed herself, in flashy dresses and her trademark black beret, on rope lines and in the path of the presidential motorcade. She studied her prey's preferences in books and accessories, and even called an antiquarian bookstore in Annapolis, where the president had browsed, to see what he had lingered over. Told it was a book about American presidents, she bought it for him. Noting his Eurotrashy taste in clothes—those double-breasted, big-shouldered suits—she bought him an Ermenegildo Zegna tie.

In old movies, girls would have to do shoe-leather investigating if they wanted to be romantic gumshoes. Now they can simply do their background checks on the Internet. Then on a date, the Googler can feign interest in all the things she already knows the Googlee likes.

Romantic Googling can be as dangerous as drunk text messaging, of course. During the Clinton administration, an office crush of mine offered to show me how to use Google and plugged in my name. The first thing that popped up was a Republican prank: a publicity head shot of mine bobbing up and down, performing a sexual act on an image of Bill Clinton.

My friend and I both turned completely red and silently went back to our work. I never had the nerve to flirt with him again (or go on Google for several years.)

Checking out a prospective date on Google, you can see a

story, blog or picture that might give an unflattering or inaccurate impression—or an unflattering, accurate one. Or you can simply get the wrong person; when I was looking up a doctor's number recently, the first citation that randomly came up was for "Man With Massive Cock Hardcore XXX."

Some singles have no urge to Google date, feeling that it short-circuits the seductive process of exploration. "It's more romantic to find things out naturally," said Campbell Robertson, a clever young reporter for the *Times*. "Then you can Google them later to find out if they were telling the truth."

Craig Bierko, an actor and musical comedy star who played one of Sarah Jessica Parker's boyfriends on *Sex and the City*, agreed that Googling a girl before a date feels creepy. "Yet," he says, "I also figure if the Internet has made it possible for me to know about some plane crash across the ocean only three seconds after it happened, then why can't I use it to prevent a plane crash across the table three hundred dollars before? Also depending on the nature of the person's past, sometimes you can Google pictures of them naked. I've heard."

Many can't resist trying to game Google, figuring out techniques for burying uncomplimentary stuff by creating their own Web sites, home pages or minimal blogs that might tip the balance in a favorable way, or even pop up first.

Bitter exes can succumb to webstalking. As the feminist writer Katha Pollitt confessed in *The New Yorker*, she went "a little crazy" after her lover left her: "I was like Javert, hunting him through the sewers of cyberspace, moving from link to link in the dark, like Spider-Man flinging himself by a filament over the shadowy chasm between one roof and another."

Or, with even more time-consuming vengeance, they can Google-bomb an ex the way Democrats do President Bush, so that when you type in the word "failure" you get connected to W.'s official White House biography. Hell hath no gigabyte fury like a woman who Google-bombs her old flame's name with a word like "impotent."

Once women cottoned on to the fact that men were evolving slowly, if at all, they went back to hunting their quarry in person and in cyberspace with elaborate schemes designed to allow the deluded creatures to think they were the hunters.

"Men like hunting and we shouldn't deprive them of their chance to do their hunting and mating rituals," says my twenty-six-year-old friend Julie Bosman, a *New York Times* reporter. "As my mom says, men don't like to be chased."

Or as the Marvelettes sang, "The hunter gets captured by the game."

My mom always told me that, too. In 1982, after I had broken up with a longtime boyfriend, she wrote me a ten-page letter filled with strategy and empathy:

"Put all his pictures in a place you won't see them, preferably the trash. The key now is indifference. Man's glory is the chase, not the conquest. This has happened to every friend I have and to me. I was a senior at Holy Cross High School and he was graduated from Catholic University. A big rush and then nothing, but during the big rush he tried to get me to come across. Then I found out he really loved a beautiful older girl and thought he was engaged. She married someone else, he got another girl (who I am sure was a casual fling) in trouble and had to marry her. For months after being dumped I lived in hell. Every face on the street might be his. Every phone call might be him. Once I saw him with a girl on the board-walk at Ocean City laughing and happy and I died.

"Years later he worked with my brother and used to ask about me all the time. He lost his leg and then died. I didn't wish it on him but he suffered, too."

In a weird postscript, that same old boyfriend of mine moved into the office next door to me as the latest *New York Times* Op-Ed columnist. Moral: Make sure you stay friends with exes. And don't throw *all* their pictures in the trash. Save a few fun, incriminating ones.

The key to staying cool in the courtship rituals is B & I, girls say—seem Busy and Important. "As much as you're wait-ing for that little envelope to appear on your screen," said Car-rie Foster, a twenty-nine-year-old publicist in D.C., "you happen to have a lot of stuff to do anyway."

If a guy rejects you or turns out to be the essence of evil, you can ratchet up from B & I to CBB, Can't Be Bothered.

In the TMI—Too Much Information—digital age, there can be infinite technological foreplay. Before dating and Googling comes "interacting"—flirtatious texting and e-mailing. *Cosmopolitan* magazine now offers tips for dirty texting, including messages like "Found my old cheerleading outfit. Still fits" and "Dont do much@the gym . . . Save energy for L8R."

Dr. Helen Fisher, a Rutgers anthropologist, concurs with Julie and my mom: "What our grandmothers told us about playing hard to get is true. The whole point of the game is to impress and capture. It's not about honesty. Both men and women, when they're playing the courtship game, deceive so they can win. Novelty, excitement and danger drive up dopamine in the brain. And both sexes brag."

Women might wear padded bras, dye their hair, apply makeup and spend hours finding a hip-slimming dress, she said, while men may drive a nice car or wear a fancy suit that makes them seem richer than they are.

The Bosman Principles, passed down to Julie from her mom, Janice, are more spontaneous than *The Rules*, which advised treating a husband as "a client or customer" they want to keep happy.

(*The Rules* abruptly went out of fashion in 2004 with the embarrassing marital breakup of one of its authors, Ellen Fein, who blamed the divorce on a dentist who allegedly botched work on her "gigantic teeth" and gave her jaw pain.)

The Bosman Principles are more Jungian than Zsa Zsa, tapping into the same sort of archetypal ritual reflected in Natalie Angier's mythic description of mating in her book *Woman: An Intimate Geography*.

"It is ancient, prehominid news," Angier wrote. "Sex is dangerous. It always has been, for every species that engages in it. Courting and copulating animals are exposed animals, subject to greater risk of predation than animals who are chastely asleep in their burrow; not only do mating animals usually perform their rituals out in the open, but their attention is so focused on the particulars of fornication that they fail to notice the glint of a gaping jaw or the flap of a raptor's wings. Momentum is chancy, and sex is nothing if not momentous. Let us not forget that. Let us not be so intimidated by overwork or familiarity or trimethylamines that we forget the exquisite momentum of sexual hunger."

Julie agrees it's all about momentum. "The way I see dating is an interplay between two clever, charming, smart people, and that interplay should be quick and deft and funny," she philosophizes. "It has nothing to do with who's being masculine or feminine. It's about the push and the pull and chasing each other around trees. It's not about women just waiting for something to happen. Courting rituals are about our best selves, our most funny, charming intelligent selves, with all our nerves on end."

For women, she contends, it means staying tantalizingly out of reach, but knowing when to dash back in and stay out of reach again.

"You appreciate something more that is slightly out of your grasp, that is alluring and mysterious," she said. (Just as, when Oscar Wilde first tasted ice cream, he was reputed to have remarked, "What a pity this isn't a sin.")

Barbara Stanwyck had the same spark-and-spurn technique with Henry Fonda in Preston Sturges's 1941 classic comedy, *The Lady Eve.*

"You have the darndest way of bumping a fellow down and then bouncing him up again," the bedazzled Fonda murmurs.

"And then bumping him down again," Stanwyck blithely agrees.

Many men I know say they were looking to marry navigators, women who would keep them from falling off the edge of the earth. So by navigating the courtship, women show their steering skills.

Julie calls her approach the best way of selecting out the narcissists and jerks. If your suitors are not willing to put in the time to play the courting game, she reasons, then they don't care enough to be good long-term prospects. (According to a 2005 study from the University College of London, men have their own way to filter out the narcissists and gold diggers. Researchers, using a mathematical formula, $P_f F_{AH} + (1 - P_f)F_{AD} < 0$, said there was evolutionary logic in offering expensive gifts to females, thus signaling serious intentions. But they calculated that men were better off investing in dinners than diamonds, so that they'd pay no cost if the invite isn't accepted.

If you don't have the patience for the Bosman Principles, simply give a guy the Cervantes test, as my girlfriend Dana Calvo used to do: "I dropped the title of a book by Cervantes I invented and raved about the imaginary piece of literature in an effort to see if my poseur date took the bait. If the guy came clean and said he had never heard the title, he passed the Cervantes test."

A gay friend of mine who lives in Manhattan proffers his Grey Goose (or "Gay Goose," as he calls them) axioms for dating:

1. Clarity beats ambiguity. If you're not sure you're communicating interest, then stop being coy. If you're not sure how your interest is being received, ask. You could lose whole, vital, pre-hormone-replacement-therapy, pre-Viagra years dithering, wondering and eating Häagen-Dazs.

2. Always err in the direction of sex. Then at least if nothing else turns out well, you've had a few minutes—or, if you're lucky, a few hours—of pleasure. But skip the

postcoital cigarette. Smoking causes fine lines around the mouth.

3. If the other person seems hesitant, troubled and tortured but worth it, the other person is hesitant, troubled, tortured and NOT worth it. There are no oxymorons—only morons—in romance.

4. Alcohol is your friend. Something has to do battle with all the guilt and inhibitions from stern parents, scary nuns and Pat Robertson. Might as well be Grey Goose.

If you go with Julie's technique, you'll need a more Zen attitude, the ability to be romantically ascetic and mentally peaceful while you're waiting.

Campbell Robertson agrees that men experience courting in an evolutionary continuum. To sum up the male-female dance, he cited a passage from *The Beak of the Finch,* a book on natural and sexual selection among the finches of Galápagos, from the chapter on Trinidadian guppies:

"A male guppy has more to do in life than merely survive. He also has to mate. To survive it has to hide among the colored gravel at the bottom of its stream and among the other guppies of its school. But to mate it has to stand out from the gravel and stand out from the school. It has to elude the eyes of the cichlid or the prawn while catching the eyes of the female guppy . . . the quieter colors of a male, the less luck he has in courting females. On the other hand he is likely to have more time to try, because the less he stands out among his own kind, the less he stands out among his enemies."

For years, Hollywood had been trying and failing to create

a male *Sex and the City*, which would give you the skinny on how men talk to each other about women. Finally, Doug Ellin came up with *Entourage*, on HBO, about a young Hollywood star named Vinnie Chase and his posse of pals from Queens who pursue women and bust on each other.

I called Ellin in L.A. to ask him what women can learn from *Entourage*.

"Men are kind of instant gratification animals," he said. "We're like animals, really, much more instinctual than women, less thoughtful. I see such similarity in all my friends, the smart ones, the dumb ones. They want what they want. I think women think there are a lot more complexities going on."

Men are driven, he says, by "the hunter-gatherer thing. Every guy I know here goes out and tries to find a woman, and holds off as long as possible without being captured, as sad as that sounds. And the successful women are the ones who act like they don't want to be captured—at first.

"Women have to know when to apply pressure, maybe after the guys hit thirty-five and start thinking about mortality and wake up horrified at being alone and hunting down twenty-one-year-olds in bars. The guys I know who are married were all pressured into it. It doesn't mean they don't love the woman, or are not happy now. It's just that they had to be told by the woman, 'It's time.' A good woman does help guide you to a place of security and comfort."

A girlfriend of mine agrees: "It's like fishing. You only begin to reel it in when you're sure you have a bite, not just a nibble. You have to make sure the fish is on the hook."

When, in 2005, neuroscientists produced brain scan images

of new love for the first time, the images backed the idea that you have to delve into the primitive, precognitive area to be successful in romance.

"New love can look for all the world like mental illness, a blend of mania, dementia and obsession that cuts people off from friends and family and prompts out-of-character behavior—compulsive phone calling, serenades, yelling from rooftops—that could almost be mistaken for psychosis," wrote Benedict Carey in *The New York Times*'s Science section.

Of course, everyone since Plato has written that love is related to frenzy, but I guess it's not official until some neurologists with a grant say it.

An analysis in *The Journal of Neurophysiology* confirmed what has been known through the ages—that Elvis's "hunka-hunka burnin' love" was literal, that passionate love scorches areas deep in the primitive brain affecting long-term attachment and spurs neural activity in the "reward and aversion system" of the brain, along with cravings for food, warmth and drugs.

"When you're in the throes of this romantic love, it's overwhelming, you're out of control, you're irrational, you're going to the gym at 6 a.m. every day—why? Because she's there," said Dr. Fisher of Rutgers, who helped write the analysis. "And when rejected, some people contemplate stalking, homicide, suicide. This drive for romantic love can be stronger than the will to live."

The passion-related region of the brain is on the opposite side from the region that registers physical attractiveness, Carey wrote, "and appeared to be involved in longing, desire and the unexplainable tug that people feel toward one person, among many attractive alternative partners."

Dr. Lucy Brown of Albert Einstein College of Medicine in the Bronx, a co-author of the study, maintains that this distinction between finding someone attractive and desiring him or her, between liking and wanting, "is all happening in an area of the mammalian brain that takes care of most basic functions, like eating, drinking, eye movements, all at an unconscious level, and I don't think anyone expected this part of the brain to be so specialized."

Julie and her girlfriends now joke that they wish there were a way to make all new dates submit to brain scans to find out who's in the throes of new love, as opposed to who's just ephemerally attracted. (That reminds me of a guy I knew who thought women should have headboards that lit up for their orgasms, like the hockey goal light above the net, so men could know for sure.)

There is also a difference between lust and love, Dr. Fisher told me, adding that the pull of romantic love is stronger than the pull of lust, and can make someone of any age feel like a teenager.

One of the most intriguing discoveries in the study had to do with what causes each sex to fall in love.

Men's brains lit up based on what they saw; women's brains lit up based on what they remembered. (As men know too well, women never forget.)

"Men needed to pick out signs of youth and health and vitality, the things that indicated she could bear him healthy babies," Dr. Fisher said. "Women spend hours on the phone with their girlfriends, talking about what he did and didn't do, or if he remembered an anniversary or birthday—signs he'd be a dependable, loving husband and father."

Men still look for the same cues on health and vitality, she said, even if they're not consciously planning to have babies, noting: "One doesn't change one's taste as one ages."

My favorite response to the brain burn was a letter to the editor in the *Times* from Karl Decker of Monroe, Connecticut: "Love like a mental illness? We do praise the contemporary research but the Elizabethans had this all figured out long ago. They knew it was.

"In *Romeo and Juliet*, poor Romeo tells of his futile love as 'a smoke raised with a fume of sighs.' The theory went thus: Being in the ecstasy (from the Greek for derangement) of love caused the blood to boil, the hot distillation to rise up and sear the brain and so affect it to madness.

"Love denied (hence those sighs) caused melancholia. The insanity of love was pretty complex, too. It is 'a madness most discreet,' concludes Romeo.

"And in *Hamlet*, Polonius knows exactly what the 'Hamlet problem' is, for he had perceived the 'hot love' between Hamlet and Ophelia. Prohibiting Ophelia from seeing Hamlet, however, has cast Hamlet into 'the madness wherein he now raves.'

"Now as for Ophelia's hysterics—but enough!"

• • •

In those faraway, long-ago days of feminism, there was talk about equal pay for equal work. Now there's talk about "girl money."

A friend of mine in her thirties said it was a term she heard bandied about the New York dating scene. She also noted a shift in the type of gifts given at wedding showers around town, a reversion to '50s-style offerings: soup ladles and those frilly little aprons from Anthropologie and vintage stores were being unwrapped along with see-through nighties and push-up brassieres.

"What I find most disturbing about the 1950s-ification and retrogression of women's lives is that it has seeped into the corporate and social culture, where it can do real damage," she complained. "Otherwise intelligent men, who know women still earn less than men as a rule, say things like: 'I'll get the check. You only have girl money.' "

Throughout the long, dark ages of undisputed patriarchy, women connived to trade beauty and sex for affluence and status. In the first flush of feminism, women offered to pay half the check with "woman money" as a way to show that these crass calculations—that a woman's worth in society was determined by her looks, that she was an ornament up for sale to the highest bidder—no longer applied.

I always hated splitting; I'd rather take turns. But if I didn't offer on a first date, the man would often insist, as though I'd been rude.

Now dating etiquette has reverted. Young women no longer care about using the check to assert their equality. They care about using it to assess their sexuality.

Going Dutch is an archaic feminist relic that young women can't believe ever happened. They talk about it with disbelief and disdain.

"It's a scuzzy seventies thing, like platform shoes on men," said one.

"Feminists in the seventies went overboard," agreed Anne Schroeder, a twenty-six-year-old magazine editor in D.C. "Paying is like opening a car door. It's nice. I appreciate it. But he doesn't have to."

Unless he wants another date.

Women in their twenties think old-school feminists looked for equality in all the wrong places, that instead of fighting battles about whether women should pay for dinner or wear padded bras they should have focused only on big economic issues.

After Googling and Bikramming to get ready for a first dinner date, a modern girl will end the evening with The Offering, an insincere bid to help pay the check.

"They make like they are heading into their bag after a meal, but it is a dodge," said Marc Santora, a thirty-year-old *New York Times* Metro reporter. "They know you will stop them before a credit card can be drawn. If you don't, they hold it against you."

Agreed one of my girlfriends, a TV producer in New York: "If you offer and they accept, then it's over."

Chimed in another young woman who worked for NASCAR: "I reached into my bag, offering to pick up our night out, knowing full well I only had six dollars. We want to come across as if we've had a good upbringing, but we'd fall off our chair if it were accepted."

A beautiful TV newsmagazine producer from L.A. sniffed:

"If he hasn't asked me about myself by the time the entrée comes, I don't even bother to thank him when he pays."

The new urban legend is about a young man who loses a girl by asking her to split the check.

Marc says it happened to a friend of his in New York: "He thought he had just gone on a great date, with clear signals that things were going to get romantic. Numbers had been exchanged and the whole business. When the bill came, she didn't offer to pay and he asked her if she would split it. She did, but never called again and didn't return messages. There may have been other reasons for the rejection, but he still blames it on his seeming cheap."

Jurassic feminists shudder at the retro implication of a quid profiterole. But it doesn't matter if the woman is making as much money as the man or more, she expects him to pay, both to prove her desirability and as a way of signaling romance—something that's more confusing in a dating culture rife with casual hookups and group activities. (Once beyond the initial testing phase and settled in a relationship, of course, she can pony up more.)

"Dating, in the proper sense of the word, has unfortunately become less and less common and too often confused with 'hanging out,' " Marc explained. " 'Hanging out' may lead to 'hooking up,' but I notice a lot of friends, men and women, looking for some basic rules of courtship they can understand and follow. That makes it all the more important that an actual date functions in the classic sense—the man paying."

His friend Lindsay Faber, a twenty-nine-year-old *Newsday*

reporter, agrees that it's a way for women to know it's a date. "It feels romantic and chivalrous and like you are being taken out on something," she said. "Otherwise it feels like you are going out with a buddy."

She recognizes that it's a double standard. "Women want to be treated like equals in the relationship, but, in the beginning, they still want the man to bring out the cash," she said. "I don't think men expect anything if they pay, but they certainly hope for something."

Some men are disgusted. "It used to be all about chivalry, but now it's more out of greed," said Brian, a news assistant in Paris. "Feminism has allowed women to be greedy—which is progress, right?"

Rick, a self-described "fat CPA" from Nashville, confessed he had to spend $10,000 on meals to land his wife.

My friend Mike, a magazine reporter in D.C. who dated in the '70s as a single guy and thirty years later as a divorced dad, is ambivalent: "It's a very bad evolution because I have to spend more money, but maybe it's worth it because I don't have to put up with all that old attitude. Women in the seventies were much more assertive, not wanting to be patronized. Now women are perfectly happy to be patronized, especially when it comes to financial matters."

Marc calls it only fair because "women have to spend a fortune to go on the date. They have to smell nice and look nice." And a bachelor pal in Manhattan chimed in: "Guys can be dogs, and they'll lead women along for a long time without making that dreaded 'commitment.' I don't think women should be both bankrupted and abandoned."

Manolo moochers may say it's about economics—they make less and they spend more to get ready—but it's really more about ritual.

"There are plenty of ways for me to find out if he's going to see me as an equal without disturbing the dating ritual," said one young woman. "Disturbing the dating ritual leads to chaos. Everybody knows that."

Carrie, a publicist in her late twenties from Long Island, told me she was not unwilling to dig into her Kate Spade bag. "He can get the jewelry, the dinners, the shoes and the vacations," she said. "I'll get the cab."

Many young women expect to be fully subsidized on romantic jaunts. When I asked a young man at my gym how he and his lawyer girlfriend were going to divide the costs on a California vacation, he looked askance. "She never offers," he replied. "And I like paying for her."

It is, as one guy says, "one of the few remaining ways we can demonstrate our manhood."

A boyfriend of mine put it this way: "I know you make a good salary, but I like the feeling of knowing I can treat you to dinner or first-class plane tickets with my black American Express card and you'll be excited."

The fem-freeloading doesn't change with marriage. Many professional women still want their husbands to pick up the checks at restaurants, pay the mortgage and get home by 6:30 to help with chores and kids.

Elizabeth Marquardt, the co-author of a report on college dating, agreed the courting rituals are in a muddle: "One Yale girl described the ridiculous situations that can come up because of all the confusion over who pays for what and when it is a date. She found herself arguing on the sidewalk with a guy over who should pay for a Slurpee. A guy will ask a girl to the movies, and she will think they are just hanging out. Then he offers to pay, changing the whole outing into a date—a trick date."

My gay friends seem just as flummoxed over modern dating etiquette. As one says: "My team could be a barometer for where your team will head: what happens when desired gender equality really happens. And you know what? It's hell. You sit there thinking: If I move too quickly to pick up the check, am I pegging myself as the dominant, aggressive daddy type? If I sit here meekly, do I send out the message: Take care of me, oh, and also, take me?"

Women say they want old-fashioned courting, even though fleeting sexual encounters are common on college campuses.

A friend of mine who has been teaching classes in the Ivy League for the last few years talked about the mass confusion caused by the uneasy blend of retro attitudes about dating with modern sexual freedom.

"These extremely powerful girls outperform boys all day in class," he says. "They're talkative, nicely dressed. Then at night, they put on as few clothes as possible, looking so skimpy it must be chilly. Very tight tank tops that show their nipples and cleavage and very short skirts that show their underpants, or if they're not wearing any. Or camisoles, which look like underwear, without bras and really tight blue jeans.

"These are girls who got double 800s on their SATs, presidents of their class, Model U.N. representatives, and on Thursday and Saturday nights they drink a bunch of pregame vodka shots with their friends, because they're actually a little scared to go out into the meat market. It's all very ritualized.

"Initially, they have tremendous power, cruising into the clubs with their bosoms hanging out. The boys who have seen these girls in class looking demure and smarter now see these incredibly hot sex objects; the boys are dumbfounded, weak in the knees, by the beauty of these nineteen-year-olds dressed as Greenwich, Connecticut, high-prep, low-class whores.

"But all of a sudden, at about midnight or 1 a.m., the power begins to shift to the boys, where it stays till 3 a.m. The girls get looped and sloppy, and the boys now have the physical power—they're groping and grinding and pawing and trying to get laid, and the girls are pathetically giving guys blow jobs. These girls aren't even getting orgasms; they're just servicing boys in dark corners.

"And when they talk about it to me later during office conferences, their intelligent eyes cloud over and sometimes they say they blacked out and don't remember what happened. And they don't know how to change it. Their general attitude is 'Boys are pigs, there aren't that many good ones' and they're kind of cranky about that."

Girls are doing everything girls did prefeminism and postfeminism. No wonder everybody's bumfuzzled.

* * *

At a party for the Broadway opening of *Sweet Smell of Success*, a top New York producer gave me a lecture on the price of female success that was anything but sweet.

He confessed that he had wanted to ask me out on a date when he was between marriages, but nixed the idea because my job as a *Times* columnist made me too intimidating.

Men, he explained, prefer women who seem malleable and awed. He predicted that I would never find a mate, because if there's one thing men fear, it's a woman who uses her critical faculties. Will she be critical of absolutely everything, even his manhood?

He had hit on a primal fear of single successful women: that the aroma of male power is an aphrodisiac for women, but the perfume of female power is a turnoff for men.

It's summed up in that famous lament from Holly Hunter's wee, wired TV news producer in the classic 1987 career-vs.-men movie *Broadcast News*. "I'm beginning to repel the people I'm trying to seduce," she wails.

It took women a few decades to realize that everything they were doing to advance themselves in the boardroom could be sabotaging their chances in the bedroom.

Evolution is lagging behind equality. So females are still programmed to look for older men with resources while males are still programmed to look for younger women with adoring gazes.

When Paul Rudnick wrote the screenplay for the 2004 remake of *The Stepford Wives,* the ultimate feminist nightmare about men preferring hot zombies to complicated career women, he told me he felt the "embedded biology" of romantic fantasies has not changed: "Men only evolve with a gun at their head. Men want a babe and don't care about her earning power. Women want a rugged poet or musician with a private jet."

For women, accruing resources has limited value in attracting men, and might even have the opposite effect of scaring them off. "There's still social pressure—everyone looking at a guy with a wife who makes more money, going, 'He's the chick,' " Rudnick said. High-powered women, especially those with children, simply have less time to lavish attention on their men.

A few years ago at a White House correspondents' dinner, I met a very beautiful actress. Within minutes, she blurted out: "I can't believe I'm forty-six and not married. Men only want to marry their personal assistants or P.R. women."

I'd been noticing a trend along these lines, as famous and powerful men took up with young women whose job it was to care for them and nurture them in some way: their secretaries, assistants, nannies, caterers, flight attendants, researchers and fact-checkers.

Steve Martin's novel *Shopgirl*, which he made into a movie, is about the affair of an older affluent man and a young girl who sells him gloves at Neiman Marcus in Beverly Hills: "Ray's former experience has been with tough-minded, outgoing, vital, ambitious women, who, when displeased, attack. Mirabelle's dull inertia draws him into a peaceful place, a calm cushion of acceptance."

Women in staff support are the new sirens because, as a guy I know put it, they look upon the men they work for as "the moon, the sun and the stars." It's all about orbiting, serving and salaaming their Sun Gods.

In all those Tracy/Hepburn movies more than a half century ago, it was the snap and crackle of a romance between equals that was so exciting. You still see it onscreen occasionally—the incendiary chemistry of Brad Pitt and Angelina Jolie playing married assassins aiming for mutually assured orgasms and destruction in *Mr. and Mrs. Smith*. Interestingly, that movie was described as retro because of its salty battle of wits between two peppery lovers.

Moviemakers these days are more interested in exploring the "calm cushion" of romances between unequals.

As a famous man I know, who was first married to a woman who did not work and then married to a woman who worked as his researcher, so memorably put it: "Deep down, all men want the same thing: a virgin in a gingham dress." (In the 2003 chick flick *Down With Love*, Renée Zellweger had to be remade from feminist author—advising women to favor career over marriage and sex over love—to a fox, wearing false eyelashes and red-and-white gingham short-shorts, to snare a good guy.)

We used to think women were trapped in the Cinderella myth, but maybe men are, too. Do men want to rescue women as much as women want to be rescued?

In James Brooks's movie *Spanglish*, Adam Sandler, playing a sensitive Los Angeles chef, falls for his hot Mexican maid, just as in *Maid in Manhattan*, Ralph Fiennes, playing a sensitive New York pol, falls for the hot Puerto Rican maid at his hotel, played by Jennifer Lopez.

Sandler's maid, who cleans up for him without being able to speak English, is presented as the ideal woman, in looks and character. His wife, played by Tea Leoni, is repellent: a jangly, yakking, overachieving, overexercised, unfaithful, shallow she-monster who has just lost her job with a commercial design firm and fears she has lost her identity.

When Sandler's chef gets a rave review in *The New York Times*, the she-monster wife pounces on him, has an orgasm without waiting for him even to get excited and starts crying about her own lost career. "What am I going to do about *me*?" she keens, as she rolls off him.

In 2003, we had *Girl With a Pearl Earring*, in which Colin Firth's Vermeer erotically paints Scarlett Johanssen's Dutch maid, and Richard Curtis's *Love Actually*, about the attraction of unequals. The witty and sophisticated British prime minister, played by Hugh Grant, falls for the chubby girl who wheels the tea and scones into his office. A businessman married to the substantial Emma Thompson, the sister of the prime minister, falls for his sultry secretary. A novelist played by Colin Firth falls for his maid, who speaks only Portuguese.

(I wonder if the trend in making heroines out of maids who don't speak English is related to the trend of guys at the gym who like to watch Kelly Ripa in the morning with the sound off?)

Art is imitating life, turning women who seek equality into selfish narcissists and objects of rejection, rather than affection.

One of the most sensational celebrity stories of 2005 was the Big Easy Bacchanalian romp of "Rat Jude" and the nanny.

Daisy Wright sold her story to the London *Mirror* of her steamy affair with Jude Law in New Orleans. She was taking care of one his kids while he filmed *All the King's Men*. His gorgeous twenty-three-year-old fiancée, Sienna Miller, was in London starring in *As You Like It*.

"I had said to Jude I didn't understand why he didn't find a wife who didn't want a career and to party all the time," recalled the nanny. "He said it is very hard to find a woman who wants this and that he would love that more than anything, but there aren't women like that in his line of work."

When Sienna confronted Jude, according to the London tabloids, he blamed her for not being devoted enough. (How could she be so selfish, spending time on her own rising career?)

It's an old story, from *Jane Eyre* to Joe Piscopo, the allure of a woman who takes care of your kids without the attendant nagging and demands of a wife.

In *Anna Karenina*, when Stepan is caught cheating with the help, he goes into a reverie: "There's something common, vulgar in making love to one's governess. But what a governess!"

New York Times reporter John Schwartz made the trend official in 2005: "Men would rather marry their secretaries than their bosses, and evolution may be to blame."

A study by psychology researchers at the University of Michigan, using college undergraduates, suggested that men going for long-term relationships would rather marry women in subordinate jobs than women who are supervisors.

Men think that women with important jobs are more likely to cheat on them. There it is, right in the DNA: Women get penalized by insecure men for being too independent.

"The hypothesis," said Dr. Stephanie Brown, the lead author of the study, "is that there are evolutionary pressures on males to take steps to minimize the risk of raising offspring that are not their own." Women, by contrast, did not show a marked difference between their attraction to men who might work above them and their attraction to men who might work below them. And men did not show a preference when it came to mere one-night stands.

So men will sleep with a woman on top once; they just don't want to live with her. It may be either because they find bossy-boots female supervisors where they work irritating, or, if you take the Darwinian explanation, they fear that upwardly mobile women will be more savvy about sneaking around and being unfaithful.

A simultaneous report by researchers at four British universities indicated that smart men with demanding jobs would rather have old-fashioned wives, like their mums, than equals. The study found that a high IQ hampers a woman's chance to get married, while it is a plus for men. The prospect for marriage increased by 35 percent for guys for each 16-point increase in IQ; for women, there is a 40 percent drop for each 16-point rise.

The problem is, a man either wants a woman's IQ to exceed her body temperature or her body temperature to exceed her IQ. What they can't seem to bear is the combination of brains and fever.

So was the feminist movement some sort of cruel hoax? Do women get less desirable as they get more successful? Women want to be in a relationship with guys they can seriously talk to—unfortunately, a lot of those guys want to be in relationships with women they don't have to talk to.

As Bill Maher crudely but usefully explained to Craig Ferguson on the CBS *Late Late Show*: "Women get in relationships because they want somebody to talk to. Men want women to shut up."

I asked the actress and writer Carrie Fisher, who has dated both older men and younger, movie stars and movie stars' staffers, about the trend.

"I haven't dated in twelve million years," she said drily. "I gave up on dating powerful men because they wanted to date women in the service professions. So I decided to date guys in the service professions. But then I found out that kings want to be treated like kings, and consorts want to be treated like kings, too."

It's funny. I come from a family of Irish domestics— statuesque, six-foot-tall women who cooked, kept house and acted as nannies for some of America's first families. I was always so proud of achieving more—succeeding in a high-powered career that would have been closed to my great-aunts.

How odd, then, to find out now that being a maid would have enhanced my chances with men.

An upstairs maid, of course.

* * *

There are many angles for romance.

In the 1957 movie *Silk Stockings,* Fred Astaire uses geography. He croons to the leggy Soviet apparatchik Cyd Charisse that he loves "the east, west, north, and the south of you."

In 1940's *My Little Chickadee,* Mae West rolls her hips and eyes and goes with arithmetic. "A man has a hundred dollars and you leave him with two dollars," she lectures a class of schoolchildren. "That's subtraction."

There's physics, of course. As an old boyfriend used to say: "It's all electromagnetic."

And then there's my favorite: the alphabetical approach.

I once had a crush on a guy who told me he was reading great works of literature from *A* to *Z*, and had gotten as far as *K*. So I went to a bookstore and picked out classics from *L* to *Z* and sent them to him. I couldn't find one for *X*, so I stuck in a tape of *The X-Files*. He liked the present, but the romance never went east, west or north. Just south.

Still, my ears perked up when I recently heard the tale of a New York journalist who gave his wife an unusual birthday present: a list of books from *A* to *Z* that would help her better understand him.

I decided to adapt the idea for Valentine's Day, and get some lucky guy the books from *A* to *Z* that would help him better understand me. I prowled Borders, but the more I looked, the more I fretted.

I could start with *All the King's Men*, but it's pretty obvious that I'm interested in the nexus between politics and dishonesty.

I love Shakespeare, but if I put in *The Taming of the Shrew*, would I send the wrong message?

Everything suddenly seemed fraught. What inferences would he draw from *The Wonderful Wizard of Oz*? Would he find me stuffy if I included *Ethan Frome*? Pretentious if I threw in Ovid? Mirthless if I chose the shame-spiraling *House of Mirth*? Hostile if I picked *Be Honest—You're Not That Into Him Either*?

High-maintenance if I selected *Empty Promises*, Ann Rule's true stories of love affairs that ended with a horrible crime? Needy if I chose the Deepak Chopra cookbook to nourish body and soul, unlock the hidden dimensions in your life and harness the infinite power of coincidence? Pandering if I stacked the deck with guy-lit like Nick Hornby, Frederick Exley's *A Fan's Notes*, and John Keegan's *The Face of Battle*? Insufferable if I put in chick lit and bride lit like Cecelia Ahern's *P.S., I Love You* and Jane Green's *Babyville*?

The more I thought about it, the more it seemed not only risky, but the height of presumption to expect someone to devote that many hours to fathoming someone else's psyche. What guy would drag himself away from ESPN's *SportsCenter* to read *Sense and Sensibility* or from beer and pizza to devour *Cakes and Ale*?

It strikes me that there must be a gender difference here. From my own unscientific sampling, I think it's far rarer for women to ask men to read their stuff than it is for men to ask women to read their stuff. Poor Condi Rice couldn't even get George W. Bush to read her presentation of his foreign policy goals in *Foreign Affairs* magazine during his 2000 campaign.

While I hardly ever hear from female readers who want me to read something, male readers are constantly e-mailing and sending me stuff to read: op-ed pieces, essays, letters to the editor or letters they've written to friends, e-mail messages their girlfriends or wives or buddies have written about me, original poetry, lists of favorite CDs and books, unpublished manuscripts, novels, jokes, business advice books, plays, TV sitcom treatments, songs, speeches, recipes for cranberry-orange nut bread. One guy even sent me his script for *George W. Bush: The Musical.* (Georgie sings to Big Daddy: "Any war you can start, I can make bigger; I can make any war bigger than you.")

Times reader Jerry Hammond of Charleston, South Carolina, e-mailed me constantly, including this comment about my mom's cameo appearances in my column dispensing wry ruminations on life: "Dowd, why don't you stay home and let your mother write the column." He signed off "Serious."

One reader e-mailed me a short movie he'd made called *White Squirrel in Tree Eating Peanut,* another e-mail about getting a publisher for his *White Squirrel Photo Gift Book* and a long list of "Ponderisms," which pondered such things as "Some people are like Slinkys. Not really good for anything, but you still can't help but smile when you see one tumble down the stairs."

Men also tell me when they're going to be on TV or giving lectures.

Sometimes, if I don't read or watch their work and write back, the authors send me snarky notes complaining about my insensitivity.

While I could never give a guy I was dating the *A* to *Z* on me, I'd love to read the *A* to *Z* that guy would choose to give me on himself. I just hope, as Diane Keaton told Woody Allen in *Annie Hall,* that all his choices won't have the word "death" in the title.

* * *

It's really enough to make a girl swear off newsmagazines.

Sixteen years after *Newsweek* issued its alarmist 1986 declaration that a forty-year-old woman was more likely to be killed by a terrorist than tie the knot, *Time* magazine chronicled the new baby bust—women who focus too much on their careers suddenly realizing they've squandered their fertility.

All that talk about forty being the new thirty and fifty being the new forty didn't apply to reproductive organs, it turned out.

Modern science can prolong the time a woman's veneer looks juicy, but the inside is desiccating at the same rate— "The Picture of Dorianna Gray."

Four decades after feminism blossomed in a giddy wave of bra barbecues, birth-control pills and unisex clothes, the ideal of having it all is a risible cliché.

Women moving up still strive to marry up. Men moving up still tend to marry down. The two sexes' going in opposite directions has led to an epidemic of professional women missing out on husbands and kids.

Sylvia Ann Hewlett, an economist and the author of the 2002 *Creating a Life: Professional Women and the Quest for Children*, conducted a survey and found that 55 percent of thirty-five-year-old career women were childless. The number of childless women age forty to forty-four had doubled in twenty years. And among corporate executives who earn $100,000 or more, she said, 49 percent of the women did not have children, compared with only 10 percent of the men.

Hewlett quantified, yet again, that men have an unfair advantage. "Nowadays," she said, "the rule of thumb seems to be that the more successful the woman, the less likely it is she will find a husband or bear a child. For men, the reverse is true."

On a *60 Minutes* report on the book, Lesley Stahl talked to two young women who went to Harvard Business School. They agreed that while they were the perfect age to start families, it was not so easy to find the right mates.

Men, apparently, learn early to protect their eggshell egos from high-achieving women. The girls said they hid the fact that they went to Harvard from guys they met because it was the kiss of death. "The H-bomb," they dubbed it.

"As soon as you say Harvard Business School . . . that's the end of the conversation," Ani Vartanian said. "As soon as the guys say, 'Oh, I go to Harvard Business School,' all the girls start falling into them."

The Washington Post reported in 2003 that record numbers of single, professional African American women had decided to adopt on their own. In D.C., black women tend to be better educated and more affluent than men their age, an independence and success that many of the women said intimidated African American men and made it harder to find spouses.

There are more recent surveys, including one by Match. com, that seem more hopeful about the ability of men to adapt to the idea of female breadwinners. Could men, jittery about their genetic viability, be trying to boost their survival chances by tapping into women's resources?

Ms. Hewlett does not buy it. She thinks that the 2005 American workplace is more macho than ever. "It's actually much more difficult now than ten years ago to have a career and raise a family," she told me. "The trend lines continue that highly educated women in many countries are increasingly dealing with this creeping non-choice and end up on this path of delaying finding a mate and delaying childbearing. Whether you're looking at Italy, Russia or the U.S., all of that is true."

Many women continue to fear that the more they accomplish, the more they may have to sacrifice. They worry that men still veer away from "challenging" women because of a male atavistic desire to be the superior force in a relationship.

"With men and women, it's always all about control issues, isn't it?" said a guy I know, talking about his bitter divorce.

Or, as my friend Craig Bierko puts it, "Deep down, beneath the bluster and machismo, men are simply afraid to say that what they're truly looking for in a woman is an intelligent, confident and dependable partner in life whom they can devote themselves to unconditionally until she's forty."

As Cher said when she slapped Nicolas Cage in *Moonstruck*: Snap out of it, guys.

Male logic on dating down is bollixed up: Women who seem in awe of you in the beginning won't stay in awe once they get to know you. Women who don't have demanding jobs are not less demanding in relationships; indeed, they may be more demanding. They're saving up all that competitive energy and criticism for when their guys get home at night.

A man I know complains that women are like a force field; the more you let them in, the more they want to take over.

But men are a force field writ large. If they would only give up their silly desire for world dominance, the world would be a much finer place. Look at the Taliban. Look at the Vatican. Look at Dick Cheney. Now look at the bonobo.

Bonobos, or pygmy chimpanzees, live in the equatorial rain forests of the Congo and have an extraordinarily happy existence.

And why? Because in bonobo society, the females are dominant. Just light dominance, so that it is more like a co-dominance, or equality between the sexes.

"They are less obsessed with power and status than their chimpanzee cousins, and more consumed with Eros," the *Times*'s brilliant biology writer Natalie Angier has written. "Bonobos use sex to appease, to bond, to make up after a fight, to ease tensions, to cement alliances. . . . Humans generally wait until after a nice meal to make love; bonobos do it beforehand."

She admires the easy sisterhood among the bonobo females and says the breed "is a sexual Olympian—males, females, old, callow, no matter—it's sex, grope, hump, genito-genital rub-a-dub-dubbing all the day long. Most of this sex has nothing to do with reproduction. It serves as the code of ethics by which bonobos survive group living. It is their therapy, their social lubricant and post-quarrel salve, a way of expressing feelings, and it's often quick to the point of perfunctory."

The males were happy to give up a little dominance once they realized the deal they were being offered: All those aggressive female primates, after a busy day of dominating their jungle, were primed for sex, not for the withholding of it.

There's no battle of the sexes or baby bust in bonoboland.

The Washington Post reported in 2005 on a far less randy but still very content matriarchy of about three dozen women in Kenya, founded by homeless women who had been raped and, as a result, abandoned by their husbands.

Their all-female community flourished, with the women running a cultural center and camping site for tourists visiting the nearby Samburu National Reserve.

In a fit of pique, the men in their tribe started a rival village of men, and also tried to build a cultural and tourist center, but were not successful and soon unraveled.

The jealous men threatened matriarch Rebecca Lolosoli with violence. As Sebastian Lesinik, the chief of the raggedy male village, explained to the *Post*'s Emily Wax: "The man is the head. The lady is the neck. A man cannot take, let's call it advice, from his neck."

But once the men were utterly defeated, even having a hard time finding wives, Lesinik softened, conceding: "Maybe we can learn from our necks. Maybe just a little bit."

* * *

After self-interestedly urging guys not to be leery of high-achieving women in my *Times* column, I was swamped with six hundred e-males chastising me for generalizing about men, and chock-full of fantasies about the minxes of MENSA.

After all, as D. H. Lawrence wrote, sex is 90 percent in the head, the head being the most important sex organ.

(I also got one terrific e-mail from a bystander in this struggle of the sexes who signed her note: "Mary Ellen, a 60-year-old, one-kidneyed, unrepentantly aggressive, abrasive but cheerful horseback-riding lesbian who found true love in the Southwest.")

Some female readers also wrote that they were concerned that men might be engaged in a sinister *Stepford* plot to get rid of uppity alpha women by refusing to mate with them and pass down their genes to their daughters.

But mostly, men wanted to defend themselves against the charge that their fragile egos resist a challenge.

"For months," wrote Yeung-Seu Yoon of Toronto, "I have been sullenly wondering if there are any women out there who have I.Q.'s that actually exceed their body temperature. What I would do to meet a woman who treats her head as more than just a frilly decorative ornament!"

Kevin Johnson from Chicago wrote me: "A woman who has qualities that put me in awe is far more likely to make me think she is worth falling for."

Wright Salisbury drily spoke up "in praise of brainy women: Shortly after we were married, my wife tearfully confessed that her I.Q., at 178, was 45 points higher than mine, that she had been salutatorian of her college class and was a member of Phi Beta Kappa. I was shocked, but divorce was out of the question. It has been terrible to live with, but there have been compensations: 1) Our children are a lot smarter. 2) She remembers people's names, places we have visited, and learns foreign languages the way I catch colds. Men, don't fear that cute little genius you have your eye on."

I also got many e-mails scorching career women as materialistic, choosy and self-absorbed.

"They want to find somebody who is as much or MORE: good looking, socially skilled and well-off," wrote Mike "not Mormon" Dropkin of Sugarhouse, Utah. "What do successful men want? Typically, a good-looking woman who is kind."

Steven Greenfield agreed: "I find that most successful women have little respect for a man who does not out-earn them. I am all too frequently made to feel as though I am the sum total of my resume, which is embarrassingly slim in their eyes."

Anthony Santelli carped about career women in their late thirties: "Despite being older and less beautiful, they are none the wiser and as picky as ever. . . . The very men whom they had rejected are now happily married to women who are less picky. Worst of all, many of these men have gone on to have successful careers and now would meet these women's standards. But it's too late."

Summing up the whole gender bender nicely, Patrick Partridge from Fort Collins, Colorado, mused that "men instinctively know that career-focused women will not be as focused on them."

Ray Lewis admitted that while smart women could fascinate, "I do find them draining at times." He revealed that he ended a romance with one because "I was worried she wasn't going to look after me as much as I would her."

It's that old saw about one person in the romance being the lawn and one being the gardener who tends to the lawn. Men would rather be hosed than hosers, emotionally speaking.

Adam Rogers, who was unhappily married to two over-achievers and undernurturers, bitterly observed: "I certainly don't want my home life to reflect the sorry state of American corporate life, where everyone thinks that he/she is so damned smart, and where very few really do anything of any consequence for anybody. . . . The more of them that are childless the better!"

My pal Arthur Gelb, the Eugene O'Neill biographer and former cultural czar of the *Times*, whose wife is the accomplished Barbara Gelb, later e-mailed me: "There's no greater turn-on than to spar with a woman who can more than hold her own, never letting herself be bullied. The smarter, stronger and more unyielding the woman, the more delectable the conquest. In my twenties, I was often bemused by some of my intelligent, achieving male friends who tended to run away from that kind of woman. They seemed to fear they would have to be constantly on their toes, giving witty responses in an endless game of repartee.

"A good friend once confided that strong women made him feel inadequate. When I asked him why he seemed perfectly at ease in the company of smart, witty men, and why he thrived on their wisecracking banter over drinks in his newspaper haunts, he admitted he was stumped."

My good friend Paul Costello had the last word. He's the director of communications for Stanford Medical School and happily married to my extraordinary girlfriend Rita Beamish. "While men say they appreciate and applaud equality, the price that it extracts from them makes them run from its reality," he wrote. "Face it, men are basically lazy. It's in our DNA. The bottom line? Men don't want it all and women do."

* * *

But maybe we don't want it all anymore, either.

The modern history of women, after all, can be summed up in three sentences:

Women demand equality.

Girls just want to have fun.

Ladies long to loll about.

Forty years of striving have tuckered women out. When the Oxygen network started, in 2000, it was full of earnest Hillary Rodham–style shows on empowerment, but no one wanted to watch; women were too tired from all their other tasks for revved-up feminist TV. "You go, girl!" had downshifted to "You go lie down, girl."

Women preferred escapist fare like Lifetime for Women's "pussies in peril" movies, as they are known. They also love the hypnotic, formulaic *Law & Order* and its endless reruns and shows like the TNT drama *The Closer* with Kyra Sedgwick as a sexy L.A. deputy police chief; prone on your couch, you can watch all those beautiful, driven cop and lawyer babes with puny personal lives kick male butt.

"If I liked being called a bitch to my face," Sedgwick tells an insolent colleague, "I'd still be married."

Geraldine Laybourne, one of the founders of Oxygen, admitted to *New York Times* TV critic Alessandra Stanley that "when we started, we thought women really needed our help. Focus groups showed us that women are not that pathetic. They want to be entertained."

Oxygen switched to reruns of *Xena: Warrior Princess, Kate*

& Allie and *Cybill*, and the sitcom *Good Girls Don't*, about the sad, sordid sex lives of two young girls from Minnesota who share an apartment in L.A. But the network may have run too far in the other direction.

Noting that *Good Girls Don't* set a new low, Stanley wrote that the show marked the moment "when it became safe to be a stupid slut on television."

Hillary Clinton, Condi Rice, Martha Stewart, Nancy Grace and Oprah continue to be steely go-getters.

But many women are doing something that didn't show up in the feminist tarot cards: lying doggo, celebrating lady chic, indulging in the old-fashioned dress and languid behavior that predated hard-charging feminism.

In the late '80s, I wrote a work-advice column for *Mademoiselle*, giving twentysomethings the word about how to clamber up the corporate ladder. I answered such questions as: "How do you end an office affair?," "Is your boss's affair your business?," "How much of one's private life is it okay to tell at the office?" and "How do you combat the office snake?" (With reptilian resourcefulness.)

Only a decade or so later, many twentysomethings were already losing interest in scampering up the corporate ladder. *Cosmopolitan* chronicled "the New Housewife Wanna-bes"— girls who wanted to jump off the fast track and shimmy down the aisle.

After just a few months at her investment banking firm, Erica, twenty-three, had a new goal, she told the magazine: "Marry that cute associate two cubicles down and embark on a full-time stint as his hausfrau."

Cosmo quoted a survey by Youth Intelligence, a market research firm in New York, that found that 68 percent of three thousand married and single young women said "they'd ditch work if they could afford to." And a *Cosmo* poll of eight hundred women revealed the same startling statistic: two out of three respondents would rather "kick back *a casa* than climb the corporate ladder."

"So why has ordering sheets and stirring sauces taken on more allure than making vice president by age 30?" *Cosmo* wondered. "Probably because so few career women do land an awesome title quickly. Work is, well, work—it's just not as glam as we're led to believe."

As *Cosmo* editor Kate White told me in the summer of 2005: "Women now want more freedom. They don't want to report to someone and they might want to be a mommy. They don't want to be in the grind. Baby boomers made the grind seem unappealing."

Women who used to abhor the idea of the Mommy Track now were praying for it. If twentysomethings were so tired of working, think how fortysomethings were dragging.

Maybe women have not evolved to the point where they want to work as long as men. Or maybe they don't want to be Mini-Mes of men—company women on an institutional track. Perhaps they'd rather work for themselves than keep grasping for that elusive managing director title. Or it could be that they just value time spent with friends and family more than time spent on office warfare.

Five years ago, you would often hear high-powered women fantasize that they would love a Wife, somebody to do the shopping, cooking, and carpooling, so they could focus on work.

Now the fantasy is more retro: They just want to *be* that Wife.

Many women I know, who once disdained their mothers' lifestyles, no longer see those lives as tedious or indulgent. Now they look back with a tad of longing. Wouldn't it be pleasant to while away time playing bridge and tennis and lunching with girlfriends and eating shrimp cocktails and taking the kids up to the beach house all summer and chilling the cocktail shaker when hubby's on his way home?

As Kristin Davis's Charlotte memorably keened to her girlfriends after several frenetic years of man-hunting on *Sex and the City*: "I'm sorry, but I've been dating since I was fifteen, I'm exhausted. Where is he?" She theorized that women like firemen so much because they really want to be rescued.

Sarah Jessica Parker, as narrator, intoned: "There it was. The sentence independent single women in their thirties were never supposed to think, let alone speak."

Women no longer wanted to become the men they wanted to marry, as Gloria Steinem once proclaimed.

Lisa Belkin of *The New York Times* did a story in 2003 on the new generation of Starbucks moms who were rejecting the workplace: "See all those mothers drinking coffee and watching over toddlers at play? If you look past the Lycra gym clothes and the Internet-access cell phones, the scene could be the '50s, but for the fact that the coffee is more expensive and the mothers have M.B.A.'s.

"We've gotten so used to the sight that we've lost track of

the fact that this was not the way it was supposed to be. Women—specifically, educated professional women—were supposed to achieve like men. Once the barriers came down, once the playing field was leveled, they were supposed to march toward the future and take rightful ownership of the universe, or at the very least, ownership of their half. The women's movement was largely about grabbing a fair share of power—making equal money, standing at the helm in the macho realms of business and government and law. It was about running the world."

Belkin interviewed eight fellow Princeton grads in Atlanta who took off their power suits and decided they didn't want to conquer the world; they wanted to stay home and raise their kids and redefine the notion of work and success.

"Maternity provides an escape hatch that paternity does not," Sarah McArthur Amsbary told Belkin. "Having a baby provides a graceful and convenient exit."

Asked why women don't run the world, Amsbary replied: "In a way, we really do."

It's a slippery slope, though. One Los Angeles agent recently went to a play group, filled mostly with stay-at-home moms, where the hostess began: "Okay. Let's go around the room and say what our husbands do."

Even that totem of women's rights, the title "Ms.," has lost its meaning, now that "Mrs." wants to crow that she's Sadie, Sadie, married lady.

In a world where many women either get divorced or never get married, it is now a status symbol to snag a married name.

Ms. was supposed to neutralize the stature of women, so they weren't publicly defined by their marital status. But nowadays most young brides want to take their husbands' names and brag on the moniker Mrs., a brand that proclaims you belong to him. T-shirts with MRS. emblazoned in sequins or sparkly beads are popular wedding shower gifts. And customized T-shirts are popular that allow you to dream of being your boyfriend's Mrs., or the mate of a celebrity.

Kitson's, the trendy L.A. store, sells tees that that fantasize MRS. DEPP, MRS. PITT, MRS. TIMBERLAKE, MRS. CLOONEY, as well as "housewife cosmetic bags" for desperate housewives from Beverly Hills, South Beach or Malibu. In the midst of the Brad-Jen breakup, Kitson's also stocked a tee that Desperate House-wife Eva Longoria bought and wore, reading, BRAD, I'LL HAVE YOUR BABY. (I had to restrain myself from ordering two T-shirts, one that said, MRS. JON STEWART and one that said, I'M CHEATING ON JON STEWART WITH VINCE VAUGHN.)

Harvard economics professor Claudia Goldin did a study that found that 44 percent of women in the Harvard class of 1980 had kept their birth names, while in the class of '90 it was only 32 percent. In 1990, 23 percent of college educated women kept their own names after marriage, while a decade later the number had fallen to 17 percent.

Time reported that an informal poll in spring 2005 by the Knot, a wedding Web site, supported Goldin's research: 81 percent of respondents took their spouse's last name, up from 71 percent in 2000. Hyphenated surnames dropped from 21 percent to 8 percent.

"It's a return to romance, a desire to make marriage work," Professor Goldin told one interviewer, adding that young women might feel that by keeping their own name they were aligning themselves with tedious old-fashioned feminists, and this might be a turnoff to them.

The professor, who kept her name when she married in 1979, was inspired to do the study after her niece, a lawyer, changed her name. "She felt that her generation of women didn't have to do the same things mine did, because of what we had already achieved," Goldin told *Time*.

Many women now do not think of domestic life as a "comfortable concentration camp," as Betty Friedan wrote in *The Feminine Mystique*, where they are losing their identities and turning into "anonymous biological robots in a docile mass."

Now they want to be Mrs. Anonymous Biological Robot in a Docile Mass. They dream of being rescued, to flirt, to shop, to stay home and be taken care of. They shop for "Stepford Fashions," as *The New York Times* once called them—matching shoes and ladylike bags and the '50s-style satin, lace and chiffon party dresses featured in *InStyle* layouts.

In the 2004 *Maternal Desire: On Children, Love, and the Inner Life*, Daphne de Marneffe, a clinical psychologist and mother of three, argued that it is in staying home and taking care of children that an identity is forged, not forsaken.

This Friedanian inversion has created a pampered tribe of upper-middle-class moms—the ones who don't need that second income to survive—and an irritating genre of twenty-first-century literature that *The New Yorker*'s Elizabeth Kolbert dubbed "a problem of not having enough problems," fraught with earthshaking dilemmas like "Should I feel guilty if I leave my kid to go get a Brazilian bikini wax?" and "Do I wear a garter belt or not when my husband gets home?"

"Choosing between work and home is, in the end, a problem only for those who have a choice," Kolbert drily observed.

Reviewing Judith Warner's 2005 dissection of modern motherhood, *Perfect Madness*, *The New Republic*'s Ruth Franklin wrote: "The women of *The Feminine Mystique* are consumed by primary doubts about their own personhood: 'I want status, I want self-respect. I want people to think that what I'm doing is important.' The doubts that consume Warner's mothers are less momentous. 'First, there was the whole debate about whether to have the whole class or just a few friends to a birthday party,' one says. 'Then there was the whole debate about whether to do the party at home or whether to go someplace that does package deals. If we stayed at home, would we have the magician, the clown, the musician, the Moon Bounce? . . . I felt great angst about whether this measured up.'

"It is more than a gulf of forty years that separates the existential crisis from the Moon Bounce," Franklin writes. "This isn't a crisis of parenting. It's a crisis of consumerism."

Writing in *The New Yorker* in 2004, Caitlin Flanagan sardonically observed: "To call these tensions a preoccupation among the mothers I know would be to commit a grave act of understatement. Last year, I went to a fund-raiser for the Los Angeles nursery school that my twin sons attended. It was a dinner dance with an auction, and the signal items up for bid were chairs hand-painted by the members of each class, a project that had been laboriously created and supervised by an ex-ceedingly earnest and energetic at-home mother. She was at the podium, a little flustered and flush with pride about the fur-niture, the decorating of which she was describing in effusive terms. Leaning against a far column watching her, with drinks in their hands and sardonic half smiles on their faces, were two of my friends: a lawyer and a movie producer. I was propelled toward them the way I was once propelled toward the cool girls in high school. And I suddenly had the bona fides to join them: my writing had recently begun to be published. We looked at the woman—think of all she'd sacrificed to stay home with her children, think of the time she'd spent dipping our own children's hands in paint so that they could press their little prints on the miniature Adirondack chairs. 'Get a life,' one of us said, and we all laughed and drank some more. And then we turned our backs on the auction and talked about work."

So are we evolving backward or devolving?

After Jane Fonda, Hillary Clinton and Donna Hanover all had to deal with the public infidelities of their husbands Ted Turner, Bill Clinton and Rudy Giuliani, Nina Burleigh wrote in *The New York Observer* that it was depressing to see those women trying to perk up careers or patch up dignity after their men took up "with younger or more pliant females."

"Feminism wasn't supposed to mean brokenhearted women in middle age," Burleigh said. Of Jane, Hillary and Donna, she asked: "Couldn't they conduct themselves with a little more spite and spirit?"

I'd had that same feeling reading the autobiographies of feminist icons Fonda and Katharine Hepburn.

I used to love Tracy/Hepburn movies. Now I find it a little hard to watch them. Here was the lithe athletic actress who presaged a bracing world where women could be the equals of men—brainy and snappy, yet sexy and stylish—admitting what a doormat she became in her romanticized romance with "Spence."

"We did what he liked," Hepburn wrote in *Me*. "We lived a life which he liked. I struggled to change all the qualities which I felt he didn't like. Some of them which I thought were my best he found irksome. I removed them, squelched them as far as I was able."

Fonda wrote that her men were attracted to her strong, independent spirit, but then tried to break it. She was reduced to procuring other women so that Roger Vadim could have threesomes with her, and she ended up deserting her movie career and slavishly staying by Ted Turner's side, because he couldn't stand to be left alone or he would cheat on her. He even went into a rage when she wanted to visit her daughter, Vanessa Vadim, who was having a baby.

When she invited Vanessa, a documentary filmmaker, to help her put together a short video of her life "to discover its different themes," Vanessa suggested drily, "Why don't you just get a chameleon and let it crawl across the screen?" Jane pondered: "Maybe I simply become whatever the man I am with wants me to be: 'sex kitten,' 'controversial activist,' 'ladylike wife on the arm of corporate mogul.' . . . Was I just a chameleon, and if so, how was it that a seemingly strong woman could so thoroughly and repeatedly lose herself? Or had I really lost myself?"

It's true that women have made some historic miscalculations.

We started out totally dependent on men. Then we thought we could be totally independent from men by imitating them. Dressing like them, in navy blue suits and little floppy ties and sensible shoes. Jousting for that big office and those stressful jobs.

But once we got far enough along to see that we could achieve male status and power, we recoiled at the idea of doing it on male terms. Why be rats on a treadmill, butting heads constantly, drinking too much, having heart attacks and falling into affairs with office playthings?

"We can't replicate men—and who wants to?" asks Natalie Angier.

In the old days, right up through Hillary Rodham, the best route to status and children was through a powerful husband. "But now, because men often don't stick around, the husband route no longer looks as good to women," Angier says.

You can make the case that women are not going backward. We're moving ahead, at home and at work—and in more elastic combinations of the two. We're just moving in less predictable and programmatic ways. We can be rescued or choose not to be. We can be alpha moms or beta career girls.

Women, Angier says, are in a new phase. "Female primates have two goals," she explains. "They want control over their reproduction and access to resources." She says that someday women in their twenties will be freed from a biological deadline by routinely freezing eggs for use at any time.

In July 2005, doctors at New York University announced that they had developed a technique for successfully freezing unfertilized eggs—and had the baby to prove it. There were also news reports that more and more healthy young women are sticking a basketful of eggs in the fridge. The number of clinics offering egg banking will double in 2005.

"This trend has the potential to rewrite the script for young adulthood, persuading women to further defer marriage and motherhood," *The Los Angeles Times* reported. "Female fertility peaks at age 27 and by age 40, the chance of getting pregnant is less than 10 percent. By freezing their eggs, women can be relatively free of their biological clock's stressful drumbeat."

Unfortunately, male primates have the same two goals as female primates: they want access to resources and control over female reproduction, too. We have a conflict of gender interest, so it turns out to be counterproductive for women to imitate men.

Freud believed that men had something that women wanted. But it wasn't what he thought.

Women don't want to be men—except in the way men often grow more attractive and powerful as they age and are so easily able to start fresh, in their fifties and sixties and even older, with younger women.

And we'd like to be like men in the way they can look good in many different ways, whereas women are expected to endlessly replicate themselves at twenty-five, à la Goldie Hawn and Heather Locklear, until they look like frozen reproductions of themselves.

* * *

$\mathcal{A}$s filtered through Hollywood's prism, the iconic woman of the '70s was Jill Clayburgh's character in *An Unmarried Woman*, a housewife who is left by her cheating husband, throws up and then picks herself up, gets a job in an art gallery, has zipless sex in SoHo and finds a cute boyfriend (a sweet, scruffy painter played by Alan Bates). Then, because she is liberated, she rejects an offer from Bates to come spend the summer with him in Vermont while he paints, choosing to concentrate on herself instead.

In the '70s, single women spent Saturday nights watching Mary Tyler Moore "light up the world with her smile" as TV producer Mary Richards. At the start of each show, she threw her beret up in the air to signal she could be independent, starting a new life and career in another city, after dumping her hemming-and-hawing fiancé.

Flash forward to the postfeminist fictional heroines, dithery singletons and desperate housewives. Bridget Jones, Carrie Bradshaw, Ally McBeal and the scheming, catfighting babes of Wisteria Lane—shouldn't it be called Hysteria Lane?—returned to the Valley of the Dolls. A gaggle of neurotic, insecure, man-crazy women indulging, variously, in too many cocktails, cigarettes, pills, shoes, kinky sex and bad affairs.

Bridget, Carrie and Ally were simply updated versions of those '50s Rona Jaffe and '60s Jacqueline Susann graduates of Wellesley and Vassar who wore gloves and hats and got low-level jobs in publishing until they could hook a man in a gray flannel suit and get that white picket fence.

The New York Times interviewed Jaffe in the summer of 2005 on the occasion of the reissuing of her 1958 novel, *The Best of Everything*, chronicling the steamy and tortured lives of five young working women in New York. She called her book "*Sex and the City* without the vibrators . . . a very universal story about the difference between what one wants and what one gets."

Ally was hugely popular with young single women—they formed viewing parties to watch the show—but David Kelley's creation, a Harvard-trained Boston lawyer played by the Modiglianiesque Calista Flockhart was cuffed around for being a bad feminist icon, a male fantasy of a liberated woman. With skirts that stopped just below the waist, the screwball litigator treated her profession as a ladder for her social life.

A 1998 *Time* cover story suggested that Ally, who began seeing visions of a dancing baby during depositions, represented a repeal of classical feminism, the degenerate conclusion of a line begun by Susan B. Anthony and achieving its apotheosis in Friedan and Steinem.

For sexy better and fluttery worse, Ally may have represented a necessary course correction in the trajectory of women.

When I first started in journalism in the mid-'70s, it was a perilous time to be a girl. You were supposed to look and behave as much like a man as possible. John Malloy's dress-for-success navy blue suits and little ties were in vogue. Any display of "female behavior"—moody, high-strung, weepy, cutesy—was frowned on, as was chatter about boyfriends or babies or clothes.

Once, at my newspaper, a cub reporter named Susan fell

into disfavor for spending too much time jabbering about shoe shopping.

As social satire, it was progress of a sort to watch Ally stand on her desk and try on jeans so her co-workers could help her decide if they were snug enough for a date.

The deeper point, when Ally admitted her fears that she'd never find a guy to rub her feet at night, was right: It was okay to admit you needed men, that you cared as much about your personal life as your work life, that men and women are, as Benjamin Franklin said, two halves of a scissors.

Women have always had a healthier attitude about the relative importance of work and personal life. In the early stages of feminism, that got obscured by the false assumption that women would be able to—and want to—replicate the male experience in the workplace in every way and do without men. "Women need men the way a fish needs a bicycle," Gloria Steinem famously said.

Ally's philosophy was really no different than that of Margo Channing in Joseph Mankiewicz's 1950 classic, *All About Eve*.

"Funny business, a woman's career," mused Bette Davis, playing the mordantly wise actress. "The things you drop on your way up the ladder so you can move faster, you forget you'll need them again when you get back to being a woman. It's one career all females have in common, whether we like it or not. Sooner or later, we've got to work at it, no matter how many other careers we've had or wanted. And in the last analysis, nothing's any good unless you can look up just before dinner or turn around in bed and there he is. Without that, you're not a woman. You're something with a French provincial office or a book full of clippings."

Ally's critics missed the point that what was cutting edge about the show was not Ally but the unisex bathroom, where all the male lawyers acted out their neuroses.

There is still the occasional business section article advising women to learn to play golf to network better. But basically, the idea that women should mimic men is now dead. Now men mimic women.

Men were afraid that the women who invaded the workplace would run around the office acting as dizzy and manipulative as Lucy and Ethel. But while women were suppressing their feminine wiles, guys were usurping those wiles. Men soon began turning traditional female modes of behavior into macho strategies to get ahead. While women were misguidedly imitating men, men were poaching the competitive tactics that women had honed at home through the centuries.

Now that it is smart office politics to share tender feelings, I see male colleagues sulking and throwing hissy fits to get their way. Now that it is smart office politics to be a sensitive family man, I see guys insisting on taking off more time and leaving early to be with their families. Now that men are supposed to bond with each other over more than sports, I see guys openly discussing their messy love lives at the office. Now that it is chic for men to confess their vulnerabilities, I see guys deciding where to sit in the office according to whether the light is sufficient to prevent seasonal affective disorder.

At *New York Times* management conferences, editors bond

by learning to cook gourmet meals like chicken stuffed with cheese, express togetherness by learning to sing "Happy Birthday" with real emotion and the "Ode to Joy" from Beethoven's Ninth Symphony in German under the supervision of a combination orchestra conductor/self-help specialist.

Any minute I'm afraid guys might start asking me for Midol. And yes, they talk about shopping. Even for shoes.

And it's not merely the office that has been feminized.

I feel a certain undeniable pride that women have taken control of the two preeminent male preserves of America—politics and sports—and ruined them.

Our two great arenas of aggressive, masculine warfare—presidential campaigns and the Olympics—have been Oprahized, turned into mawkish soap operas and personal sagas of redemption instead of mere muscular, gladiatorial contests.

It has to count as progress in our gender games.

Alan Dundes, the late folklorist and professor of anthropology at Berkeley, wrote in his essay "From Game to War" that all contests and sports are based on one theme that "involves an all-male preserve in which one male demonstrates his virility, his masculinity, at the expense of a male opponent. One proves one's maleness by feminizing one's opponent. . . . No male wants to be considered a 'sissy' (from 'sister'). Thus males must aggressively seek to parry any such threatened thrusts."

Now to win, men have to feminize themselves. Match, set.

· Two ·

WHY PANDORA'S BOX IS NO TENDER TRAP

T here is a growing school of thought among those who study the American political landscape that men may be biologically unsuited to hold political office and leadership positions.

In the past, it was felt that manly discourse worked in the service of "ambition, business and power," as Hugh Blair, an eighteenth-century theorist, put it. It was, unlike the feminine chatter in the parlor, thought to be impersonal, unemotional, forthright and reasonable.

For centuries, it was widely believed that women's physical makeup made them emotionally unfit to be leaders.

Aristotle observed that women's minds should be kept free from exertion because "children evidently draw on the mother who carries them in the womb, just as plants draw on the soil." Darwin said that while the female spent her energy forming her ova, the male spent "much force in fierce contests with rivals, in wandering about in search of the female, in exerting his voice."

Even as late as 1970, Dr. Edgar F. Berman, Hubert Humphrey's personal physician and an official on a national policy-making committee of the Democratic Party, declared that his "scientific position" was that "women are different physically, physiologically and psychically."

"If doctors do not know that there is such a thing as premenstrual tension," he huffed, "they'd better go back to medical school."

Dr. Berman learned his lesson. When his words caused a furor among women and he was forced to resign, he ruefully observed: "Pandora's box is no tender trap."

But at long last, the tables have turned. Now it is male temperament and illogic that are causing alarm—making us wonder if the sensitive little dears are just too emotional and unstable to be left in charge running the country and the globe.

Politics, after all, is rife with male diva fits, mud wrestling, gossipmongering, feline backbiting, teary confessions and grooming obsessions. (And this happens all over the world; look at *les luttes de chats* among European leaders over who would have the best plumbers in the European Union and who would have the best restaurants for the 2012 Olympic site.)

Men are engaging in shrewish, scolding, clawing, vengeful, sneaky, vain behavior that is anything but reasonable and impersonal. Women are affected by lunar tides only once a month; men have raging hormones every day.

Running for president and running the Democratic Party, Howard Dean has had many outbursts that, if he were a woman, would certainly be labeled hysteria (from the Greek for womb).

In his presidential campaign, Al Gore seemed to spend more time worrying about earth tones in his wardrobe than Earth in the Balance. John Kerry fiddled with cosmetic facial fillers and acted as submissive as a French maid with President Bush.

Once men dismissed women for having loose lips that could sink ships. But what a devious little gossip Karl Rove turned out to be, spilling the beans about undercover CIA agent Valerie Plame. Liz Smith dubbed Rove the "foremost fishwife" and Samantha Bee noted on *The Daily Show* that Rove and Cheney chief of staff Scooter Libby were like Chatty Kathy sorority girls on a *Bye Bye Birdie* party line.

The Bush administration's invasion and occupation of Iraq was anything but impersonal. W. was spurred in part by vengeance against Saddam for trying, as he said, "to kill my daddy." And he and Dick Cheney sold it to the American public with feverish, irrational warnings over nonexistent weapons and Al Qaeda–Saddam links.

Male critics accused Anita Hill and Monica Lewinsky of having erotomania—fantasizing that a man is in love with you. But isn't empire-mania—fantasizing that occupying a country will be a cakewalk—a more dangerous malady?

Chris Rock says that men lie about small things—"I'm out

with the guys"—and women lie about big things—"It's your baby."

But the Bushies were doing that female big-lie thing of "it's your funeral if that maniac makes a mushroom cloud."

The Iraq attack sparked world-class catfights between Colin Powell and Dick Cheney, and Powell and Rummy.

The Pentagon played the carnivorous tiger batting aside the State Department's timid kitten, forcing Colin Powell to provide a diplomatic fig leaf to predetermined war plans, snatching away State's prerogatives and junking State's exhaustive postwar planning even though the scatterbrained neocons had no coherent occupation plans of their own.

Male catfights, it turns out, go pretty much like female ones. As Uma Thurman told John Travolta in *Pulp Fiction*, when tough-guy scamps get together, they're worse than a sewing circle.

The Hollywood fur flew the June night in 2005 when Lindsay Lohan barred Jessica Simpson from a post–MTV awards party at the Standard Hotel on the Sunset Strip; just so, the Washington fur flew when Rummy had a diplomatic party celebrating the fall of Baghdad for "the coalition of the willing" at his Embassy Row home and didn't bother to invite— or even inform—the top diplomat, Colin Powell.

And what about Rummy's hot flashes over "Old Europe"? His diva fits, once refusing to shake hands with the German foreign minister who didn't support the Iraq war, outdiva-ed J.Lo.

Cheney's hormonal mood swings are so terrifying, all you can do is duck as the guy goes to his secure underground lair to plot which countries he wants to preemptively invade next.

One month when he was feeling sulky and shrewish, he threw out half a century of American foreign policy in one sitting. And all those menopausal memory lapses, when the vice president would totally forget—even after evidence contradicting him came out—that Iraq had nothing to do with 9/11 or Al Qaeda?

People tend to think Cheney is calm and reasonable, because of his monotone baritone, but he has hissy fits all the time. Talking to Sean Hannity on Fox News about Democratic chairman Howard Dean, the vice president bitchily purred: "Maybe his mother loved him, but I've never met anybody who does."

The man who got to run Halliburton with the help of friends and then anointed himself vice president meowed that Dean had "never won anything as best I can tell." (Dean was elected governor of Vermont five times.)

And did you see *Fahrenheit 9/11*? That tape of Paul Wolfowitz preparing for a TV interview by spitting on his comb and then letting an aide spit as well, so he could slick back his hair?

No wonder Wolfie could never remember how many American kids died in Iraq, and got it completely backward about how Iraqi oil revenues would pay for reconstruction there. No wonder he and Rummy left our troops so stretched and vulnerable that they were reduced to using cardboard cutouts to stand sentry, and to jury-rigging Humvees that had not been properly armored, resulting in so many lost limbs and lives and a complete security mess in Iraq today.

Wolfie was just too caught up in his feline grooming practices to count straight.

They thought a woman couldn't be president because she couldn't handle the military. But the Bush men actually broke the military.

And our president. Have you noticed that, like a *Cosmo* girl, he's always trying to wear clothes that are over-the-top sexy to work? Tight hottie jeans at the ranch, or that one memorable day he showed up on the aircraft carrier strutting in that *Top Gun* flight suit with the ejection harness between his legs that drove all the Republican pundettes wild?

The teenage terrors in *Mean Girls* had nothing on Tom DeLay, Richard Perle, Doug Feith and the inimitable John Bolton, the stapler-throwing, staff-abusing Naomi Campbell of the Bush team who always appears to be frothing at the mustache.

The Mean Girls had arbitrary rules like: On Wednesdays, you have to wear pink. On Fridays, only jeans or track pants.

The Mean Guys of the Republican Party had much worse rip-out-their-eyeballs rules: If you didn't gin up evidence against their foes every day of the week, you were out. The GOP vixens have been so ruthless about making up their own draconian rules as they go along, ripping rivals and excluding and punishing independent thinkers—and even using government spy satellites to gather intelligence on them—poor Lindsay Lohan never could have survived.

Male pols, who once deemed women unsuitable for the Oval Office because they might cry, now can't turn off the faucet.

First, in June 2005, Republican senator George Voinovich grew teary on several subjects as he talked to reporters, including the Bolton nomination to the U.N. "My emotions are a little bit closer to the surface than maybe they should be," he wept.

Shortly after that, Democratic senator Dick Durbin went to the Senate floor to offer a tearful apology for his gaffe comparing the abuses at Guantánamo Bay to techniques used by the Nazis, the Soviets and the Khmer Rouge.

And what about those emo Bush boys? W. came close to breaking down at the end of his national address televised from Fort Bragg in June 2005 urging Americans to continue supporting the sinkhole he has created in Iraq that has already claimed more than 1,800 American lives, cost $200 billion and was eating up another $1 billion every week.

Poppy and Jeb Bush also mist up without embarrassment. Unlike Greenwich Granite matriarch Barbara Bush and cool-as-ice Laura, the Bush men feel free to show their feminine side.

W. even shared with Al Roker that, like Paris Hilton, he talks baby talk to his fur muff of a dog, Barney.

And think about money for a minute. Harvard president Lawrence Summers said women were not as good at math. And it was long thought that women could handle the budget at home but not for the nation.

So how on earth did we get such flibbertigibbet spendthrifts in charge of the federal budget?

My finances are a mess, but at least I'm only dunned for a few thousand by American Express. W. took over with a $100 billion–plus surplus from Bill Clinton, and now the Congressional Budget Office is forecasting a $1.3 trillion deficit over the next decade, plus the billions for Katrina cleanup. America has a huge trade deficit, and foreign countries like the Japanese, Chinese and Saudis own trillions of our debt. What if the Saudis decide to foreclose on us? Burkas for everyone?

In 1973, when the White House was trying to figure out the Deep Throat mystery and shut down the leaks to Woodward and Bernstein at *The Washington Post*, FBI director L. Patrick Gray told President Nixon that a lot of the gun-toting macho guys in the FBI were "like little old ladies in tennis shoes. They've got some of the most vicious vendettas going on."

Nothing has changed. As far as I can see, the efforts of the male-dominated preserves of the FBI and CIA to play nice and cooperate have been no more successful since 9/11 than before, and no more successful with the Homeland Security office in place than before and no more successful with the new intelligence czar in place than before. The more turf you create in Washington, the more men will claw each other's eyes out— no matter what color alert we're wearing this fall.

Women are alleged to be the technologically backward sex, yet the FBI has spent over a decade struggling—and failing— to get a computer system that can link the words "flight" and "schools." Little girls can Google, why not G-men?

Hopefully, the semantic stereotypes will begin to change at long last. Maybe now women will be decisive and men will be intransigent; women will be forceful and men will be shrill;

women will engage in the free flow of information and men will gossip. Women will be tough and rigorous and men will be harpies, harridans, magpies and termagants. Women will have nuclear showdowns, and gunfights at the O.K. Corral, act as gladiators and prizefighters, and engage in Maverick-and-Goose dogfights. And men will have catfights.

We desperately need leaders to run for office who are not so flighty, spendthrift and emotionally labile, and who are not such ninnies with our money. We need true warriors with real testosterone—or at least testosterone patches.

We need more manly candidates like . . . Hillary and Condi.

Just think: these two women have similar nicknames. Hillary is known as "the Warrior" by her staff and Condi is known as "the Warrior Princess."

Both can be steely by day and shimmer at night in their Oscar de la Renta gowns. Condi even set a new standard for dominatrix diplomacy when she reviewed American troops in Wiesbaden wearing a long black *Matrix* jacket and black leather stiletto boots. "It was cold out there," she told me afterward, with a sly smile.

As they said of Kathleen Turner's flinty babe in *Body Heat*, Hillary and Condi share a special talent: They are relentless.

· Three ·

WHIPPING THE PANTS OFF THE WOMEN WHO WEAR THEM

t was December of 1995.

I'd covered the Clinton White House with him. I'd even been on overseas trips with him. He seemed funny and charming and bright, but I couldn't shake this weird feeling that something was off. My suspicions were overpowering. I had to find out the truth.

I asked him for a face-to-face in the White House press briefing room one morning. We sat amid a sea of empty chairs below the podium, and I looked into the perfectly green eyes of the perfectly elegant and eternally tanned NBC correspondent.

"Are you an android?" I asked Brian Williams.

He was surprised, but recovered quickly. "Not that I'm aware of," he said, in a perfect android response delivered in his perfectly enunciated baritone. "I can deny the existence of a factory in the American Midwest that puts out people like me."

Of course, he might have been programmed to fend off this kind of query with deadpan humor.

At thirty-six, Brian was already the hair apparent to Tom Brokaw, a man hailed by Jay Leno as "NBC's stud muffin." He looked exactly like the love child of Brokaw and Peter Jennings. I was struck by this remarkable bit of morphing the first time I saw him manning the NBC anchor desk on a Saturday night.

Then I tuned in to CBS on Sunday night and saw the young man that network was grooming as an anchor, John Roberts. He looked exactly like Dan Rather, minus that mesmerizing don't-take-your-eyes-off-me-'cause-I-might-crack aura.

But I really began to get those *Invasion of the Body Snatchers* chills when I realized that the substitute anchor on *Entertainment Tonight*, Bob Goen, was a dead ringer for square-jawed, white-toothed John Tesh. Definitely a pod person.

I mean, weren't we supposed to have TV news anchors who looked more like America as we hit the millennium?

Instead of NBC's aggressive State Department reporter, Andrea Mitchell, or CNN's topflight, unglamorous, bespectacled Pentagon reporter, Barbara Starr, we were overrun with sleek male anchor clones.

I got a copy of Goen's official biography, which included his astrological sign (Sagittarius) and shoe size (9½). His personal life philosophy: Never have seconds of three-bean salad before interviewing Janet Jackson.

That could not have been the résumé of a real person.

John Roberts, the former co-host of *Canada A.M.*, laughed off the accusation that he was a yuppie replicant of Dan Rather. "I don't think they're casting by looks," he told me. Did he think there was any chance I would buy that? He persisted: "I think they're casting serious, type A, aggressive personalities."

Brian was low key on the road trips we went on with President Clinton—always willing to pick up a bar tab for ten—and courteous to fans. When they couldn't quite remember his name, he'd helpfully prod, "Oprah Winfrey."

He claims to have gone to Catholic University in Washington, where I went, but had anyone actually ever seen him on campus? He did, however, make a far better case for being human than Roberts.

"My nose is crooked from a high school football accident, so I've always used that to refute the android theory," he said. "I'm losing my hair. I have to do miles on the treadmill to keep my weight from ballooning to three hundred pounds. And I spend Sundays, my day off, the way most Americans do, as an unshaven slug on the floor of the den, watching football and playing with my kids."

Howard Stringer, the former CBS president, vainly tried to fight against clones on TV. "In the old days, the Collingwoods and Sevareids were recruited from radio," he said. "Cronkite was a wire-service reporter. It didn't matter what they looked like. But that pool is drying up. Everyone's now got it glued in their minds that an anchorman or -woman must look like a Greek demigod."

Couldn't he or somebody else just send a memo and unglue it?

Searching for idiosyncrasy, he called me for a lunch to discuss whether I would want to work as a political reporter on TV. "I'm tired of these gorgeous cookie cutter types," he said, which I took as a dubious compliment. I told him I couldn't be on TV because I talked like a Valley Girl. Stringer, an extremely charming Welshman, demurred. But later in the conversation, after I'd uttered the words "you know" and "like" about a hundred times, he asked me, "So, what part of California are you from?"

Deflated, I explained that I was "like, from D.C., you know?"

Stringer did not succeed in making TV look less beautifully homogenized, and eventually he moved on to be the chief of Sony, where his responsibilities include the movie division, home of a lot of beautifully homogenized actors and actresses.

Joe Angotti, a former NBC vice president and retired broadcast chair of the Medill School of Journalism, reassured me that we were not suddenly being invaded by anchor clones from outer space.

"Cloning is a proud television tradition," he said. "Successful entertainment formats are almost always cloned. Seinfeld's roots go all the way back to Danny Thomas. Mary Tyler Moore begat *Murphy Brown* and *Friends.* In the minds of television executives, newscasts are the same as sitcoms. So Dan Rather got the same considerations as *Beavis and Butt-head.*"

I was working up to a good diversity fit when John Tesh, who would move on to being some sort of a musician, told me that even he was tired of "vanilla" and wished the networks would get some "really wild-looking people to do the news—like Howard Stern."

That stopped me. Maybe those soothing, sonorous replicants weren't so bad after all.

· · ·

Nine years later came the End of an Era. A momentous change.

On the evening of December 2, 2004, on NBC, one tall and handsome white male anchor with bespoke clothes replaced another tall and handsome white male anchor with bespoke clothes.

Even Tom Brokaw was a little surprised at this *plus ça change* anticlimax. "I honestly thought, eight or nine years ago, that when we left," he said, referring to himself, Peter and Dan, "that it would be the end of white male anchor time."

Nah. White males are hard to dislodge. Indeed, they're ascendant in Red State America.

As my mom said, discussing her belief that Martha Stewart had been railroaded by jealous guys, "If men could figure out how to have babies, they'd get rid of us altogether."

The networks don't even give lip service to looking for women and blacks for the job of anchor—they just put prettyboy clones in the pipeline.

"I think we're still stuck in a society that looks at white males as authority figures," Brokaw conceded.

Bill Carter, the chief TV reporter at *The New York Times*, agreed: "Katie Couric may be a much bigger star and even more experienced than Brian Williams. But when the next 9/11 happens, it'll be Brian, not Katie, in the central role. The attitude still seems to be, 'We want a daddy in that chair.'

"You'll only know that a woman has really achieved parity with the anchor dudes when they are the centerpiece of a network's coverage during a national crisis."

Roger Ailes, the sly Fox News chief, said he teases Williams about having too many shirts, but thinks he's perfect because "he has that Tom Brokaw look of somebody every mother wants her daughter to marry."

And then there's biology. Asked why there couldn't be an anchorette as we enter 2005, Brokaw, the father of three accomplished daughters and the husband of one strong, cool wife, Meredith, replied: "You know, honestly, what happens is career interruptus by childbirth and a couple of other things. It's unfair to women that they have to juggle all this stuff, but it plays some role, I think."

I don't get it, really. It seems like sitting in a chair behind a big desk for a half hour a day and reading the news, with loads of staff support, would be the perfect job for a glowing pregnant woman. Especially, given that the evening news nowadays is often about such airy matters as diet, dermatology, plastic surgery and whether some college girls on a championship lacrosse team meeting with the president should have worn flip-flops to the White House.

At CBS, the cozy Bob Schieffer filled in when Rather limped away, leaving Rather look-alike John Roberts vying with Rather sound-alike Scott Pelley to be the permanent anchor.

At NBC, Conan O'Brien is signed up to succeed Leno in

2009, and CBS executives only considered four guys—three of them white—to replace Craig Kilborn on *The Late Late Show*. They replaced one tall, white, nice-looking Craig with another tall, white, nice-looking Craig—albeit a far more charming and appealing one.

Even if I felt like raising a ruckus about Boys Nation, who would care? Feminism lasted for a nanosecond, but the backlash has lasted forty years.

We are in the era of vamping, self-doubting *Desperate Housewives*, not the strong, cutting *Murphy Brown*. It's the season of prim, stay-in-the-background First Lady Laura Bush, not assertive two-for-the-price-of-one First Lady Hillary. Where would you even lodge a feminist protest these days?

"You ought to call the Lifetime network, or, as we say, the 'Men Are No Damn Good Network,' and protest it," Ailes drolly suggested.

I know that women have surpassed men, in many respects, by embracing their femininity and frivolity. Katie Couric and Diane Sawyer, who mix news with dish, cooking and fashion in the morning, are the real breadwinners of their news divisions, generating more ratings and revenue than the replicant men of the night.

Yet, as Ailes says, "network anchoring is still Mount Olympus."

When the sad news came that the dashing Peter Jennings had lung cancer, which would claim his life, Elizabeth Vargas was one of the two temp fill-ins. But most of the talk about permanent replacement centered on the other temp, Charlie Gibson, the one who was considered to have more heft, even though he could often be found doing cooking and gardening segments at breakfast time and light features like the one about the gorilla named Coco who had a nipple fetish and liked to see his female caretakers with their shirts off. Or, if Gibson was too valuable to ABC's effort to try to topple Katie Couric, they could turn to generically handsome young anchor replicant Bob Woodruff.

Even though Vargas's ratings were only slightly lower than Gibson's, ABC officials hustled her out of the anchor chair and left Gibson in charge when terrorists attacked twice in London in July 2005.

I asked a top executive in charge of ABC whether Vargas had a chance, and he said, certainly. But as soon as it was out of his mouth, he began to worry about it.

"I know this is going to sound really sexist, but if there were another 9/11, I'm not sure if she has the gravitas to hold that anchor chair for ten hours in a national crisis," he conceded. "Maybe it's not even sex. Maybe it's age. I just think we'd need someone with a little gray in their hair."

I point out that Brian Williams is only forty-five.

"He's not fifty?" the executive asks. "But doesn't he have some gray?"

If they're waiting for women to show their gray, they'll never get a woman anchor.

"Maybe," he mused, "we could let Elizabeth do it Monday through Friday and then someone else could do it if there was a crisis."

So in other words, a woman can be the network news anchor as long as news doesn't break out?

I checked around for feminist outrage, but couldn't find

any. The institution had actually become a dinosaur in the time networks were stewing about whether a woman could handle it.

My girlfriends felt that if the evening news was an anachronism, why shouldn't the anchor be?

"Caring about having a woman in the showcase or figurehead role seems so eighties," one of my girlfriends said.

My friend Jane Mayer, a *New Yorker* writer, said she prefers to devote the "one little ounce of feminist annoyance" she has left for the excess of "young fluffs" on cable news—as opposed to substantial newswomen on CNN like Candy Crowley and Barbara Starr at the Pentagon, "who looks like she could hit those generals with a handbag if they didn't give her answers."

But she admits that she watched Brokaw partly because he was "eye candy," and declares women are at fault in this matter: "Women like to read books about men and go to movies about men. But men don't like to read books about women or go to movies about women. The only way this is going to change is if women refuse to watch men. And the problem is, women like watching men."

● ● ●

It's funny that the networks cling to the idea that Daddy has to give the news even as they admit people don't think Daddy Knows Best anymore.

Les Moonves of CBS said that with the end of the era of Dan, Tom, Peter and Ted, viewers would no longer be interested in "voice-of-God, single-anchor" formats.

But who knew they would prefer the voice of Frank? A ring-a-ding Sinatraesque "one for my baby and one more for the road" network voice?

In the free fall of TV news, ABC's attempt to create a successor for Ted Koppel's *Nightline* will go down as one of the most hilariously embarrassing moments.

One show tested was set in a nightclub with male and female hosts. The club had white tablecloths, candles, a jazz quintet, a live audience seated at little tables and—this is not a joke—faux fog.

We've gone from the fog of war to the fog of news.

The nightclub segments that were tested had Gen X hosts and guests and red-blue debates on Michael Jackson and the Olsen twins' "dumpster chic," along with "mad as hell" rants.

ABC decided not to go with the smoke machine. Still, Koppel—who vowed to leave *Nightline* before he was forced to cover "wet burka" contests—must be spinning in his country home.

In 2004, Rupert Murdoch echoed Moonves in giving the American Society of Newspaper Editors some bad news about young people in the age of the Internet, blogging and cable news: "They don't want to rely on the morning paper for their up-to-date information. They don't want to rely on a Godlike figure from above to tell them what's important. They certainly don't want news presented as gospel."

And at a Las Vegas meeting of affiliates, CBS News president Andrew Heyward said that when Schieffer moved on, the next anchor should "get off the pedestal and out from behind the big desk."

"The theme is team," Heyward said. (What's next? A revolving set with Howard Beale and Sybil the Soothsayer?)

It's interesting that media big shots are moving away from patriarchal, authoritarian voice-of-God figures, even as voice-of-God figures, such as the Catholic Church and elected officials, are building up their authoritarian patriarchies.

The white smoke in April 2005 signaled that the Vatican thought that what it needed to bring it into modernity was the oldest pontiff since the eighteenth century. (The only other job this pope would have been qualified for was *60 Minutes* anchor.) The new Holy Father was Joseph Ratzinger, a seventy-eight-year-old hidebound archconservative who ran the office that used to be called the Inquisition and who was a youthful Hitler Youth.

For American Catholics—especially women and Democratic pro-choice Catholic pols—the cafeteria has officially closed. Cardinal Ratzinger, nicknamed "God's Rottweiler" and "the Enforcer," approved of denying Communion rights to John Kerry, Tom Daschle and other Catholic politicians in the 2004 election, and regards women who use birth control or men who use condoms, even to prevent the spread of AIDS, as sinners. By contrast, the Vatican did not get militant about the president going to war, even though it officially opposed the war.

President Bush has long acted as if he channeled the Lord's message. And Tom DeLay and Bill Frist pandered to the far-right-wing and evangelical Christians by implying that God spoke—and acted—through them as well.

Bush's subtler obeisance to the evangelical right is no longer enough. Puffed up with its electoral clout, the Christian right now wants politicians to genuflect openly.

The doctor who would be president is down on both knees. He was happy to exploit religion by giving a video speech on a Christian telecast that portrayed Democrats who blocked the president's judicial nominations as being "against people of faith."

And, of course, Democrats were apoplectic. "I cannot imagine that God, with everything He has—or She has—to worry about, is going to take the time to debate the filibuster in heaven," Senator Richard Durbin of Illinois said.

Hasn't anyone ever told him that God is in the details?

As they toy with less lofty multiple-anchor formats, the networks may be more open to women. But at the Vatican and in the Christian right's vanguard, we can be sure that the voice of God is not female.

* * *

I got my tween friend Emma Specter one of the latest pink change purses with the legend, BOYS ARE STUPID. THROW ROCKS AT THEM. "

In return, she asked me if I wanted to see her Glare.

She'll need that glare if she decides to be an alpha girl, or an RMG (Really Mean Girl).

Alpha girls ruthlessly rule junior high school, à la *Mean Girls* and *Heathers*, with cold shoulders, hot clothes and withering looks known as "deaths," jettisoning pathetic wannabes from their popular Queen Bee cliques. There have been growing efforts in schools to tame pushy alpha girls.

In *The New York Times Magazine* in 2002, Margaret Talbot wrote that the consensus that girls were less aggressive and more empathetic than boys began to change in the early '90s, when researchers found that girls outmaneuvered rivals with nastiness instead of fists.

There had been earlier signs that females were not necessarily the softer sex. Jane Goodall reported in the '60s that some female chimpanzees in Tanzania killed the offspring of their rivals to stay on top.

Marion Underwood, a psychology professor at the University of Texas, told Talbot: "Girls very much value intimacy, which makes them excellent friends and terrible enemies. They share so much information when they are friends that they never run out of ammunition if they turn on one another."

In *The Washington Post*, Laura Sessions Stepp delineated three groups: alphas, stars who define teen life and determine who will be excluded; betas, who worry that they're not in the in crowd; and gammas, student council president types who care more about what they do than how they appear.

But here is what puzzles me: If schools are overrun with alpha girls, why isn't America run by alpha women? Besides Oprah, it's hard to think of lots of alpha women who steadily soared up. Meg Whitman shines at eBay, Anne Mulcahy has made good progress turning around Xerox, Judy McGrath rocks at MTV, Indra Nooyi is carbonating Pepsi and two women—Sallie Krawcheck of Citibank and Zoe Cruz of Morgan Stanley—are rising very high in the Wall Street boys club.

But Hillary Clinton and Martha Stewart had to survive serious humiliation before they could start rappelling back up the cliff.

Carly Fiorina flamed out at Hewlett-Packard. Tina Brown

stumbled at *Talk* and on CNBC. Linda Wachner at War-
naco tumbled. After helping to develop *Desperate Housewives*
and *Lost*, Susan Lyne was forced out as president of ABC Entertainment by her backstabbing alpha-male colleagues.

Leona Helmsley and Lizzie Grubman, the Queen and
Princess of Mean, went to jail. Sotheby's Diana Brooks ended
up, like Stewart, under house arrest with an ankle bracelet, albeit in an Upper East Side town house.

Bernadine Healy got pushed from the Red Cross, Geraldine Laybourne lost altitude at Oxygen and Mattel's Jill Barad
got evicted from Barbie's dream house.

The closest thing we have to *Heathers*-style predatory face-
offs are Hillary Clinton versus Jeanine Pirro in the New York
Senate race and the alpha blondes of the morning, Katie and
Diane, who fight over who will get the Brad Pitt "get" instead
of the captain of the football team.

Maybe there would be more alpha women in the working
world if so many of them didn't marry alpha men and become
alpha moms, armed with alpha SUV's, which they drive in an
alpha, overcaffeinated manner down the freeway while clutch-
ing a venti skim latte. They're equipped with alpha muscles
from daily workouts and alpha tempers from getting in teach-
ers' faces to propel their precious alpha kids.

New York magazine chronicled "The Rise of the Alpha
Moms" in the summer of 2005. The story profiled Isabel Kall-
man, a Columbia graduate, former hyperaggressive vice president at Salomon Smith Barney, wife of a co-chairman of
Atlantic Records and mother of Alpha Boy, four-year-old Ry-
land. She has started a channel, out of her Upper East Side

apartment, broadcast on Comcast, called Alpha Mom TV. It's designed to show other hyperaggressive parents how to raise the perfect child.

"They'll be told what to do and what not to do and how to do it better," the magazine said, "discover how to boost their newborn's coordination and strength; learn massage that 'can help babies eat and sleep better'; hear 'research-based explanations of how children separate and attach'; and obtain guidance on 'raising overachievers.' "

And what if all this scary alpha parenting produces scary alpha children who refuse to do as they're told? In 2005, *The New York Times* had a story that detailed the proliferation of picky eaters among toddlers. Across the country, guilty and "battle-worn parents" were giving up after repeated attempts of begging the kids to eat fruit, veggies, milk and fiber and "surrendering, serving macaroni and cheese, chicken nuggets, grilled cheese, pasta and hot dogs rather than endure the mealtime stress of having their children eat well-balanced meals."

A study, underwritten by Gerber Products, found that among children aged nineteen to twenty-four months, one-third did not eat any fruit servings on a given day, and 18 percent did not eat any vegetables.

"By fifteen to eighteen months, the most common vegetable consumed is French fries," said Dr. Barbara Devaney, lead author of the study. Researchers advised begging kids ten times to eat something before giving up, noting that most parents gave up after five. I saw a woman at Starbucks give up after three fruitless shouts to her little son, who was engrossed in the baked goods section, "Aaron, it's yogurt or *nothing*."

If alpha moms are rolling, professional alpha women are stalling. Over and over, you see alpha males, who would otherwise be plotting to crush one another, forming alliances to crush the uppity alpha woman in their midst.

The corporate culture still reeks of testosterone. Could it be that alpha men do not want to share their alpha zone with alpha women? At Enron, executives ditched wives for secretaries, like the secretary dubbed simply "Va-Voom." As Marie Brenner wrote in *Vanity Fair*, one vice president openly displayed a "hottie board" to rank the sexual allure of Enron women. (It was poetic justice that it was women at Enron who fingered the guys for their excesses.)

Women will never match men in the corporate world until they learn the black art, à la Michael Ovitz at Disney and Peter Purcell at Morgan Stanley, of failing at a job and still walking off with a $110 million–plus bag of cash to soothe their wounded egos. (Carly Fiorina got a mere $21 million severance package when she was forced out of her job at Hewlett-Packard.)

The Washington political culture is also full of vintage testosterone and gender gaps.

Some female White House correspondents were put out at what they saw as gender bias exhibited by the president at a June 2005 press conference. They asked Bush press secretary Scott McClellan afterward why, even though 25 percent of the journalists at the news conference were women, and many female hands were up, the president had only taken one question from a woman reporter?

"The president looks forward to taking questions from a

wide variety of people, and I don't think that's a reflection on the president," McClellan replied. "I think that's a reflection on maybe the media and the diversity within the media. So I think that's a question you ought to direct to the media, not us."

The National Journal reported that women in the top tier of the Bush administration were five times more likely to be single than their male counterparts; the magazine found that only 7 percent of men were single, compared to 33 percent of women.

When W. first came in, there were stories chronicling the "family-friendly" White House and interviewing the top officials Karen Hughes and Mary Matalin.

"Matty," Matalin said of her little girl, "knows who Osama bin Laden is."

By the end of the first term, the women had left their demanding jobs, at least partly to please their husbands.

Hughes, who came back to help out with the administration's P.R. effort in the Muslim world, told me when she moved back to Texas in 2002, "I want my son to know where his home is when he comes home from college. I want to see my stepdaughter and granddaughter."

She actually meant it. When a man says he's quitting a big political job, or he's decided not to run for office because he wants to spend more time with his family, it's always taken as code for: the DNA test has come back positive, a multicount indictment is about to come unsealed or the twenty-one-year-old has given eight-by-ten glossies to *The National Enquirer.*

Condi Rice rose to secretary of state because, as a single woman without kids, she had the time and freedom to stick close to W.'s side in exercise rooms from Crawford to Camp David. And Condi is a gamma, not an alpha. She helpfully coached W. on foreign affairs, and congenially went along with the world domination plans of Dick Cheney and Rummy.

Hillary Clinton, once an alpha First Lady, put on a gamma routine as Senator, networking and joining forces with everyone, even with dread former foes of her husband like Newt Gingrich.

Could it be that alpha men still don't want women to challenge them, question them or, heaven forbid, outmaneuver them? Could it be that they prefer the less competitive and more appreciative company of beta, gamma, housewife and va-voom girls?

• • •

Arabs put their women in veils. We put ours in the stocks.

Every culture has its own way of tamping down female power, be it sexual, political or financial. Americans like to see women who wear the pants beaten up and humiliated. Afterward, in a gratifying redemption ritual, people like to see the battered women be rewarded.

That's how Hilary Swank won two Oscars. That's how Hillary Clinton won a Senate seat and a presidential frontrunner spot. And that's how Martha Stewart won her own reality TV show and became a half billion dollars richer while she was in prison.

We've come a long way, baby, from the era of witch trials, when women with special powers who knew how to curse were burned at the stake. Now, after a public comeuppance, they are staked to a lucrative new career. These days, the scarlet letter morphs into a dollar sign.

Maybe temperamental, power-mad divas always needed to be brought down a peg. They used to do it to themselves. Judy Garland and Marilyn Monroe were gorgeous monsters, but were so self-destructive that there was no need to punish them further.

But Hillary and Martha—the domestic diva with the new ankle bracelet echoed Judy Garland on her Web site when she got out of jail that "there is no place like home"—are not self-destructive. They are fair-haired predators who elicit both admiration and an enmity that Alessandra Stanley memorably dubbed "blondenfreude."

From pornography to *Desperate Housewives,* women being degraded has an entertainment value far greater than men being degraded. People liked Hillary and Martha a lot more once they were "broken," like one of Martha's saddle horses, ice queens melted into puddles of vulnerability.

Maybe it's because both women sometimes overreached, treated the help badly and displayed an unseemly greedy streak. Maybe it's because a dichotomy about their roles made them seem disingenuous: they gained renown for traditional feminine roles, and apron-and-hearth books, assuming domestic guises to achieve male power and taking a route to the mahogany epicenter through the kitchen.

Hillary was America's First Lady, photographed smiling in her designer dress as she oversaw table settings and placement for state dinners, writing a book on East Wing style, complete with recipes, like the one for hot pumpkin soup, and details on place-card calligraphy, even though we knew she did not care about such domestic piffle and was instead maneuvering to take over huge chunks of domestic policy.

Martha was America's first lady of filigreed lifestyle nesting, even though we knew that her über-nest was so scary that her husband flew the gold-leaf coop.

So when strong women are brushed back, alpha men can take comfort in knowing that alphettes are not threateningly all-powerful and have to soften those sharp edges.

I learned covering Geraldine Ferraro's vice-presidential bid that the reaction of women to extraordinarily successful women is also ambivalent, with as much hostility as sisterly pride. An Icarus crash can mitigate the jealousy while intensifying the feminist attachment.

After her husband's philandering with Monica, Hillary played the victim card all the way to the Senate. After her own bad judgment about her stocks, Martha metamorphosed from jailbird to phoenix.

Why don't we need to see Oprah, another titan known by her first name, slapped back? (Except for that odd moment at the Hermès store in Paris, when Hermès shot itself in the Birkin bag by refusing to let Oprah shop at closing time.)

Probably because Oprah has never had an icy or phony side to her public persona and because her struggles with abuse and molestation in her childhood and with her weight as an adult take the edge off any animus that might be leveled at her for a net worth of $1.3 billion.

And what about Condi, the first African American woman to be touted for a presidential run on a Republican ticket?

Perhaps she does not need to play the victim to make people feel better about her power because she has never been seen as a termagant, pushing people around and bending them to her will. She always seems subservient to her president and vice president, a willing handmaiden and untiring spokeswoman for their bellicose bidding.

• • •

It took Hollywood awhile to figure out how to turn the Enron scandal into a TV movie.

How could they take all the stuff about "the contingent nature of existing restricted forward contracts" and "share-settled costless collar arrangements," jettison it like the math in *A Beautiful Mind* and juice it up?

Enron was such a mind-numbing black hole, even for financial analysts, that if you tried to explain all the perfidious permutations you'd never come out the other end.

A movie executive asked Lowell Bergman, the former *60 Minutes* producer who is now an investigative reporter for *The New York Times*, for the most cinematic way to frame the story. (Bergman had the ultimate Hollywood experience of being played by Al Pacino in another corporate greed-and-corruption saga, *The Insider.*)

"It's about the women up against the men," he replied.

Before you knew it, Enron was Erined. Texas good ol' girl,

fast-talking, salt-of-the-earth whistle-blower Sherron Watkins was the new Erin Brockovich. The intrepid *Fortune* reporter Bethany McLean, an Alicia Silverstone look-alike who was the first journalist to sound an alarm about Enron's accounting practices, was a great character, as was Loretta Lynch, the tough California utilities czarina and Yale-trained litigator who questioned whether what Enron did was of any value to consumers.

"From the beginning of the California energy meltdown, women were not afraid to point a finger at the seventh-largest corporation in the U.S. and say 'You can't do this,' " Bergman told me. "And the electric cowboys at Enron, where the culture had a take-no-prisoners, get-rid-of-any-regulation, macho perspective on the marketplace, was aggressive when it came to shutting them up."

As a Texas writer says: "This was Jeff Skilling's club and there weren't a lot of women in his club."

At first, the slicked-back Gordon Gekko of Houston and his arrogant coterie in the company skyscraper—where men were wont to mess around and leave wives for secretaries—dismissed female critics.

Some privately trashed Lynch as "an idiot" and coveted McLean, calling her "a looker who doesn't know anything." But when they realized the women were on to them, the company that intimidated competitors, suppliers and utilities tried to oust Lynch from her job and discredit McLean and kill her article.

When Watkins confronted Kenneth Lay with her fears, he knew the cat was spilling out of the beans, as Carmen Miranda used to say. Within two months he had to fess up to $600 million in spurious profits.

(In Houston's testosterone-fueled energy circles, many men watched Kenny Boy's wife, Linda, crying on TV and muttered that in Texas there is nothing lower than sending your woman out to fight your battle.)

As a feminine fillip, there was Maureen Castaneda, a former Enron executive who revealed the shredding shenanigans there. Castaneda realized something was wrong when she took some shreds home to use as packing material and saw they were marked with the galactic names Chewco and Jedi, which turned out to be quasi-legal partnerships.

Only ten years after Mattel put out Teen Talk Barbie whining "Math class is tough," we had women unearthing the Rosetta stone of an indecipherable scandal.

What did this gender schism mean? That men care more about inflating their assets? That women are more caring about colleagues getting shafted?

It is men's worst fear, personally and professionally, that women will pin the sin on them.

At Enron, it was men who came up with complex scams showing there was no limit to the question "How much is enough?" And it was women who raised the simple question "Why?"

There has been speculation that women are more likely to be whistle-blowers—or tattletales when they are little—because they are less likely to be members of the club. Some men suggest that women, with their vast experience with male blarney, are experts at calling guys on it.

Sherron Watkins and Coleen Rowley at the FBI were like grown-up Nancy Drews, piecing together clues and ferreting out criminal behavior and management cover-ups. Along with Worldcom whistle-blower Cynthia Cooper, they were the 2002 *Time* Persons of the Year.

First, male superiors often tell female whistle-blowers to shut up. And if the women point fingers anyhow, they end up being painted by their status quo colleagues as wacky, off-the-reservation snitches with dubious futures.

"I think your statements demonstrate a rush to judgment to protect the FBI at all costs," Rowley told FBI chief Robert Mueller in a classic understatement. She wrote a thirteen-page memo detailing the screwups of superiors who blew off her attempts to get a search warrant for Zacarias Moussaoui, and who found the Minneapolis and Phoenix warning memos in the in-box and put them in the out-box. Then she shot the memo not only to Mueller, who immediately tried to bury it with a CLASSIFIED stamp, but also to two lawmakers on a congressional intelligence panel.

By contrast, Kenneth Williams, the prescient Phoenix agent who wrote the vivid memo about Osama's thugs ominously congregating at American flight schools like Hitchcock's birds, stayed inside the family. He was the organization guy who went through channels and put the bureau in the best light before senators.

If it were not for Rowley's courage, Mueller and other Bush officials would still be insisting they couldn't possibly have known or imagined or hindered the terrorists' grand plan.

She brought us the truth: That the 9/11 terrorists could have been stopped, if everyone in the FBI had been as hardworking and quick-witted as she, or if the law enforcement agencies had not been so inept, obstructionist, arrogant, antiquated, bloated and turf-conscious—and timid about racial profiling. (As *The Economist* noted, "There is a big difference between policemen picking on speeding black drivers and spies targeting Arabs who might harbor plans to set off nuclear bombs.")

Rowley retired from the FBI in 2005 and is now running for Congress as a Democrat in Minnesota on a platform that the war on terror is being screwed up by the Republicans.

"We took our forces out of Afghanistan, where the true threat was, and sent them to a country that, at that time, was not linked to Al Qaeda," she told CNN.

Her male superiors, the brainiacs who never followed up on clues that could have cracked the Al Qaeda plot, stayed on without ever being penalized.

Once women were pleased when men whistled at them. Now men are displeased when women blow whistles on them.

* * *

When I need to work up my nerve to write a tough column, I try to conjure up an image of Emma Peel in a black leather catsuit, giving a kung fu kick to any diabolical mastermind who merits it.

I try not to visualize the witches in *Macbeth*, sitting off to the side over a double, double, toil and trouble bubbling cauldron, muttering about what is fair or foul in the hurly-burly of the royal court.

There's been an intense debate about why newspapers have so few female columnists. Out of eight *New York Times* Op-Ed columnists—nine, counting the public editor—I'm the only woman.

In 1996, after six months on the job, I went to Howell Raines, then the editorial page editor, to try to get out of my column. I was a bundle of frayed nerves. I felt as though I were in a *Godfather* movie, shooting and getting shot at in wars that were always escalating.

As a woman, I told Howell, I wanted to be liked—not attacked. He said I could go back to city news, which I had done in Washington and New York for many years. I decided to give it another try. Bill Safire told me I needed Punzac, Prozac for pundits.

In my experience, guys don't appreciate being lectured by women. It taps into myths of carping Harpies and hounding Furies, and their distaste for nagging by wives and mothers. The word "harridan" derives from the French word *haridelle*—a worn-out horse or nag.

The angry, male-hating female monster is a staple of mythology (Medusa and the Furies) and movies (Glenn Close with raised knife and Sharon Stone with raised ice pick).

The subtext here is that men like to put fear in the hearts of others. It is a sign of their power. Women don't. Eric Van Harpen, who was Anna Kournikova's tennis coach, speculated that women need different motivation: "Men play to win. Women play not to lose."

Many women are already afraid that, as they get more powerful, they get more scary, and this will repel men. Women are attracted to male power. Men are threatened by female power.

A friend of mine called nearly in tears the day she won a Pulitzer: "Now," she moaned, "I'll never get a date!"

I've found, in decades of dealing with political aides who could get lethally nasty, that men take professional criticism more personally when it comes from a woman. When I wrote columns about the Clinton impeachment farce, Chris Matthews said that for poor Bill, it must feel as though he had another wife hectoring him.

In all the years I wrote about Colin Powell, the secretary of state never agreed to an interview with me, even though he regularly invited the *Times*'s male columnists over to chat, some of whom had written far more critically about him than I.

"They're scared of you," explained the *Times*'s diplomatic correspondent, as though I should be flattered.

While a man writing a column taking on the powerful may be seen as authoritative, a woman doing the same thing may be seen as castrating. I'm often asked how I can be so "mean"— a question that Tom Friedman, who writes plenty of tough columns, doesn't get.

Even the metaphors used to describe my column play into the castration theme: my scalpel, my cutting barbs, my razor-sharp hatchet, my Clinton-skewering and Bush-whacking. "Does she," *The L.A. Times*'s Patt Morrison wondered, in a review of my book *Bushworld*, "write on a computer or a Ronco Slicer and Dicer?"

In 1998, President Clinton described me as a castrating word-that-rhymes-with-rich at the annual White House correspondents' dinner. He did it in a joking way, during his stand-up routine, but, as Freud noted, humor is simply hostility masquerading as wit.

Clinton entertained the room by reading a list of mock headlines by or about real journalists. "George Mitchell writes about the prospects of lasting peace between Barbara Walters and Diane Sawyer," he said. " 'Buddy Got What He Deserved,' by Maureen Dowd." (He was referring to his chocolate lab, Buddy, getting neutered.)

As the audience laughed, I ducked down, praying the C-SPAN cameras were still on Paula Jones.

"Now everyone will think I'm a castrating witch," I complained to my male colleagues at the table.

"Now?" they replied in unison.

My friends said I should be happy the president mentioned me. But I hadn't even wanted poor Buddy, who later perished after getting run over by an SUV in Chappaqua, to go under the knife.

Although I had written that some restraint might be needed at the White House, I was never talking about the pooch. It was the hound dog I was after. Buddy had plenty of room to roam, and the Secret Service was there to make sure he didn't grope unsuspecting females.

I understood Clinton's remarks were all in the service of satire, a cause I cherish. Yet I wondered. Would the same joke have worked if Clinton had put a scalpel—or whatever they use to deprive dogs of their manhood—into the hands of Frank Rich?

Marlin Fitzwater, Bush 41's press secretary, recalled the public temper tantrum and private invective of the first President Bush's chief of staff, John Sununu, toward the late Ann Devroy, the flinty White House reporter at *The Washington Post*. Devroy broke the story of "Air Sununu," the aide's profligate use of military jets for personal trips, including ski vacations and dentist appointments in Boston.

The raging-bull chief of staff also epically cursed me after reading one of my stories about his arrogant behavior. "I will destroy her," he told Fitzwater, who was stunned and scared by his venom. "If it takes me the rest of my life, I will destroy her. I don't know where or when, but I'll get her."

Fitzwater speculated to me that "men tend to judge criticism from men on the content, but they assign different motives to women—probably related to centuries of tradition about motherhood and male-female prejudices. Men are still learning what equality means. Deep down in the darkest part of our hearts, male superiority still exists."

With men, sharp give-and-take tends to be seen as a natural part of the prizefight, the art of war—all in the name of professional duty.

If a man writes a scathing piece about some gaffe a politician has made, no one accuses him of hostility toward men. If a woman writes the same scathing piece, the politician or his male aides will often suggest that her criticism is a reflection of some psychological problem. She is bitter about men. She hates men. She needs to get . . . a better love life. She is hormonally grumpy.

Men are used to verbal dueling with other men, according to Alan Dundes, the late folklorist at Berkeley. "But they are worried about being put down by a woman," he told me. "Women are supposed to take it, not dish it out. If a woman embarrasses a man, he feels inadequate, effeminate. He wants her to go back to the kitchen."

Or the store. I've been caught off guard a couple of times when men I'm friendly with have reacted to columns on politics or the media that they didn't like with sarcastic remarks about shopping. In a decade of columnizing, I've written only a handful of columns that mention shopping. Yet once with a famous anchor and again with a well-known conservative columnist, their visceral way to belittle me was to snap, Get thee to a mall.

In sport and war, the big fear of men is to be feminized. In the workplace, the big fear of women is to be diabolized. So when a man kids a woman about being castrating, it is never more than half a joke. It's discouraging. Can men and women ever meet in a place that's not about sex? It's enough to make a girl reach for a sharp object.

The kerfuffle over female columnists started in the spring of 2005 when Susan Estrich, the former Dukakis campaign manager and brash Fox TV analyst, launched a crazed and nasty smear campaign against my brilliant friend Michael Kinsley, the former *L.A. Times* editorial page editor, trying to force him to run her humdrum syndicated column.

Given the appalling way she's handled herself, Susan—an

acquaintance for many years—was the last person Michael should have hired.

Estrich, an expert on rape law and the first woman president of the *Harvard Law Review*, once cowrote a screenplay about a prostitute who teaches her two girlfriends how to lure and hang on to men by learning erotic techniques (practicing with whipped cream and anatomically optimistic food items) while wearing Wonderbras, garter belts and Victoria's Secret lingerie.

When asked by *The New York Observer* in '97 how her screenplay squared with her feminism, Estrich replied that she had wanted to explore the issues of feminism through the "classic male form" of the hooker, not "the hooker as victim, but the hooker as a person who is possessed of great power and knows how to use it."

Huh?

Kinsley conceded in a piece in the *L.A. Times* that "everyone involved should be trying harder, including me" to close the gender gap on op-ed pages.

"There cannot be many places where 'diversity' is less a euphemism for reverse discrimination and more a commonsense business requirement than on a newspaper op-ed page," he said. "Diversity of voices, experiences and sensibilities is not about fairness to writers. It is about serving up a good meal for readers."

Gail Collins, the first woman to run *The New York Times*'s editorial page and the author of *America's Women: Four Hundred Years of Dolls, Drudges, Helpmates, and Heroines*, told me: "If the gender imbalance in the letters to the editor and unsolicited op-eds we get every day is any indication, there are about four men waving their hands for every woman. Obviously, there are a lot of women who could be great columnists, but the pool of opinion writers still seems to be heavily male. That's not surprising if you compare the millennia in which women were told they had no right to have opinions on public matters to the few decades that they've been encouraged to speak out. Things will even out—it's just a matter of time."

There's a lot of evidence that Papa likes to preach more: Male shouters predominate on TV political shows, as do male bloggers. Teenage boys trash talk much more on the basketball court than teenage girls. Men I know and men who read *The New York Times* write me constantly, asking me to read the opinion pieces they've written. Sometimes they'll e-mail or fax me their thoughts to read right before I have lunch with them. Women hardly ever send their own rants.

My friend Zofia Smardz, a *Washington Post* Outlook editor whose job it is to find contributors for the *Post*'s opinion pages, wrote an intriguing piece for the *Post* on "Opiniongate."

"I know who's constantly beating on my door to be heard, and who's a little more inclined to hang back," she said. "I took an informal count while writing this, and over a recent span of seven days, unsolicited manuscripts to our section were running seven to one in favor of, yes, those pesky, ubiquitous men."

Why, she asked, can't all the smart, knowledgeable, opinionated women out there muscle their way into print?

Zofia recalled what she learned when she ghostwrote a book a few years back for a female neuropsychiatrist.

"Did you know that men are generally oriented toward the left brain, the mind's intellectual and linguistic power center, while women tend to use both sides of the brain?" she said. "But the left brain is the dominant side. It likes to run things, be in control. So that (plus the testosterone, of course) makes men more assertive. Unafraid to take risks and willing to take a shot at anything, anytime. Women, being tuned in to the more cautious (and more creative) right brain, are more reluctant to do something unless they're sure they're going to get it right.

"Here's how the neuropsychiatrist put it: Think of a man as carrying a quiverful of arrows. When he spies a target, he lets fly with the whole caboodle. Most of his arrows will miss the bull's-eye, but one is likely to hit. And that's the one people will remember—and applaud. A woman, though, proceeds slowly and considers carefully. Only when she's pretty sure she has a perfect shot does she send off a single arrow. And she hits the mark! Amazing! But . . . too bad. The guy's already walked off with the prize."

Zofia explained that this dovetailed neatly with what she observed at the *Post*. "If opinions were really arrows, I'd look like a bristling porcupine thanks to all the male views fired into my hide in any given week. But if I relied mostly on women, I'd be a pretty scrawny hedgehog. So I feel like the brain researchers may be seriously on to something."

She said they have a running joke in her office: "Call a man on Monday, say you're from Outlook and he blurts, 'How many words and okay if I get it to you by 5 o'clock?' Call a woman, spell out the idea, have a nice long conversation, ask her if she'll write, listen to the long pause, she says, 'I don't know, I have to think what I'd say (!),' you press a little, tell her she can have till Thursday, she says, 'Well, I have class and faculty meetings, my husband's out of town, I have to take kids to soccer practice, it might be hard,' you press some more, she says again, 'Let me think about it, can I call you tomorrow?'

"See? He's already emptying his quiver and she's weighing the pros and cons of shooting the arrow."

There's been a dearth of women writing serious opinion pieces for top news organizations, even as there's been growth in female sex columnists for college newspapers—from "Between the Sheets" at Tufts to "Sex at the Beach" at California State University at Long Beach—opining on vibrators, cross-dressing, multiple orgasms, bondage, oral sex and masturbation.

Going from Tess Harding to Carrie Bradshaw, Dorothy Thompson to Candace Bushnell, is not progress.

I wrote a column in the *Times* acknowledging that the private cost of never flinching from a public fight in print with powerful officials (and dealing with their nasty, vengeful aides) was high for me. My father—fearless about everything—had tried to toughen me up when I was little. But I was shy and oversensitive, then and now, so I find the level of vituperation coming back at me draining.

Some other women columnists disagreed with my premise, asserting that women do enjoy mixing it up just as much as men.

"Some of us love fights," Barbara Ehrenreich, the author of *Nickel and Dimed,* who wrote a guest column in the summer of 2004 in *The New York Times*, told *The New York Ob-server.* "I think that's complete bullshit."

Whether they fancy fighting or find it wearing, there's no doubt women have the nerve and authority to ruminate and rant as well as men. And many kinds of columns don't involve such jousting. There are plenty of brilliant women who would bring grace and guts to our nation's op-ed pages, just as, Larry Summers notwithstanding, there are plenty of brilliant women out there who are great at math and science.

We just need to let the ladies dish it out in the paper and get at those petri dishes in the lab. (Instead of merely washing those Laura Petrie dishes.)

*   *   *

In fact, no one else brought as much grace and guts to the newspaper business as two women who died in the last few years.

At long last, when Deep Throat outed himself, there were only two people I was dying to dish with about the revelation of Washington's juiciest—and oldest—secret.

But they were both gone.

Katharine Graham, the late publisher of *The Washington Post,* and Mary McGrory, star columnist of *The Washington Star* and the *Post,* would have been deliciously entertaining on the subject of Mark Felt scooping Bob Woodward, three decades after the FBI number two man led him to the big scoops that made him Bob Woodward.

In an era when many male journalists were cowering at the

vengeful Nixon, both of these dazzling dames stood up to the corrupt president.

During Watergate, Kay was threatened with unspecified retaliation if the *Post* published an article that said John Mitchell, as attorney general, controlled a secret fund used to spy on Democrats. Mitchell warned Carl Bernstein that "Katie Graham" would have her breast "caught in a big fat wringer if that's published." Woodward later presented Mrs. Graham with an old-style wooden laundry wringer, which she proudly kept in her office.

Mary blazed a path for newspaper women—she was often the only one on the campaign trail in the early days. She won the Pulitzer in 1974, after being audited by Nixon's IRS and making Nixon's enemies list as a "syndicated columnist of the new left."

In a column about Nixon's "you won't have me to kick around anymore" news conference after he lost the 1962 California governor's race, Mary wrote: "For Richard M. Nixon, it was exit snarling." She called him "the joyless Californian."

"He was eternally coming and going," she wrote. "He was finished, he was back. He was always changing his persona, but it was always the same. He was mawkish, snide, savage, full of rage and grievance. I found him a preposterous politician—awkward, angry, aggrieved. He gave politics a bad name."

Mary and Kay were swell—true originals who lived through history others could only read about, women who got more stylish as they got older, while staying just as tough on pols who abused power.

At dinner in 2001 with Mrs. Graham and Michael Kinsley

at Kinkead's, a Washington restaurant, I told her that C-SPAN radio, which had been broadcasting Lyndon Johnson's phone tapes from the Oval Office on Saturdays, had just played one where LBJ flirted with her.

The most powerful man in Washington was trying to get the most powerful woman in Washington to denounce his congressional enemies in her newspaper, and he was dripping Southern honey.

"Hello, my sweetheart, how are you?" the Texas rancher drawled to the Widow Graham. "You know the only one thing I dislike about this job is that I'm married and I can't ever get to see you. I just hear that sweet voice and it's always on the telephone and I'd like to break out of here and be like one of these young animals down on my ranch. Jump a fence."

How did the classy, shy publisher react to that on the tapes? She laughed. He laughed. "Now that's going to set me up for the month, Mr. President," she said, her proper lockjaw accent sounding positively saucy.

When I told Mrs. Graham it had been played on air, I thought she might blush and demur, as she often did when she was the subject. But instead she smiled, almost slyly. "Yes," she recalled. "Lyndon had a sneaker for me."

She went on to talk about her "flirt" with Adlai Stevenson and how no one had expected John Kennedy to become president because he just seemed like "a callow playboy."

For four decades, until her death in 2001 at eighty-four, she was The Man in the quintessential man's town, so imposing and respected that even though she told people to call her Kay, they always ended up calling her Mrs. Graham. On occasion even her son Don, who took her place as publisher, called her that behind her back.

When she finally wrote a memoir, it was so searingly honest and beautifully written about her life and the capital through the decades, that she won a Pulitzer for it at eighty.

Mrs. Graham described the awful story of losing her charismatic but mentally ill husband Phil twice, once to a mistress and then to suicide. She wrote about how she transformed herself from a timorous doormat for her publisher husband—"I increasingly saw my role as the tail to his kite and the more I felt overshadowed, the more it became a reality"—into a publisher herself whose brave decisions joining *The New York Times* in printing the Pentagon Papers and beating the *Times* on Watergate transformed the *Post* and American journalism.

She had an arc that echoed the evolution of women: Raised to be a milquetoast, her confidence undermined by her domineering mother and philandering husband, she somehow made herself over into a figure of greatness.

But the really cool thing about America's most powerful woman was that she was a girl. Our grande dame was not at all stuffy. She loved ice cream and chocolate desserts. She loved to flirt with powerful men and seek their counsel and chat about clothes and perfume with women. She was the little brown hen who blossomed into a swan, looking more glamorous every year in Oscar de la Renta and Armani. She took only the best advice—about journalism from Ben Bradlee, about finances from Warren Buffett and about clothes from Anna Wintour.

She loved movies, even silly ones. She and her best pal, Meg Greenfield, the wondrous editorial page editor of the *Post* who died just two years before Mrs. Graham, used to sneak off in the middle of the workday to see movies—*Police Academy* movies, ninja movies, teen romance movies.

One time, Meg called Kay and said, "Do you want to go see the French president?"

"Where's it playing?" Kay asked.

"I meant Pompidou," Meg replied drily.

Once, in the '70s, after Kay had refused an invitation to attend the then all-male Gridiron Club, which put on an annual evening of skits for press and pols, she and Meg drove down to the Capital Hilton where the show was going on, just to watch the tuxedoed male guests and the female picketers outside, ducking down in their seats as they drove by.

She was painfully insecure. She learned to stand up to presidents but she never stopped looking shy at big black-tie Washington dinners. "I hate these things," she whispered to me at one. "I never know what to say to anyone." And before the dinner she held at her Georgetown home welcoming George W. Bush to Washington, she told friends she was a basket case.

Mrs. Graham was always shocked when young women of all classes flocked to hear her speak. She told me how moving that was for her. She had inherited her position, and yet, emotionally, she had to start at the bottom and work her way up.

LBJ had it right. She was a woman worth jumping over a fence for.

The irrepressible President Johnson, who knew a prize filly

when he saw one, also flirted with McGrory. She told me that he pounced on her once in the Oval Office, murmuring that if she loved the Kennedys she should love him just as much.

I first realized that writing a column could be a good gig when I saw all the cute guys clustered around Mary's desk in the back of *The Washington Star* newsroom, hard-boiled political reporters acting as adoring as Las Vegas chorus boys.

But while my status changed over the decades, as I slowly clambered up from *Star* clerk to *Times* columnist, Mary's status never changed. She was always the same *bella figura*: She Who Must Be Obeyed. As the erudite daughter of an erudite Boston postman, she was the last person who loved the U.S. Postal Service. She signed her handwritten notes Maria Gloria, an homage to her beloved Italian.

I tried to learn from her. Not about cooking. Her Jell-O Surprise was frightening and her meatloaf worse. And it was impossible to write as she did. It was a truth universally acknowledged, as her idol Jane Austen wrote, that nobody could write with the sense and sensibility, the luminous prose and legendary reporting, of McGrory.

But I emulated her other talents:

Her uncanny ability, even in remote parts of New Hampshire or Ireland, to find some sucker to carry her bags or drive her car.

The way she nobly resisted the passing fad called technology, often writing in longhand when her laptop—or "that fiendish little gadget," as she called it—gave her fits.

The way she acted helpless like a barracuda.

From Joe McCarthy to Henry Kissinger to Robert McNamara to Linda Tripp, every public figure learned to beware when Mary started asking confused and innocent-sounding questions, like some Capitol Hill Columbo.

She became a star at the *Star* with her courageous coverage of the Army-McCarthy hearings in 1954. It was my father, Mike Dowd, a D.C. police inspector who was in charge of Senate security for twenty years, who got Mary her big break by giving her a front-row seat for the spectacle. "I wanted to help out a nice Irish girl," he told my brother Michael, then a nineteen-year-old working in the Senate post office (and sorting the mail for senators John Kennedy, Richard Nixon and Prescott Bush, W.'s grandfather.)

Her deadline coverage of the assassination and burial of her beloved JFK was remarkable. One story began: "Of John Fitzgerald Kennedy's funeral it can be said he would have liked it. It had that decorum and dash that were his special style. It was both splendid and spontaneous. It was full of children and princes, gardeners and governors. Everyone measured up to New Frontier standards."

Afterward, she instructed admiring reporters: "Write short sentences in the presence of great grief."

Mary always got her way—one way or another. When her editor at the *Post*—where she moved after the *Star* folded— told her he did not have an extra pass for her to get into the Anita Hill–Clarence Thomas hearings, Mary was displeased. Shortly thereafter, the editor was watching the hearings on TV and suddenly saw Mary being escorted to a front-row seat by the committee chairman, Joe Biden.

Mary loved the *Star* and Rome and rogues and children and

losers and underdogs and Jack Kennedy. "He walked like a panther," she told me. She was on the phone with Kennedy when he decided to make an impromptu stop in Vegas, the trip where Frank Sinatra fatefully introduced JFK to Judith Exner. (Mary went to bed early that night.)

She did not love, as her nephew Brian McGrory, the *Boston Globe* columnist, said, pomposity or self-involvement or bullies or blowhards or Nixon.

Once she wanted to get away from John Volpe, who had been in the Nixon cabinet, when he was droning on at her during a party at the Shoreham Hotel. "Hey," she interrupted him finally, "you were the Secretary of Transportation. Where are the elevators?" And away she went.

Mary treated the powerful and the powerless the same, with what her *Post* editor Bill Hamilton called an exasperated "good help is hard to get" manner.

She was, for many years, one of few Democrats not hiding from the label *liberal.* "I still think it's a respectable word. Its root is *liber,* the Latin word for free, and isn't that what we are all about?"

When I was a cub reporter at the *Star,* she invited me to one of her A-list Sunday brunches. Only twenty-five, I thought, sashaying up to her apartment in my best outfit, and I have already entered the sanctum sanctorum of Washington politics.

When Mary pointed me toward the blender and told me to make a daiquiri for Teddy Kennedy, I realized I was not there as a guest. At least I was in good company. Years later, at another party, I saw George Stephanopoulos, a Dick Gephardt staff member who would later become a top Clinton aide and

Sunday ABC talk show host, passing canapés. I saw Mark Gearan, who would go on to head the Peace Corps in the '90s, playing the piano. And I saw Phil Gailey, who would become the editorial page editor of the *St. Petersburg Times*, clogging and playing the Autoharp.

Mary's servants had an excellent record of upward mobility.

She also shanghaied me to come swim with the kids from her favorite charity, St. Ann's Infant and Maternity Home, in Ethel Kennedy's pool at Hickory Hill in McLean, Virginia, on Wednesday afternoons. At the time, I was working in a different suburb in a different state, Rockville, Maryland, and I didn't know how to swim.

But Mary didn't let me weasel out of it. Mangling, intentionally perhaps, my editor's name, she instructed him to give me Wednesday afternoons off. "Yes, Mary," he replied, humbly, gratefully.

Over the years, she called me with other offers I couldn't refuse. She wanted me to come to Ireland in May 1998. We would cover the peace referendum and have a fun girls' bonding trip, she said. There was no chance to bond, of course. On the train from Dublin to Belfast, after staying up all night on the plane, Mary interviewed everyone at the station, everyone on the train, including the lame woman whom she got to carry her bags, the cabdriver on the way to the hotel, the waitress at the hotel coffee shop, the room-service waiter carrying our tea and the priest at Sunday Mass.

Another time, in the Clinton years, she telephoned and said in a chirpy voice, "Let's go see Yasir Arafat at the White House!" When I hesitated, she chimed in with another inducement: "And then go shopping!" Only Mary would think of pairing those activities.

Like Mrs. Graham, she blossomed as she got older, developing a taste for nice clothes; I would run into her at Neiman's or Saks on a Saturday, pawing through the racks, looking for a spiffy suit to wear on her pal Tim Russert's *Meet the Press* the next morning. (Sometimes we would also see Condi Rice out shopping, with her Secret Service agents standing as stiff as mannequins amid the designer mannequins, looking chagrined if you caught their eye.)

Mary continued to call me and have me over after she had a stroke in March 2003. You could understand a bit here or there—"casserole" or "Cheney." It broke my heart to hear the words coming out so jumbled, from lips that never uttered a less than perfect sentence.

Once, in a private diary of the *Star*'s final days in 1981, Mary had written, "I do not want anyone to think I have collapsed under calamity." She never did. She took on life and sickness and death with the same Yankee pluck she developed at Girls' Latin School in Boston.

Whenever I get nervous, I think of Mary and the invaluable advice she once gave her nephew Brian at a stuffy Washington party: "Always approach the shrimp bowl like you own it."

Four

WHY THE WELL-HUNG Y IS WILTING, EVEN AS THE X IS EXCELLING

Men have a perfect right to be insecure.

They're doomed, poor darlings.

It won't be next Thursday or anything, but men, says Brian Sykes, a leading British researcher on sex chromosomes, "are now on notice."

Some are resigned to it. Tough guy Norman Mailer told Katie Couric that his "terror theory" was that "women are going to take over the world. . . . You know, men, no matter how bad they were to women over the years, over the centuries, needed women for the race to continue. But all women needed were about a hundred semen slaves that they could milk every day, you see, and they could keep the race going. So they don't need us. And—there's a real possibility in my mind, about one in ten, that a hundred years from now there will be a hundred

men left on earth, and the women will have it all to themselves."

Are men necessary? I asked Dr. Sykes.

"Clearly not," he replied.

Are men necessary? I asked British geneticist Steve Jones.

"You don't even need the sex slaves," Dr. Jones assured me.
"You just need their cells in a freezer. You'd have to have a
very good electricity supply."

Some guys I know have been fretting for years that they
may be rendered obsolete if women get biological and financial independence, learning how to reproduce and refinance
without them.

The latest research on the Y chromosome shows that my jittery male friends are not paranoid. They are in an evolutionary pratfall.

In a wry twist of fate, Mother Nature appears to have decided to demote men to the weaker sex. It's only a matter of
time before we will be judging guys by their hourglass figures,
pliability and talent for gazing raptly at their dates, no matter
how bored.

The Y chromosome has been shedding genes willy-nilly for
millions of years and is now a fraction of the size of its partner, the X chromosome. Size matters, and experts are suggesting that, in the next one hundred thousand to ten million years,
men could disappear, taking *Maxim* magazine, March Madness
and cold pizza in the morning with them.

The Y chromosome is "a mere remnant of its once mighty
structure," wrote Dr. Jones, a professor of genetics at University College in London and the author of *Y: The Descent of*

Men. "Men are wilting away. From sperm count to social status and from fertilization to death, as civilization advances, those who bear Y chromosomes are in relative decline."

Males have always been a genetic "parasite," he said, marveling that if Simone de Beauvoir or anybody else were writing *The Second Sex* today they'd have to make it, biologically speaking, about men.

"There are elements of *The Picture of Dorian Gray*," he said, ominously. "The Y's picture is fading away."

It is degenerating at such a fast rate that men face an "inevitable eventual extinction" and steadily falling male fertility, with nearly all men completely sterile in about 125,000 years, warned Dr. Sykes, a science adviser to the British House of Commons, in *Adam's Curse: A Future Without Men.*

A sky-is-falling, or Y-is-falling, type, Dr. Sykes believes in the brutality of masculinity, that the Y has pushed its host bodies into a lot of violent and authoritarian behavior throughout history. Men have been "driven on by the lash of their Y chromosomes," he wrote, and men and women have been forced to submit "to its will."

"Driven on and on by the crazed ambition of the Y chromosome to multiply without limit, wars began to enable men to annex adjacent lands and enslave their women," he continued. "Nothing must stand in the way of the Y chromosome. Wars, slavery, empires—all ultimately coalesce on that one mad pursuit."

Having spent years reporting on George W. Bush and his willful impulses toward war and empire building, I'm wondering if W. should more aptly be nicknamed Y.

"The reason men wanted empires in the first place was to distribute their sperm as widely as possible," Dr. Sykes said. "The emperors kept huge numbers of women for their own use—thousands, not just half a dozen. The harems were great breeding factories."

All imperialism is not stud-ism, of course. I can't imagine W. or Dick Cheney lounging among the odalisques in a harem, enjoying erotic delights that could, as Alfred Drake sang in *Kismet,* "drive a man out of his Mesopotamian mind." And it is simply impossible to use the word "harem" and "Wolfowitz" in the same sentence.

"We've never had a woman emperor surrounded by ten thousand sex slaves," Dr. Sykes said. "Very wealthy women rarely accumulate harems. There's no point. The motivation isn't there, since women can only have a small number of children in their lifetime."

A healthy, fit man still pumps out 150 million sperm a day, but the global potency of the Y may have peaked back with Genghis Khan. Dr. Sykes said that there's circumstantial evidence, based on an Oxford study, that sixteen million men now carry the Khan Y chromosome. The geneticist didn't seem to be sure who had the whip hand, the Mongol Emperor of all Emperors or his Y.

"Is the Khan chromosome's achievement owing to the sexual exploits and military conquests of the Mongol emperor?" he wrote, suggestively but simplistically, marveling about the conqueror's loins. "Or was the Great Khan himself driven to success in war, and in bed, by the ambition of his Y chromosome?"

Surely there is an element of wishful thinking when men

depict women as less driven by desire. History has shown that once they get the power, women can be just as sexually capricious and demanding as men.

When Bette Davis played Elizabeth I, she was always sending her lovers off to the Tower of London when they made eyes at her pretty ladies-in-waiting. Catherine the Great was hardly known for her restraint. And how about Agrippina or Cleopatra or any of those other sexually rapacious ancient babes?

"Isn't it touching that they think we are so under control?" said anthropologist Helen Fisher. "But every time a man is sleeping around, he is sleeping around with a woman. It's basic math that women are 50 percent of the problem here. Men want to delude themselves into thinking that women are Madonnas and pristine and in control of their sexuality because men have a terrible fear of cuckoldry."

The news that Dolly the sheep had been cloned without a ram ramming, and the South Korean cloning factory's success in making a dozen human embryos and duplicate puppies, have sent frissons through the Y populace, geneticists say, because men began to fear that science would cause nature to return to its original, feminine state and men would fade from view.

"Japanese scientists last year created a perfectly normal female mouse without using a male at all," Dr. Sykes told me. "It's not cloning. They took the egg from one mouse, and then instead of mouse sperm, they took the DNA from another egg. Bingo!"

Perhaps that's why some men in Western societies are adapting, becoming more feminized and turning into over-therapied, over-sharing, over-emoting "emo boys," and metrosexuals who get facials and buy wrinkle cream and wear pink flowered shirts.

Better to be an X chromosome than an ex-chromosome.

In September 2005, *Men's Vogue* hit the stands, and there's a new shopping magazine for men called *Cargo*.

The New York Times Styles section, with its exquisite gaydar, declared a "gay vague" vogue, noting it's harder and harder to tell who is gay. Straight men, it said, "are adopting looks—muscle shirts, fitted jeans, sandals and shoulder bags, that as recently as a year ago might have read as, well, gay. . . . What's happening is that many men have migrated to a middle ground where the cues traditionally used to pigeonhole sexual orientation—hair, clothing, voice, body language—are more and more ambiguous."

My witty friend Frank Bruni, the *New York Times* restaurant critic, provided me with the gay (as opposed to gay vague) point of view: "It used to be that if you saw an unwrinkled, well-moisturized guy prowling the Clinique counter or Clarins counter, you could safely assume three things—he was vain, he appreciated a hypoallergenic cleansing lotion and he was on your team. Now you assume only the first two."

French sociologists unveiled a study in spring 2005 that found that American and European men are no longer so macho, though Chinese men still are. "The masculine ideal is being completely modified," said Pierre François Le Louet of the French marketing and style consultant group Nelly Rodi. "All the traditional male values of authority, infallibility, virility and strength are being completely overturned." Instead, he said, in fashion and life, men are turning more toward "creativity, sensitivity and multiplicity."

In June 2005, the *Hindustan Times* broke the story of a teenage boy in India who had been having what seemed to be periods for a year, leaving doctors flummoxed. The fifteen-year-old bled from his penis in the second week of every month, the paper reported, and suffered nausea, stomachaches and mood swings.

Dr. Jones told me that the "all-pervasive battle of the sexes goes back thousands of millions of years. It's all because one partner makes large cells called eggs and one partner gets away with making smaller and more abundant sex cells.

"Every time a man has sex, he makes enough sperm to fertilize every female in Europe. And that is a divergence of interest because males have taken the tactic of high-risk behavior in spreading lots of their cells around in the hope of fertilizing a lot of females.

"And that now pervades their entire being all the way from sperm cells to being struck by lightning, which happens more to men than women because of their risk-taking behavior—showing off to peers by playing on an expensive golf course or climbing mountains."

My friend Leon Wieseltier gets very irritated with evolutionary biologists whose theories on male evolution don't evolve.

"There are many problems with the biological explanation of human feelings," he says. "Biology cannot even explain human sexual behavior adequately. Take promiscuity. In Western societies, the most salient feature of promiscuity is that it is decidedly not about procreation. In our way of heterosexual life, which has been in existence now for centuries, we have dissociated male pleasure from the spreading of the male seed. Libertinism, high or low, is not about family making. There is male pride, to be sure, in male promiscuity, but not chromosomal pride. And worse, the simplifications of the Darwinists take all the fun out of promiscuity. They make promiscuity seem like a solemn biological obligation rather than an exercise of freedom and imagination."

To save the Y chromosome, Dr. Sykes suggested, scientists may need to transfer its contents onto another gene. He said that if the Y vaporizes, reproduction would need to be assisted in some way.

"What I think'll happen within my lifetime," he said, "is that some lesbian couples will have children, and they will both be parents, an egg from one and a fertilized egg from the other will produce a perfectly normal girl. You could have a new species of human reproduced without men at all."

He fantasized about "a world without men," a version of the mythological "cult of Diana" hunter-gatherer societies where women were in charge and men were just there for entertainment, where there would be "no Y chromosomes to enslave the feminine, the destructive spiral of greed and ambition fueled by sexual ambition diminishes and as a direct result the sickness of our planet eases. The world no longer reverberates to the sound of men's clashing antlers and the grim repercussions of private and public warfare."

Dr. Huntington Willard, the director of the Institute for

Genome Sciences and Policy at Duke University, doubts that a planet without men—and with women leaders festooned with testosterone patches, hailed by some doctors as female Viagra—would be so peaceful.

"Remember all those B movies that end up with Amazons developing all those aggressive traits?" he said. "There's always a subgroup that becomes the aggressors."

Whether or not the predicted demise of the well-hung Y is correct, there's no point in idealizing a world composed exclusively of women.

Reading about the amoral cruelty of female guards and interrogators in Guantánamo, Abu Ghraib and Bagram, it's easy to believe it wouldn't be that different. And anybody who's attended an all-girls Catholic high school knows that Xs can act as territorially, brutally and thoughtlessly as Ys.

"Historically, men have made most of the political errors," Dr. Sykes agreed. "But look at Mrs. Thatcher. She was pretty bloody awful."

He speculates that Adam will end up causing his own curse by accumulating wealth and property and toys and polluting the planet. "It would be very ironic," he said, "if the polluted planet exacted revenge by hitting back at sperm production and making all those men sterile."

The scientists predicting the demise of the Y get furious e-mails from men denouncing them as "man-haters." One Web site that pelts Dr. Jones, AngryHarry.com, rants that men will prevail over women, who are described as Marxists and Nazis.

Dr. Willard recommends to flustered men that they take the

long view, because "most species eventually mutate themselves out of existence. Sex determination as we know it is only a couple hundred million years old, so if the Y chromosome degrades itself out of existence, some other mechanism will turn up. Worms reproduce with females and hermaphrodites. They've gotten rid of the stand-alone male."

Dr. Jones, an expert on the sex life of slugs, agrees, calling hermaphrodite sex, like Woody Allen onanism, "sex with somebody you really love."

"Plenty of creatures don't bother with sex at all," he says. "Sea anemones just cut themselves in half indefinitely and make copies again and again and again."

He says that bananas—"despite their suggestive shape"— and potatoes are entirely female. And that alligator eggs become male if they're warmed and female if they're cooled, and turtles the other way around.

"There are many, many ways to make males," he says, citing the mole vole, which has males with no Y chromosome, and the North American blue-finned wrasse.

"If you take the male wrasse out of the aquarium, after a few days one of the females begins to look a bit shifty and more brightly colored and she turns into a male and makes sperm and fertilizes her female partners. Social pressure changes the hormonal balance, just as it can with humans. Men in extreme pressure in battle, females training for a marathon, the sex hormone patterns change."

(I wonder if it works the same way if you take the female out of the fish tank. When I took a leave from my column at the *Times,* I noticed that some male columnists were suddenly writing on women's issues.)

Men may save themselves simply through "the healing power of lust," Dr. Jones said. "People carry on having sex because it's fun—insofar as I remember.

"Even if women make men sex slaves, they'll find some conscience-stricken women to bring them out of slavery, as happened with slavery. I'd be very, very surprised if technology takes over the old-fashioned methods we're so used to. People only turn to the test tube when the double bed has failed. I can't think of anybody who goes to the lab first."

Although he does think sperm freezers are a good idea—for everybody.

"Boys and girls age sixteen are well advised to produce quantities of sperm and eggs and freeze them because the quality is far better than the stuff thirty-five-year-olds can make," he said. (This is the best argument I've ever heard for frigidity.)

As a confirmed pessimist, Dr. Jones concludes that men are more likely to be wiped out in a devastating SARS-like epidemic or in a nuclear war they start, clashing antlers, long before the Y gets around to degenerating.

And that conjures up the image of the Y as Slim Pickens in *Dr. Strangelove,* straddling the hydrogen bomb as though it were a rodeo steer and waving his cowboy hat, yelling "YEE-HAW!" as he sets off the destruction of mankind.

Why, oh Y, am I not surprised that the Y is not going gently into that good evolutionary night?

. . .

Coldplay's CD *X & Y* refers to algebraic unknowns, but the lyrics of the title song about fixing something that's broken could just as well apply to the Y chromosome unknowns:

The most promising survival mechanism for the battered Y involves, naturally, self-love. The unflinching narcissism of men may send women into despair at times, but it could save their sex for the next few million years.

Nicholas Wade reported in *The New York Times* Science section on a remarkable discovery that biologists in Cambridge, Massachusetts, made in 2003.

"The decay of the Y stems from the fact that it is forbidden to enjoy the principal advantage of sex, which is, of course, for each member of a pair of chromosomes to swap matching pieces of DNA with its partner," he explained, adding that researchers had found that "denied the benefits of recombining with the X, the Y recombines with itself."

The ultimate guys' night out. Simply put, the Y chromosome figured out a Herculean way to save itself from extinction by making an incredibly difficult hairpin turn and swapping molecular material with itself—like one of those tortuous Christy Turlington yoga positions.

Dr. Jones isn't so sure it will work: "Narcissism tends not to last." (Spoken like a man who's never met a narcissist.)

Olivia Judson, science's answer to the sensual British cook Nigella Lawson, agrees that men may need more than solipsism to survive.

Dr. Judson, a thirty-five-year-old evolutionary biologist at

Imperial College in London who wrote a book about animals under the pen name Dr. Tatiana, says the worm has turned.

"For a long time, it was assumed that promiscuity was good for males and bad for females in terms of the number of kids they could have," she told me. "But it wasn't until 1988 that it really started to become evident that females were benefiting from having sex with lots of males, with more promiscuous females having more and healthier offspring."

In her book, Dr. Judson wrote about powerful leech babes, noting that females in more than eighty species, like praying mantises, have been caught devouring their lovers before, during and after mating.

"I'm particularly fond of the green spoon worm," she told me. "The male is two hundred thousand times smaller, effectively a little parasite who lives in her reproductive tract, fertilizing her eggs and regurgitating sperm through his mouth."

And then there's the tiny female midge, who plunges her proboscis into the male midge's head during procreation. As Dr. Judson pithily put it: "Her spittle turns his innards to soup, which she slurps up, drinking until she's sucked him dry."

The Economist reported on a variation of the creepy-crawly, girl-eats-boy love stories. The male orb-weaving spider kills himself before the female has a chance to kill him. Biologists now believe that the male orb weaver dies when he turns himself into a plug to prevent other males from copulating, thus ensuring his genes are more likely to live on.

Slug or plug—which would you rather date?

In a development that should make men shudder, some Chesapeake Bay watermen fished something stunning out of the water in the summer of 2005: a dual-gender crab, a "bi-lateral gynandromorph," the right side female and the left side male. (The nice thing about being a bilateral gynandromorph is that you never have to look your best.)

Before turning the crab over to scientists, the watermen conducted their own experiment into its sex life. "They dropped a female crab, which was just about ready to mate, into its tank," *The Washington Post* reported. "First, the half-and-half crab cradled the female under his legs, as a male crab would do in preparation for mating. Then, the crab seemed to lose interest in the female and let her go."

A day later, the female side of the freaky, he-she crab emerged and ate half of the poor eager-to-mate female—something female crabs do to other females when they feel vulnerable, after shedding their shells.

The watermen gave the nasty crab to scientists and said they were going fishing for a merry mermaid.

*   *   *

Not only is the Y shrinking, the X is excelling.

Research published in the journal *Nature* in 2005 revealed that women are genetically more complex than scientists ever imagined, while men remain the simple creatures they appear.

"Alas," said Duke's Dr. Willard, a coauthor of the study, "genetically speaking, if you've met one man, you've met them all. We are, I hate to say it, predictable. You can't say that about women. Men and women are farther apart than we ever knew.

It's not Mars or Venus. It's Mars or Venus, Pluto, Jupiter and who knows what other planets?"

Women are not only more different from men than we knew. Women are more different from each other than we knew.

"We poor men only have forty-five chromosomes to do our work with because our forty-sixth is a second X that is working at levels greater than we knew," Dr. Willard said, adding that their discovery may help explain why the behavior and traits of men and women are so different. They may be hard-wired in the brain, in addition to being hormonal and cultural.

The researchers learned that a whopping 15 percent—two hundred to three hundred—of the genes on the second X chromosome in women, thought to be submissive and inert, lolling about on an evolutionary Victorian fainting couch, are active, giving women a significant increase in gene expression over men.

As the *Times*'s Nicholas Wade, who is writing a book about human evolution and genetics, explained it to me: "Women are mosaics, one could even say chimeras, in the sense that they are made up of two different kinds of cell. Whereas men are pure and uncomplicated, being made of just a single kind of cell throughout."

So maybe that *Seinfeld* episode is right, where George Costanza tries to prove that man's passions can all be fulfilled at the same time if he can watch a handheld TV while "pleasuring" a woman while eating a pastrami on rye with spicy mustard.

This means men's generalizations about women are correct, too, to extend the metaphorical approach to a chromosomal reality. Women are inscrutable, changeable, crafty, idiosyncratic, a different species.

"Women's chromosomes have more complexity, which men view as unpredictability," said David Page, an expert on sex evolution at the Whitehead Institute for Biomedical Research in Cambridge, Massachusetts.

Known as Mr. Y, Dr. Page calls himself "the defender of the rotting Y chromosome."

"I prefer to think of the Y as persevering and noble," he said, "not as the Rodney Dangerfield of the human genome."

He drolly conjured up a picture of the Y chromosome as "a slovenly beast," sitting in his favorite armchair, surrounded by a litter of old fast-food takeout boxes and curled pizza crusts: "The Y wants to maintain himself but doesn't know how. He's falling apart, like the guy who can't manage to get a doctor's appointment or clean up the house or apartment unless his wife or girlfriend does it."

Dr. Page said that the Y—a refuge throughout evolution for any gene that is good for males and/or bad for females— has become "a mirror, a metaphor, a blank slate on which you can write anything you want to think about males." It has inspired cartoon gene maps that show the belching gene, the inability-to-remember-birthdays-and-anniversaries gene, the fascination-with-spiders-and-reptiles gene, the selective-hearing-loss-"Huh?" gene, the inability-to-express-affection-on-the-phone gene.

"The Y married up," Dr. Page concluded. "The X married down."

The discovery about women's superior gene expression may answer the age-old question about why men have trouble expressing themselves: Because their genes do.

•   •   •

Speaking about a planet without men, what about those fruit flies who, with the change of one cell, were turned into lesbians? (Not that there's anything wrong with that.)

The New York Times reported on the front page in June 2005 that scientists were stunned when they watched the behavior of a female fruit fly that researchers had artificially endowed with a single male-type gene:

"When the genetically altered fruit fly was released into the observation chamber, it did what these breeders par excellence tend to do," Elisabeth Rosenthal wrote. "It pursued a waiting virgin female. It gently tapped the girl with its leg, played her a song (using wings as instruments) and, only then, dared to lick her—all part of standard fruit fly seduction."

The story startled because, in an era when Americans are trying to control their environment and every aspect of their lives, it was a reminder that one gene can reverse everything. As first reported in the journal *Cell*, it took only that one "master sexual gene" to create patterns of sexual behavior.

"In a series of experiments, the researchers found that females given the male variant of the gene acted exactly like

males in courtship, madly pursuing other females," Rosenthal
wrote. "Males that were artificially given the female version of
the gene became more passive and turned their sexual attention to other males."

The paper's lead author, Dr. Barry Dickson, senior scientist
at the Institute of Molecular Biotechnology at the Austrian
Academy of Sciences in Vienna, noted: "It's very surprising.
What it tells us is that instinctive behaviors can be specified by
genetic programs, just like the morphologic development of
an organ or a nose."

Even though it's not clear if there's a similar master gene
switch for humans that can influence and determine behavior,
thrilled scientists sanguinely predicted that the remarkable results would move the debate about sexual preferences out of the
realm of morality into the realm of science.

Have they met Jerry Falwell and Rick Santorum? (Senator
Santorum memorably said that marriage should not be open to
homosexuals or others who have "man on child" or "man on
dog" sex and also said it was no surprise that the Catholic
Church pedophilia scandal flared up in Boston because the city
was a liberal seat of "sexual freedom.")

"You won't persuade the religious right," laughed Hunt
Willard. "But certainly, maybe this is the first time we have a
clear demonstration that there can be real genetic control over
sexual tendencies. Humans have adapted to homosexuality.
Think of Greeks in the old days. Homosexuality is not necessarily a bad thing genetically. It's an unproductive thing genetically. But as long as homosexuality is mixed in with
heterosexuality, nature moves on."

There is no push for this sort of research because the issue cuts both ways.

"Both conservatives and liberals love and hate this research," Dr. Page explained. "Let's say we find incontrovertible evidence that genes determine sexual preference, that a gay lifestyle isn't a matter of choice. Liberals would say, 'We've been telling you for years there's no choice about it. How can you discriminate against gays based on genes?' And gays might say, as people in the deaf community do, 'If you find a gay gene running through a family, are you going to abort us and eliminate babies with gay genes?' "

Another *Times* story on pheromones confirmed the notion that homosexuality may be innate.

"Using a brain imaging technique, Swedish researchers have shown that homosexual and heterosexual men respond differently to two odors that may be involved in sexual arousal, and that the gay men respond in the same way as women," Nicholas Wade reported. The two chemicals in the study "were a testosterone derivative produced in men's sweat and an estrogen-like compound in women's urine, both of which have long been suspected of being pheromones. . . . The estrogen-like compound, though it activated the usual smell-related regions in women, lighted up the hypothalamus in men. This is a region in the central base of the brain that governs sexual behavior and, through its control of the pituitary gland lying just beneath it, the hormonal state of the body.

"The male sweat chemical, on the other hand, did just the opposite; it activated mostly the hypothalamus in women and the smell-related regions in men."

Even comic Dennis Miller, conservative on so many issues, thinks the religious right has to give it up its attempts to help "misguided" brothers and sisters overcome the "sin" of homosexuality. "If you're a guy who's fireman-calendar-on-the-fridge gay, you can't talk yourself out of it," he told Jon Stewart.

Scientists used to think that it would be too hard to control behavior genetically. But now they're beginning to think it would be possible. If you can control homosexuality with one gene, you may also be able to control monogamy.

Researchers from Emory University reported in the June 2005 issue of *Science* that, depending on a single gene, some male prairie voles—mouselike rodents—are devoted fathers and faithful partners while others are deficient in both arenas.

The scientists said they had detected the same DNA sequence in humans but do not know how it would influence human behavior.

As Wade explained in the *Times*, male voles with a long version of this section of DNA are monogamous and devoted to their pups, while voles with shorter versions of the DNA strand are less so: "People have the same variability in their DNA, with a control section that comes in at least 17 lengths detected so far."

So size matters again: This time the bigger you are, the truer you are.

Wade asked researchers the gazillion-dollar question: "So should women seek men with the longest possible DNA control region in the hope that, like the researchers' voles, they will display 'increased probability of preferences for a familiar-partner female over a novel-stranger female'?"

Dr. Larry Young replied that the genetic effect in men would be influenced by culture, "and thus hard to predict on an individual basis." It was refreshing to hear a scientist finally mention the power of culture.

Wade noted that the same DNA control mechanism is also present in humans' two closest cousins, the chimpanzee and the bonobo, and bears on a controversy about which of these two species humans more closely resemble: "Chimpanzees operate territorially based societies controlled by males who conduct often-lethal raids on neighboring groups. Bonobos, which look much like chimps, are governed by female hierarchies and facilitate almost every social interaction with copious sex."

Dr. Page told me that the various behaviors of men encoded in DNA are meant "to ensure our adaptability over the long term," and that both sexes should stop having Henry— or Henrietta—Higgins fantasies of remaking the other sex to get rid of irritating traits.

From cave drawings to text messaging, the sexes, he says, have been getting along with each other, and accommodating each other, for billions of years, since the primordial soup.

"If we start tweaking the behavior of the sexes," he cautioned, "it will lead to chaos."

• • •

Do male nipples prove evolution?

Not at all, according to a Web site for a planned Creation Museum—AnswersinGenesis.org—devoted to showing that the Bible is literally true and that the temptress Eve actually brought the Garden of Eden crashing down around poor Adam's head.

While nipples may be biologically de trop for men, a creationist "expert" on the site noted, that doesn't mean they resulted from natural selection. They could just as well be a decorating feature of the Creator's (like a hood ornament). Who are we to question His designs, the expert asked, since we cannot presume to comprehend His mind?

In an America more obsessed with legislating religion than advancing science, where high schools are increasingly afraid to teach evolution and many IMAX theaters are even shying away from showing movies that mention evolution, the evolution-vs.-creationism debate rages on issues like male nipples and female orgasms.

Both are vestigial by-products of the fact that male and female embryos have the same characteristics, except for different chromosomes, in the first six to nine weeks of life until the Y kicks into gear.

"We are left with nipples and also with some breast tissue," *Best Life* magazine explained to confused male readers. "Abnormal enlargement of the breasts in a male is known as gynecomastia. (Some people call them 'bitch tits.') Gynecomastia can be caused by using anabolic steroids. So if Barry Bonds shows up at an old-timers game with 44DD man boobs, then I think we will finally have our answer to the steroid controversy."

Donald Symons, an anthropology professor at the University of California at Santa Barbara who wrote *The Evolution of Human Sexuality*, posited that natural selection favored female nipples, because women needed them for reproductive success. Male nipples just came along for the evolutionary ride.

(Although a 2005 article in *The Times* of London suggested that in the absence of mom, a man's nipple may be just as comforting to a crying baby.)

Similarly, natural selection favored a male orgasm, because men use contractions of orgasm as a way to deliver sperm. Female orgasms came along for the ride because women got the erectile and nerve pathways in the early parallel body plan.

As Dr. Elisabeth Lloyd wrote in her book *The Case of the Female Orgasm: Bias in the Science of Evolution*, since male nipples and female orgasms were not needed for reproduction, they may have survived just for the sake of, as George Costanza might put it, pleasuring.

"To continue the parallel, I would add that either embryological bonus—the male nipple or the female orgasmic equipment—can be used by the gifted parties," she wrote. "Males often inherit not only the nipple structure but also the pleasurable and sexual sensitivity of the female nipple, and they can make use of this in their sexual practices. Similarly, females inherit the clitoral organ and the structural erectile tissues and neural pathways needed to experience orgasm and can make use of them in their sexual practices."

Dr. Lloyd, a philosopher of science and professor of biology at Indiana University, created a stir with her 2005 book, which examined all the theories about the evolutionary purpose of the female orgasm.

She said she was certain that the clitoris was an evolutionary adaptation, selected to create excitement, leading to sexual intercourse and then reproduction. But since the orgasm had no direct line to fertility or reproduction, she said that it must have survived simply "for fun."

In the '70s and '80s, *Cosmopolitan* regularly published articles about "the big O." There was an intense debate driven by the fluffernut opinions of male experts who suggested that mutual climaxing was common and superior, and that "clitoral" orgasms were nonexistent or inferior to "vaginal" orgasms, ones achieved simply through intercourse, without separate clitoral stimulation. Traditionalists refused to believe that an orgasm could be purely for pleasure, without a reproductive underpinning.

Dr. Lloyd noted that most of the orgasm theories in scientific "cliterature," to borrow writer Christopher Buckley's coinage, were developed by men who did not understand the nature of female orgasm and had false expectations based on the dynamics of male orgasms. These cockeyed theories ended up making women feel inadequate and abnormal when their experiences did not measure up.

In a way, it's analogous to what happened to women with clothes in the '70s. Just as they thought equality meant aping male corporate dressing, they thought equality meant aping male orgasms. Now women can dress—and climax—in their own style.

Dr. Lloyd analyzed thirty-two studies, conducted over seventy-four years, about the frequency of female orgasm during intercourse. She found that when intercourse was "unassisted"—not accompanied by stimulation of the clitoris—only a quarter of the women studied experienced orgasms often or very often during intercourse. Five to 10 percent never had orgasms, yet many became pregnant.

As Natalie Angier pointed out in her book *Woman*: "Marilyn Monroe, the most elaborated sexual icon of the twentieth century and surely the source of auto-eruptive glee for thousands of fans, confessed to a friend that despite her three husbands and a parade of lovers, she had never had an orgasm." In her come-hither look, Marilyn was better at the hither than the come.

The Los Angeles Times revealed in 2005 that Marilyn did at long last learn to have orgasms from her shrink, who taught her how to stimulate herself so she could go on to have them with men. "I never cried so hard as I did after my first orgasm," Marilyn said on her psychiatrist's secret tapes. "How can I describe to you, a man, what an orgasm feels like to a woman? I'll try. Think of a light fixture with a rheostat control. As you slowly turn it on, the bulb begins to get bright, then brighter and brighter, fully lit. As you turn it off, it gradually becomes dimmer, and at last goes out."

Angier neatly addressed the question of whether women are supposed to have clitorises in the first place.

"Maybe you've pondered along these lines yourself," she wrote. "Maybe you've idly rolled the old sexual chestnuts around in your mind and wondered why it is that women are the ones with the organ dedicated exclusively to sexual pleasure, when men are the ones who are supposed to be dedicated exclusively to sexual pleasure. Men are portrayed as wanting to go at it all the time, women as preferring a good cuddle; yet a man feels preposterously peacockish if he climaxes three or

four times in a night, compared to the fifty or hundred orgasms that a sexually athletic woman can have in an hour or
two. Maybe you thought it was some sort of cosmic joke, in the
same category of sexual dissonance as the fact that a man is at
his libidinous peak before he is quite a man, by age eighteen
or twenty, while a woman doesn't reach full flower until her
thirties or even forties (about the time, a female comedian
once put it, that her husband is discovering that he has a favorite chair)."

Angier takes issue with evolutionary biologists who reduce
X and Y relations to the stereotype of a coy female and ardent
male, as illustrated in the "familiar ditty variously attributed
to William James, Ogden Nash and Dorothy Parker":

Hoggamus, higgamus
Men are polygamous
Higgamus, hoggamus
Women monogamous

(Or as the poet Elizabeth Bishop wrote in 1944, "I'm going
to go and take the bus and find someone monogamous.")

"A raft of epidemiological studies have shown that marriage adds more years to the life of a man than it does to that
of a woman," Angier asserted. "Why should that be, if men are
so 'naturally' ill-suited to matrimony?"

Rejecting Darwinian rationales for the behavior of Bill
Clinton, she said women's behavior may be shaped more by politics and culture—from *Sister Carrie* to Carrie Bradshaw—
than sexual mores:

"Would a man find the prospect of a string of partners so appealing if the following rules were applied: that no matter how much he may like a particular woman and be pleased by her performance and want to sleep with her again, he will have no say in the matter and will be dependent on her mood and good graces for all future contact; that each act of casual sex will cheapen his status and make him increasingly less attractive to other women; and that society will not wink at his randiness but rather sneer at him and think him pathetic, sullied, smaller than life? Until men are subjected to the same severe standards and threat of censure as women are, and until they are given the lower hand in a so-called casual encounter from the start, it is hard to insist with such self-satisfaction that, hey, it's natural, men like a lot of sex with a lot of people and women don't."

She suggests that younger women might be drawn to mature men not, as the evolutionary biologists insist, because the men have more resources, but because they deplete less oxygen than young studs on the rise.

Could it be, she asks, "that an older man is appealing not because he is powerful but because in his maturity he has lost some of his power, has become less marketable and desirable and potentially more grateful and gracious, more likely to make a younger woman feel that there is a balance of power in the relationship? The rude little calculation is simple: He is male, I am female—advantage, man. He is older, I am younger—advantage, woman. . . . Who can breathe in the presence of a handsome young man whose ego, if expressed as a vapor, would fill Biosphere 2? Not even, I'm afraid, a beautiful young woman."

Angier also disputes the assumption that women have a lower sex drive than men. "Yet it is not low enough," she reasoned. "There is still just enough of a lingering female infidelity impulse that cultures everywhere have had to gird against it by articulating a rigid dichotomy with menacing implications for those who fall on the wrong side of it. There is still enough lingering female infidelity to justify infibulation, purdah, claustration. Men have the naturally higher sex drive, yet all the laws, customs, punishments, shame, strictures, mystiques and antimystiques are aimed with full homonid fury at that tepid, sleepy, hypoactive creature, the female libido."

We can see this all the more vividly now that we are tilting against a radical Islamic culture that obliterates, stones, rapes and executes women in order to suppress their sexuality, that suffocates women's human obligation to contribute to society, wasting their brains and hearts and skills because of inane, obscene fears that civilization will fall at the sight of a female ankle or clavicle.

Honor killings only go one way. "It seems premature ... to attribute the relative lack of female interest in sexual variety to women's biological nature alone in the face of overwhelming evidence that women are consistently beaten for promiscuity and adultery," the primatologist Barbara Smuts said. "If female sexuality is muted compared to that of men, then why must men the world over go to extreme lengths to control and contain it?" So what do women want? Liberty and emotional parity, Angier believes.

At the same time that Dr. Lloyd's book came out, a London study of twins suggested that the ability of a woman to have an orgasm is one-third genetic. In what *The New York Post* called "a genetic anti-climax," one in three respondents said they never or hardly ever reached orgasm during intercourse and 21 percent said they rarely, if ever, came during mastur-bation.

Scientists at St. Thomas's Hospital in London said their findings didn't mean that women with logy orgasm genes were screwed, so to speak, but rather that more patience and atten-tion would be required. (Like the scene in *American Gigolo*, when Richard Gere tells Lauren Hutton he spent three hours pleasuring a seventy-year-old woman. "Who else would have taken the time?" he wondered, patting himself on his Armani-clad back.)

And another study, by researchers at the University of Groningen in the Netherlands, showed that women could fake orgasms with their mates, but not in their heads. Brain scans showed when the orgasm was real, the parts of the brain in-volving fear, emotion and consciousness were deactivated. (So if you want to fake it, ladies, don't sleep with a neurologist.)

I appreciate Dr. Lloyd's feminist spin on the orgasm, but I'm not sure I agree with her about the orgasm having no role as an "adaptive" mechanism in evolution.

I tend more to the view of one Harriet Lindbeck of New Orleans, who wrote a letter to *The New York Times* after read-ing an article about Dr. Lloyd's book. I like to imagine that Har-riet, whoever she is, composed her saucy missive at Galatoire's, over turtle soup and a Sazerac, between steamy liaisons in the Big Easy before it became the Big Uneasy.

"Although I'm not a biologist, I propose a commonsense

theory that explains why female orgasm has been adaptive in our species," Lindbeck wrote. "Men who regularly help women reach orgasm are in some combination more empathetic, fonder of their partner, emotionally savvier and perhaps better seducers.

"The first three characteristics are attractive to women; they also make men better fathers, thus somewhat more likely to engender children and more likely to raise them successfully.

"The last two characteristics, savvy and seductiveness, are by definition very likely to attract partners, even if they are not associated with good child-rearing skills.

"In fact, the less female orgasm is attached to intercourse, the more emotional skill and intelligence our male ancestors must have had to foster female orgasm—whether for altruistic or self-serving reasons.

"Thus, women choosing men who are better lovers has helped produce savvier and more sensitive human beings."

So there may even be a biological imperative for generosity in bed.

Five

OF PUSSYCATS, BOOTY CALLS, ROAD BEEF AND SLUMP BUSTERS

went to the West Fifty-seventh Street offices of *Cosmopolitan* once in the early '80s, looking for freelance work. An editor gave me some red binders filled with story ideas that were oddly reversible.

You could choose "I Had an Affair With My Best Friend's Father" or "I Had an Affair With My Father's Best Friend."

You could choose "My Fling With My Gynecologist/Psychiatrist/Dentist" or "My Year of Celibacy."

There was: "I Am a Puerto Rican *Cosmo* Girl," "I Am a Black *Cosmo* Girl" and "I Am a Handicapped *Cosmo* Girl."

I felt a little provincial. I hadn't had a fling with my dentist or my father's best friend. So I chose a story called "On Turning 30." I'd read so many *Cosmo*s that I assumed I understood the formula perfectly. (In my twenties, I'd religiously followed *Cosmo*'s advice on such things as buying satin sheets and putting them in the fridge in summer, or taking a book with a provocative title on the bus or subway so a guy would have an excuse to talk to you. I used *Crime and Punishment*, which never worked so well.)

I peppered my story with exclamation points and italics, in the *Cosmo* manner. But the edited version came back with a handwritten comment from Helen Gurley Brown herself in the margin: "Pure pablum."

Like every great trendsetter, the original *Cosmo* girl knew the difference between real and faux. I did a total rewrite, minus the italics.

Brown always understood that you stick with a winning formula. She put that formula in amber all through the feminist revolution and politically correct era, and eventually women swung back around to courtesan wiles.

She has the integrity of her fishnets, peddling the same seductress philosophy prefeminism, postfeminism and postmenopause. She is the perfect twin to Hugh Hefner. They started in the '50s, before ideologies about feminism and the Pill, and were willing to be ridiculous at times in order to consecrate their whole lives to the question of sex—who, when, why, where and how.

She was the editor of one of the most successful magazines of all time but never won a prize for editorial content at the National Magazine Awards. In 1996, she was honored for her commercial success and named to the editors' Hall of Fame. I went over to her office on that occasion to chat with her.

She had put the glass award on a table, underneath a picture of the young Christie Brinkley glistening in a gold bikini. Her lair was exactly what you might imagine for the editrix who has spent her life urging young women to unleash the inner tiger. There was a leopard rug, pink flowered wallpaper, makeup mirrors on the wall, a candle on the desk, Chanel perfume by the window and *Sammy Davis Jr.'s Greatest Hits* by the CD player.

Even then, at seventy-three, Brown was relentlessly girlish, green-bean thin, beehive-teased. She and her magazine had arrested development. She had been running the same stories ("How Big Should the Big O Be?," "How to Hold a Man by Giving Him His Freedom" and "Just a Good Friend or Is She After Your Man?") since I was in college. The only difference was now they added arbitrary numbers for shock effect in headlines in the spirit of "1,213 Ways to Please a Man Without Waking Him" and "346 Ways to Lean Over at Dinner and Tell Him You're Not Wearing Any Underwear."

Brown was chipper, hiding whatever hurt she felt that the Hearst Corporation was giving the magazine she had run for thirty years to a younger editor, Bonnie Fuller, who had made her name aping Brown running *YM* magazine.

It was a more P.C. era, in the wake of Anita Hill, and Hearst fretted that Brown's unreconstructed version of the *Cosmo* girl, fond of lingerie and married men, was as passé as the *Playboy* bunny. Her downplaying of the AIDS threat for women and her pooh-poohing of sexual harassment embarrassed the company.

"I parted company with the feminists in the seventies when it was thought that you had to wear charcoal gray turtleneck sweaters and no makeup," said Brown, wearing Adolfo and jangly gold jewelry. "I was accused of hurting the cause because I was still talking about women as though they were sex objects. But to be a sex object is a wonderful thing, and you're to be pitied if you aren't one."

She did give "the radical feminists," as she calls them, credit, though: "Gloria Steinem and her group went over to *Time* magazine and demanded that women be allowed to be reporters as well as stenographers. It had to be established that women were quite equal in terms of both stupidity and of brains with men."

In the midst of the hurricane over harassment unleashed by Anita Hill, when grizzled senators were being hounded by feminist Furies making them promise never to be insensitive again, Brown wrote a hilariously out-of-sync piece for *The Wall Street Journal* titled "At Work, Sexual Electricity Sparks Creativity."

She explained that she refused to run articles on sexual harassment in *Cosmo* because "I have this possibly benighted idea that when a man finds you sexually attractive, he is paying you a compliment . . . when he doesn't, that's when you have to worry."

She also reminisced fondly about her salad days at a Los Angeles radio station KHJ, as she worked her way through secretarial school, when the men played "a dandy game" called "Scuttle."

"Rules: All announcers and engineers who weren't busy would select a secretary, chase her down the halls, through the music library and back to the announcing booths, catch her and take her panties off. Once the panties were off, the girl could put them back on again. Nothing wicked ever happened. Depantying was the sole object of the game.

"While all this was going on, the girl herself usually shrieked, screamed, flailed, blushed, threatened and pretended to faint, but to my knowledge no scuttler was ever reported to the front office. *Au contraire,* the girls wore their prettiest panties to work."

As for her, she said that "alas, I was never scuttled . . . too young, too pale, too flat-chested. Clearly unscuttlable."

She insisted that "some of the best creative work ever to come out of offices I've worked in (seventeen before I got to *Cosmo*) has been produced by teams of men and women showing off for each other," and concluded with a moral out of Aesop's would-be erotic fables: "I think indeed we should come down hard on the bullies and the creeps but not go stamping out sexual chemistry at work."

This was the exactly same philosophy she propounded in her 1964 book, *Sex and the Single Girl,* now marketed as "a cult classic." "I'm convinced that offices are sexier than Turkish harems, fraternity house weekends, Hollywood swimming parties, Cary Grant's smile or the *Playboy* centerfold," she wrote, "and more action takes place in them than in a nymphet's daydreams." (Clearly, she's never been to the Washington bureau of *The New York Times*.)

"Far from being minor, transient, pippypoo associations," she bubbled, "romances and affairs starting through work can be some of the most cliff-hanging, satisfying, memorable episodes in any two persons' lives."

But Hearst needn't have worried. The *Cosmo* girl, once scorned by feminists, outlasted feminism. She permeated the culture; she is, after all, just a tarted-up Cinderella, always believing happiness is just one makeover—or sex trick—away.

When young editors started lipstick feminism "zines" for "girls" in the mid-'90s, they mocked "Helen Girly Brown," saying she was stuck in a *Valley of the Dolls* world.

Debbie Stoller, the editor of *BUST*, told Geraldine Baum of the *L.A. Times* that the early feminists were "women" who wanted to be like men, while latter-day grown-up "girls," like Madonna and Courtney Love, wanted the freedom to be "girly" for their own pleasure.

But Stoller's postfeminist philosophy sounded exactly like Brown's prefeminist philosophy. "Even when we grow up, we are all girls," Brown liked to say. "Girl is the feminine side, the playful side, the hopeful side."

Brown hung in there long enough to see women circle back her way, yearning to be endlessly illuminated about "The Three Kinds of Sex Guys Crave." The Age of Aquarius dissolved into the Age of Collagen and Fake Curves. The sultry fabrics Brown always promoted—zebra, leopard, satin—are now common at the office and even on nightly newscasts.

Cosmo is still the best-selling magazine on college campuses, as it was when I was in college, and the best-selling monthly magazine on the newsstand:

The June 2005 issue, with Jessica Simpson on the cover, her cleavage spilling out of an orange croqueted halter dress, could have been June 1970. The headlines are familiar: "How to turn him on in 10 words or less," "Do You Make Men M-E-L-T? Take our quiz," "Bridal Special," *Cosmo*'s stud search and "Cosmo's Most Famous Sex Tips; the Legendary Tricks That Have Brought Countless Guys to Their Knees."

(Sex Trick 4: "Place a glazed doughnut around your man's member, then gently nibble the pastry and lick the icing . . . as well as his manhood." Another favorite *Cosmo* trick is to yell out during sex which of your girlfriends thinks your man is hot.)

At any newsstand, you'll see the original *Cosmo* girl's man-crazy, sex-obsessed image endlessly, tiresomely replicated, even for the teen set. On the cover of *YM*: "Go Get HIM! Guy-Snagging Moves That Really Work," or *Mademoiselle*: "Make Love With the Lights On!"

"There has been lots of copying—look at *Glamour*," Brown sighed about the catfighting women's magazines. "I used to have all the sex to myself."

In the summer of 2005, *Glamour*'s covers blared "What everyone you know is *really* doing in bed: The sex survey that'll shock you," "Men's 99 Unspoken Sex Secrets" and "The 8 Worst Things You Can Say to a Man." *Marie Claire* went with "Be Gutsy in Bed" and the inspirational first-person confessional: " 'Prostitution Gives Me Power.' " And *Jane* revealed "Sex Tips from Celebs."

Before it curdled into a collection of stereotypes, feminism had fleetingly held out a promise that there would be some precincts of womanly life that were not all about men. But it never quite materialized.

It took only a few decades to create a brazen new world where the highest ideal is to acknowledge your inner slut. I am woman, see me strip. Instead of peaceful havens of girl things and boy things, we have a society where women of all ages are striving to become self-actualized sex kittens. Hollywood actresses now work out by taking pole-dancing classes.

Female sexuality has been more a zigzag than an arc. We had decades of Victorian prudery, when women were not supposed to like sex. Then we had the Pill and zipless encounters, when women were supposed to have the same animalistic drive as men. Then it was discovered—shock, horror!—that men and women are not alike in their desires, and that you couldn't squander all your fertility years playing at the sexual fair. But zipless morphed into hookups, and the more one-night stands the girls on *Sex and the City* had, the grumpier they got.

Then came "a silent epidemic," as CBS called it, of dysfunctional female libidos, with researchers showing as many as four in ten American women experiencing some form of sexual dissatisfaction.

Newsweek offered this insight in its 2000 search-for-female-Viagra cover: "For women, the relationship and the context of sexuality can be even more critical to satisfaction than the majesty that is orgasm."

Women aspire to the majesty of the cuddle? Who knew?

To go with that *Newsweek* cover, Brown wrote a sidebar urging superannuated *Cosmo* girls to pick up the pace. "I had sex last night," she wrote, not burying the lead. "I'm 78 and my husband, movie producer David Brown, is 83. . . . Sex is one of the three best things there are, and I don't know what the other two are."

If older men can attract nubile sweeties with trips and baubles, she said, why can't older babes go the *American Gigolo* route? "If there's a man who might be up for having sex with you, take him to Gucci," she instructed.

The thought of being with a man who wants to go to Gucci, much less having to pay for him to go there, is a little daunting. Next he'd be asking you to buy him a little white dog.

Brown conceded that after sixty or seventy, some shyness might set in. "Here's the biggie: How you can possibly undress in front of a man who's never seen you naked," she wrote. "That cellulite, those folds, those pooches!"

But she had some tips: "Wear something up to the last minute before getting into bed; turn off the lights if that makes you less nervous and back out of the room when it's over if you think your front is better than your back."

I called Brown in 2005 to see if she agreed that not much had changed since her first issue in July 1965. She was at the Hotel Bel-Air with her husband.

Jessica Simpson met her standards. "The girl on the cover should always have cleavage," she said, "always a pretty girl, but not the girl next door, not a librarian, not that they're not wonderful people, but someone more sexy and exciting."

The cover blurbs, she said, were even raunchier than when she had her husband writing hers. "My *Cosmo* was not as sexual," she recalled. "We always had one major sex article in the middle. We always ran an article on masturbation once a year to tell girls, 'Honey, it feels good, an orgasm is an orgasm.' But I also cared more about writing. I got Gore Vidal, Truman Capote, Irwin Shaw, Dominick Dunne. Now the sex in *Cosmo* never stops. They have stories like 'Finding his G-spot and five places he should touch you he hasn't discovered.' "

She has, er, put her finger on something. We live in a society that is so derangingly sexualized, it's not a sexy society. You can't think about sex clearly if all you're thinking about is sex, whether it's an obsession over celibacy or nymphomania. The more we analyze it, medicate it, demystify it and deconstruct it, the more we make it the incessant subject of movies, music, magazines, novels, memoirs, TV shows, online female sexual dysfunction quizzes, the less clarity we attain.

We're saturated—from the tweens sporting T-shirts with messages like MY DAD THINKS I'M A VIRGIN and YOU WERE HOTTER ONLINE to vibrators hidden in rubber duckies, lipsticks and brushes at Bendel's designed for the traveling gal who wants to bring sex toys secretly through airport security.

America has always been conflicted about sex, its puritanical side clashing with its prurient side.

But now, with the ascendance of the prudish religious right and the numbing oversexualization of commerce and culture, America seems positively bipolar about sex.

As former attorney general John Ashcroft was throwing a blue curtain over the breasts of the classical statue representing Justice in the Justice Department lobby, women's and men's magazines were going blue with cleavage shots and raunchy sex tips and teenage stars were getting breast implants.

As Amazon.com began selling sex toys, a public radio station in Kentucky briefly canceled the venerable Garrison Keillor's show *The Writer's Almanac* because he read a poem with the word "breast" in it.

An art dealer in New York captured the schizoid insanity of the moment perfectly, confiding that he gets calls from wealthy private collectors in places like Texas saying that they don't want Rubens or Monet nudes because they have small children at home. They'd rather stick with impressionist landscapes and old Dutch masters.

The current *Cosmo* editor, my friend Kate White, says that *Cosmo* is more lascivious now because society is. "If I had Helen's headlines now," she said wryly, "*Cosmo* would look like *Reader's Digest.*"

Just as I did, Kate went to *Cosmo* back in the day to look through the red binders for freelance work, and was asked to do a feature on "How to tell what a man is like in bed by what's in his refrigerator."

"I thought, okay, if he has beef jerky, does that mean he's a beefy jerk?" she recalled, laughing. "I gave up."

She said her goals in college were "to be cute, get cute guys and be the editor of a magazine," all of which she has done with panache, looking gorgeous in leopard skin in her editor's letter picture. "But the feminists made you feel that if you wanted to have your cake and eat it, too, if you wanted to be pretty and sexy and like guys you couldn't be a feminist," she said.

Still, Kate worries about the Barbie effect, and says she publishes no articles advocating plastic surgery. In August 2005, she ran a story about the attack of the Barbie clones, from Pamela Anderson to Carmen Electra, asking "Has Plastic Surgery Gone Too Far?"

The story pointed out that there's been a 118 percent increase in cosmetic surgery since '97, and wondered "Is this quest for bodily perfection leading us to look like a nation of plastic dolls?"

Well, yeah.

Her predecessor still holds the title of editor in chief, Cosmopolitan International. "I'm eighty-three and I'm a working girl from 1940 'till right this minute," Brown said. "*Cosmo* is now in fifty-five countries, with thirty-five new editions—one in Beijing that is so full of ads you can hardly lift it."

It's also in Estonia, Latvia, Lithuania, Croatia and Serbia, and in three countries with large Muslim populations: Indonesia, Turkey and India.

I was curious about foreign *Cosmo* editions. Do they offer freelances stories like "I'm a Lithuanian *Cosmo* Girl—a Member of the Coalition of the Very Willing" and "I'm a Siberian *Cosmo* Girl—No Ethnic Cleansing Jokes," and, for the Muslims, do they have red binders with stories like "I Had an Affair With My Mullah's Falconer or With My Falconer's Mullah"?

Kate explained, "In these countries we have to use nuance and innuendo when writing about sex. The words 'pleasure' and 'passion' are used more than 'lust' or 'orgasm.' The how-to sex and relationship articles are geared toward couples who are in a serious relationship and not just casually dating. In Thailand, for instance, a penis is referred to as 'the master of the universe,' or 'the little brother.' The vagina is simply called 'there.' "

I asked Helen to sum up what she has learned.

"Pussycat," she purred. "You can have a better life if you work at it, but, honey, there's no free lunch. You've got to do it yourself."

What could be more feminist than that?

● ● ●

As women's magazines tarted up, men's magazines dumbed down.

While *Cosmo* offered features like "I Had an Affair With My Father's Best Friend," *Maxim* offered ones like "I've Shagged Your Mum." ("She had hands like sandpaper," the writer recalled.)

This was a source of great irritation to my late friend Art Cooper, the editor of *GQ* for twenty years, who was bemused by what this revealed about the state of mind of American men at the turn of the century.

Art was no prude. He had edited *Penthouse* letters to the editor in the mid-'70s. He would call to propose stories I could write for him. "Do you want to *do* Russell Crowe?" he'd ask, a genial leer in his voice.

Art was a bear of a man who strode around in a cloud of Ralph Lauren Safari, an old-school sybarite who loved wine, women, cigarettes and sexy chat. He died at sixty-five of a stroke right in the place he had most enjoyed all those things simultaneously—New York's Four Seasons Grill Room.

He wanted *GQ* to have IQ, to be literary and voracious in its interests, and he felt the image of American men should be more adult and cosmopolitan than nearly naked babes, beer, gear, bathroom humor, scoring tips and a core philosophy that men are incapable of talking to other men unless they are making jokes. Art yearned for an America that was more Bogie than Pauly Shore, more Steve McQueen than Adam Sandler, more James Bond than Austin Powers.

He could not fathom the explosive popularity of British imports *Maxim, Stuff* and *FHM,* and fought a failing battle to keep *GQ* from being engulfed by the immature laddie-book tide of flesh-peddling and articles like "50 Things Women Don't Want You to Know." (No. 46: "If she tries to kill herself, she will probably botch the job.")

Dismissing *Maxim* as "visual junk food" and "a joke book with T & A," he told me: "I think it's a reaction against political correctness. It's a reaction against the women's movement. It's for guys who really want to be fourteen again."

But it didn't really make sense that the frat-boy mags were thriving because men were confused and threatened by feminism, since women's mags had gotten all retro and sex-drenched, too. (Just as Wal-Mart bans laddie books, Kroger's hides *Cosmo* behind plastic blinders.)

Oddly enough, Felix Dennis, who created the top-selling *Maxim,* said he stole his laddie "us against the world" attitude from women's magazines like *Cosmo.*

Just as women didn't mind losing *Cosmo*'s prestigious fiction writers, plenty of guys were happy to lose the literary pretensions of venerable men's magazines and embrace simpleminded gender stereotypes, like the *Maxim* manifesto instructing women: "If we see you in the morning and night, why call us at work?"

Jessica Simpson and Eva Longoria move seamlessly from showing their curves on the covers of *Cosmo* and *Glamour* to *Maxim*, which dubbed Simpson "America's favorite ball and chain!" In the summer of 2005, both *GQ* and *FHM* featured Pamela Anderson spilling out of their covers. ("I think of my breasts as props," she told *FHM*.)

A lot of women now want to be *Maxim* babes as much as men want *Maxim* babes. So women have traveled an arc from fighting objectification to seeking it.

"I have been surprised," *Maxim*'s editor, Ed Needham, confessed, "to find that a lot of women would want to be somehow validated as a *Maxim* girl type, that they'd like to be thought of as hot and would like their boyfriends to take pictures of them or make comments about them that mirror the *Maxim* representation of a woman, the Pamela Anderson sort of brand. That, to me, is kind of extraordinary."

The luscious babes on the cover of *Maxim* were supposed to be men's fantasy guilty pleasure, after all, not their real life-affirming girlfriends. With so many women dressing and acting like *Maxim* girls, men get a little confused.

Dave Chappelle did a hilarious stand-up routine about how this trend makes it very hard for guys in bars trying to discern between a slut and a wholesome girl dressed like a slut. "All right, lady," he tells a girl in a bar who objects to a raunchy pickup line. "You are not a whore but you are wearing a whore's uniform."

Needham agreed it's a bit baffling. "Men used to think women were completely passive and inert and only came to life sexually when men could stir them into action through their fantastic chat-up lines and cheesy dance routines in the bedroom," he said. "But the joke is, women have made up their minds exactly what they want to do and whether they're interested or not, long before the guy has got into his routine."

Magazines like *Men's Health* convey a tonier image of an evolving male "striving toward self-improvement, mastery and control," according to David Zinczenko, the editor in chief. And good abs, of course. "Men want to wake up at forty and feel the way Johnny Depp feels, or seventy-five and feel the way Paul Newman feels, with a successful career, marriage, family and a life that includes excitement, adventure and charity.

"Men like to eliminate the unknown as much as possible. That's one of the reasons men like SUVs, because they can stick to their schedule even if it snows. They don't have to give up control to the elements."

He mused that men are in a muddle: "Society sends men confusing signals. Society tells men to be more like women, more sensitive, more caring, more thoughtful. And you know what happens then? They end up in 'Styles of the Times' in stories about why men are becoming more like women, ordering wine by the glass as well as the bottle."

Si Newhouse felt the laddification of men's magazines had gone so far that an antidote was needed. So he created a new men's magazine and put a woman in charge. Anna Wintour supervised the 2005 fall launch of *Men's Vogue*, which hopes to win back some of the readers who want more out of life than breasts and beer, the sort of man, one executive of the new magazine said, who escorts a woman to the Met ball.

Needham said the laddie philosophy is that men are not the noble, heroic creatures conjured up by the classic men's magazines "who are superb at golf or excellent at marlin fishing. That's an even more wayward and absurd stereotype than *Maxim*'s stereotype of the spineless man, that man is driven by failings and weaknesses and never overcomes them, but deals with them through the medium of humor. Men are incapable of talking about their inner world the way women are."

He defends the oafish laddie approach to the male psyche: "Eating, sex and sports are the Europe, Asia and Americas of the male mental map. That doesn't leave a lot of room for much else.

"There is this endless fascination and infinite appetite for knowledge about women and their motives and how to understand them better for purely selfish reasons. Men's appetite for titillation, sex, sexual imagery, sexual references and anecdotes has no bounds."

Needham thinks a lot of the advice that women get from the sex-crazed women's magazines is "absurd." For instance, the September 2005 *Cosmo* advises women on the "tactile moves that are sure to send him running," including treating him to a walking back massage in four-inch stilettos and dripping hot wax on him. (Sounds like an old Madonna movie.)

I'm pretty certain, however, that I read in the August *Cosmo* that dripping hot wax in stilettos was sure to bring him running. Either way, many men get alarmed at the tips in *Cosmo*. "If they're *not* supposed to drip hot wax on you," said one terrified and confused man reading the September issue, "are they *not* supposed to pour scalding water on your member?"

And certainly the counsel women are getting from *Glamour* and *Cosmo* does not dovetail with the counsel men are getting from *Maxim* and *Stuff.*

When you read women's magazines, they're all about trying to please men. When you read laddie books, they're all about trying to please men, too.

Are the sexes meshing? In magazines, not so much.

Cosmo Style in the summer of 2005 offered earnest tips for being sexy for him, while *Maxim* offered tongue-in-cheek tips for dumping her:

Cosmo: "Do your chores (like mowing the lawn) in your bikini."

Maxim: "It seemed like a good idea at first, but she just never regained her figure after that fourth baby. . . . Be noble, gradually reducing eye contact, then slink away in the night."

Cosmo: "Kissing after applying a minty lipgloss packs an explosive passion punch."

Maxim: "Ignoring a girl you've just started seeing can actually spare her feelings—hell, that's what caller ID is *for.*"

Cosmo: "Lick your fingers while you're eating for an erotic edge."

Maxim: "Repeat after us: 'It's not you; it's me.' It's the gold standard cliché for a reason. She refuses to admit you're inferior? Prove it by sleeping with everyone she knows, starting with her mother."

Cosmo: "Hide a booty call box underneath your bed. Fill it with . . . tea light candles, scented massage oil, a jaw-dropping bra and panty set."

Maxim: "Stick to your decision: One booty call and you're back in her web."

• • •

For an even more brutal glimpse into the primitive thinking of a certain segment of the male species, there was Jose Canseco's 2005 best seller, *Juiced*.

"As everyone knows, baseball players are very superstitious," the former Oakland A's slugger wrote in a segment called "Slump Busters." "Players who are struggling start talking about how they need to go out and find something to break their slump. And often enough it comes out something like this: 'Oh my God, I'm 0-for-20. I'm going to get the ugliest girl I can find and have sex with her.' "

Canseco nobly pointed out that he never stooped to this tactic. "I'd rather go 0-for-40," he protested. But he tattled that many of his fellow athletes did seek out "slump busters." What a lovely term used by our sports heroes, our boys of summer.

"It could mean the woman was big, or ugly, or a combination of both," Canseco explained. He said that golden boy Mark Grace, the former Chicago Cubs first baseman who seems like the kind of nice guy and good sport you'd want to bring home to mom, defined a slump buster as making out with the "fattest, gnarliest chick you can uncover."

Grace has talked about slump busters himself in interviews over the years, telling the sports radio talk show host Jim Rome that if a team was enduring a losing streak, the guys would persuade one player to break the curse by going out and rounding the bases with an ugly woman. Grace called it "throwing himself on the grenade" for the good of the team. Canseco agreed: "However you slice it, it was bound to be unpleasant."

With steroid-infused sensitivity, he also explained a couple of other words in the baseball argot: Any girl you met on the road and went to bed with was referred to as "road beef," and any road beef you flew in was known as an "import."

Even some men I know felt awful for the unwitting slump busters who would read *Juiced* and realize that the best night of their lives was actually the worst. Those really cute baseball players they thought liked them just as they were, as Bridget Jones liked to say, were really holding their noses to break a curse. Harsh.

At the dawn of feminism, there was an assumption that women would not be as severely judged on their looks in ensuing years. Phooey. It's just the opposite. Looks matter more than ever.

Pretty soon, we'll be back to the era when flight attendants—or should I say stewardesses?—were canned if they gained a few pounds. *The New York Post* reported in 2005 that the Borgata Hotel Casino and Spa in Atlantic City decided to start weighing all its waitresses—known as "Borgata Babes." "Any who plumped up by more than 7 percent had to lose their jobs or the weight."

Consider this gender differentiation: A gorgeous, fit guy who sleeps with an overweight, unattractive woman is "throwing himself on a grenade" for the team. A gorgeous, fit girl who sleeps with an overweight, unattractive man is lucky to have found romance in movies like *Sideways* and *Hitch*.

In Neil LaBute's play *Fat Pig*, the lead character—played by Jeremy Piven—drops an overweight woman he likes—even after she offers to staple her stomach for him—simply because he can't bear his friends' mockery.

TV is brimming with *Beauty and the Beast* pairings in sitcoms featuring fat, lazy husbands and foxy, impressive wives.

On the other hand, I have a male friend who had a season of thinking man's slump busters.

Some years ago, he recalled, he began to feel guilty about his unthinking association of beauty with sex, of physical perfection with erotic attraction, and so he resolved that for several months he would sleep only with unattractive women.

"Except, of course, that some of them turned out to be attractive indeed, except to the eye," he told me about what he had discovered. "The eye is just one of the human senses, and vanity is finally the enemy of sex. Lust must be as blind as love, if it is to attain to its heights."

· Six ·

THE DRAG OF
GOING STAG

As a Catholic and the daughter of a cop in Washington, I grew up caught in a triple play of patriarchal culture.

The Church was run by men. The nation's capital was run by men. The law was run by men. Besides that, I had three older Irish brothers who liked to be waited on.

When I first got into journalism, I covered sports, then politics—also male-dominated fields.

I learned early that I was a serf in a feudal society where men made the rules and set the tone. Once, in first grade, I was late, and afraid to go in and face the wrath of Sister Hiltruda.

The handsome and charming Father Montgomery found me crying in the schoolyard and offered to bring me in. As I entered the classroom, holding his hand, I smiled triumphantly at a glowering Sister Hiltruda. She would not be able to utter a word to me, or raise a ruler.

Even though there's plenty of evidence that organizations run like male secret societies don't work—look at the inept FBI, the disastrous CIA, the Bush team that screwed up the Iraq occupation—it's surprising how slowly things change for women in some precincts.

In December 2004, the Pentagon inspector general found that successive commanders at the Air Force Academy had failed over the course of a decade to acknowledge the severity of—or even put checks in place to stop—sexual assault and harassment at the Colorado Springs campus.

Thom Shanker of *The New York Times* wrote that: "Sexual assaults against women were reported almost 150 times over 10 years but that little action was taken until the accusations became public in 2003. . . . Eight Air Force officials were found to share responsibility for 'creating, contributing to or abiding the unique sexual assault reporting program' at the academy and for 'the resulting problems.' "

The Air Force vice chief of staff, General T. Michael Moseley, concluded that "true cultural change takes time."

Right.

Women are breaking male barriers, slowly, even in Hollywood, where actresses are often cast as girlfriends, wives, hookers or strippers. By the summer of 2005, in the flesh-peddling dream factory built by men, four of the six major studios had women in the top creative decision-making roles. (Even though they're running a devalued Tinseltown that can't seem to muster the originality to pull out of its box office slump.)

At twenty-three, Sergeant Leigh Ann Hester, a retail store manager from Bowling Green, Kentucky, became the first woman since World War II to win the Silver Star for her heroism fighting her way through an enemy ambush south of Baghdad.

Thirty-year-old Captain Nicole Malachowski was named the first woman pilot to fly an F-16 in the Air Force's famous Thunderbirds' flying diamond formation.

And the petite hundred-pound Danica Patrick, the twenty-three-year-old who was sponsored by David Letterman's racing team, became the highest female finisher to race in the Indy 500 in June 2005.

Patrick was feted by *Sports Illustrated* as its cover athlete, inspiring little girls everywhere. And as *New York Times* sports columnist Selena Roberts noted drily, "Usually, women do not achieve such a prized position on *S.I.*'s cover unless they pose with their bikini strings falling down."

Once men controlled the votes and purse strings of women. Now women have enormous power as voters and consumers. Each successive presidential campaign I've covered, the candidates have tried harder and harder to woo the female vote, until some, like Al Gore, are practically lactating.

Gradually, women have infiltrated the seats of Washington power.

As the late Georgetown social queen, Susan Mary Alsop, once told me about the decades of male WASP ascendancy in Washington, a time of "Let's make a pitcher of martinis and overthrow the government of Guatemala" panache: "If women were smart, they'd shut up. You simply could not sit between Isaiah Berlin and Jack Kennedy and talk about children."

Even as late as the '90s, the first President Bush belonged to four men's clubs, including the Alibi Club, which featured a sign over the telephone that read: "If you pay the steward 25 cents, he will say you're not here. If you pay him 50 cents, he will say you're in a meeting. If you pay him $1, he will say you are on your way home." Male officials bonded with Bush Sr. by telling him dirty jokes, and women in the White House avoided wearing pants to work.

As Sandra Day O'Connor told Judy Woodruff in 2003, "Things move very slowly for women in terms of having equal opportunity. . . . Let me tell you one reason why I think it's important, and that is for the public generally to see and respect the fact that in positions of power and authority that women are well represented. That it is not an all-male governance, as it once was, as it was when the Constitution was framed."

When W. chose the first woman to be White House chef, but a man to be chief Supreme Court justice, O'Connor commented that John Roberts was a fine choice, except that he was "not a woman." (Only a man gets promoted *before* he gets the job.)

"Roberts Vows to Be Most Generic White Male in History of Supreme Court," humorist Andy Borowitz announced in his daily bulletin. "With a beaming President Bush at his side, Judge Roberts said that if he serves on the nation's highest court, 'The nondescript American white male, who is woefully underrepresented in this country at present, will finally have a voice.' "

A monsoon of sickening stories in the last few years illustrate how twisted societies become when women are either never seen, dismissed as second-class citizens or occluded by testosterone: the Catholic Church subsidizing pedophilia; the implosion of the macho Enron Ponzi scheme; the Taliban's obliteration of women; the Afghan warlords' resumption of pedophilia; the brotherhood of Al Qaeda and Mohamed Atta's misogynistic funeral instructions; the repression of women, even American servicewomen, by our allies the Saudis; the Bush administration's failure to follow up on its insistence that the Saudis give women rights. (Women there still can't even drive.)

In their limited 2005 elections, a Saudi monarchy spokesman explained that the women could not yet vote because the men had not yet built them separate voting booths. (And we suspect the Saudis can afford it.)

Egyptian authorities still pursue suspects by pressuring their female relatives and by taking a wanted man's wife or daughter into custody. In June 2005, Michael Slackman reported in *The New York Times,* women were groped and beaten "as part of an attack on political protesters by a crowd of men chanting support for the ruling party, all while the police stood by and watched."

Societies built on special privileges are far too invested in preserving those privileges. They will never do the soul-searching and housecleaning on their own that will examine the nature of such privilege.

Even after the pedophilia scandal, the Church hierarchy stubbornly persisted in its allergy to modernity, remaining a men's club, shrouded in hoary mists and incense.

The Catholic Church says priests must be male because

Jesus' apostles were male. So should women have stayed out of U.S. government because the founding fathers were male?

And suppose, as some female scholars believe and Dan Brown conjures in *The Da Vinci Code*, Mary Magdalene was a Madonna rather than a whore, an influential apostle who was defamed and reduced to a metaphor for sexual guilt by the men who ran early Christianity. Then the Church loses its fig leaf of justification for male domination and female exclusion.

The Vatican may have blamed Americans for overdramatizing the sex scandal and Irish priests for perpetrating it, but it was clear for years that the Church was in a time warp, arrested in its psychosexual development.

Back in the twelfth century, celibacy may have provided priests some extra mystique. Wrapped in purity and secrecy, they became, as one priest put it, "sacramental studs." But now we have a perp walk of sacramental pervs. The vow of celibacy became a magnet for men trying to flee carnal impulses they found troubling. In some cases this meant homosexuality, in others pedophilia.

The last happy, hetero, celibate parish was run by Barry Fitzgerald and Bing Crosby. (Or was it?)

In a weird way, celibacy italicizes sex and installs an obsession with sex at the very heart of the identity of the priesthood. The one place the Church needs to go to save itself—shedding its dysfunctional all-male, all-celibate, all-closed culture—is the one place it's unwilling to go. (The Vatican even tried to renege on altar girls not that long ago.)

We all knew boys who were pounced on in the rectory by priests. On a road trip to the beach, my brother and his friends had to play "pink bellies" with a priest—a game the priest devised that entailed the boys' pulling down their pants and slapping their stomachs until they turned pink.

While teaching us not to lie or cheat, the Church simply covered up its own sins, recycling abusive priests and putting parish after parish of children at risk, paying off victims and demanding their silence, refusing to admit that sexually assaulting children was a destructive crime and not merely a moment of moral weakness.

The Church was hoisted on its own ritual. The age of confession moved from the little box to the TV box, and victims began to feel free to unearth their buried pain.

When a seventy-nine-year-old rector at St. Patrick's Cathedral in New York was caught canoodling with his shapely forty-six-year-old secretary in the summer of 2005, many Catholics were relieved that at least it was an adult and a woman. (Although David Letterman wondered if Catholics would mind their collection money being spent on Viagra.)

After his election, Pope Benedict reiterated to African bishops the inane policy that they should fight AIDS through fidelity and abstinence rather than condoms. And he reaffirmed misguided Church doctrine that priests must continue "embracing the gift of celibacy."

As a cardinal, the pope wrote the 2004 letter to bishops on the role of women in the Church that read like a big KEEP OUT! sign.

"A certain type of feminist rhetoric makes demands 'for ourselves,' " he said, disapprovingly, when women should be more concerned with "the others." A woman, he said, has "roles inscribed in her own biology," motherhood and virginity, "the two loftiest values in which she realizes her profoundest vocation."

Pope Benedict holds fast to excluding women from the priesthood. And he said that women should not seek so much power that their identities and roles are emphasized to the disadvantage of "the other"—presumably men, unless he means space aliens—or make themselves "the adversaries" of men.

How can a Catholic political columnist do her job if she's damned for eternity if she takes an adversarial position to men?

In *Time,* Andrew Sullivan wondered: "So a woman is less a woman if she is a scientist or journalist or Prime Minister?"

Gay people, Pope Benedict has argued, are beset by an inherent tendency toward an "intrinsic moral evil" and are thus by nature "objectively disordered."

Sullivan, a conservative gay Catholic, objected: "A whole class of human beings naturally more disposed to evil than others?"

Like the Church, the Arab world cannot flourish without taking full advantage of the talents and capabilities of women.

Among the misogynistic Islamic terrorists, and in fundamentalist Middle Eastern countries (some our allies, some our foes), men are so afraid of female sexuality that they turn their women into ghosts, squandering their brains and skills because of insane fears that skin is a sin.

When I visited Saudi Arabia in 2002, I came down to the lobby of my hotel in Riyadh to go to an interview with the Saudi education minister wearing a long pink silk skirt with fringe on the bottom. I felt that I was an American, and a guest of the government, and should not have to dress to repress like Saudi women and off-duty American servicewomen stationed in the desert kingdom. But I instantly knew something was terribly wrong.

All the men in the lobby stared, a frozen tableau of horror. I was frozen, too, terrified that they would pick up their lemons and dates, en masse, and stone me to death.

"GO PUT ON YOUR ABAYA!" my Saudi government minder screamed at the first flash of pink.

It wasn't until I donned the suffocating black abaya provided by the government for meetings with Saudi Arabian officials—including Crown Prince Abdullah—that I understood what it meant to be obliterated because of my sex.

Women in fundamentalist Islamic countries are disappeared by their men, buried alive and swathed in black shrouds like mummies. Driven through Riyadh on the Friday I arrived, I saw no women in the streets anywhere. The Muslim holy day had turned the capital into a city of men in white robes, fathers hurrying to mosques with their sons. Saudi women and girls were quarantined indoors.

Under the abaya, and behind the wooden screens and separate rooms in restaurants where women were relegated, even at McDonald's, I began to shrink into a passive, cowed creature, a second-class human in a world of men.

When I went to the coffee shop in our hotel with CNN's

Christiane Amanpour, and the waiter instructed us to go to a back room segregated for women and children, I meekly began to follow orders.

Christiane never looked up from her newspaper.

"Bugger off and bring us our coffee," she barked at the waiter. He knew the voice of authority when he heard it and scuttled off.

With the loss of interest in the abilities of women, the cradle of civilization that produced the remarkable Cleopatra fell behind economically and culturally, simply proving that societies need the participation of women to prosper in every way.

The Bush administration preaches about the rights of women in the Middle East, and uses repression against Muslim women as a rationale for war, while curbing the rights of women in America and often turning a blind eye to the repression of Muslim women in countries that are U.S. allies.

W. has a feminist foreign policy, but not a feminist domestic policy. The only women whose equality he's interested in are women who wear burkas there. Women who wear low-slung jeans here are losing rights in an administration where faith trumps both science and facts.

American politicians and Islamic terrorists both hide behind women's interests, grotesquely making women responsible when it suits them to make war. The five leading spokesmen for democracy in the Middle East are women: Condi Rice, Laura Bush, Liz Cheney (number two in the Near East bureau under Rice and majordomo of a Middle East democracy project), the new undersecretary of state for public diplomacy Karen Hughes and her deputy, Dina Powell.

And yet before the Bush administration began trying to justify its rush to invade Iraq, the only highly placed White House official coming to the defense of Muslim women in countries where we keep military bases was press secretary C. J. Cregg on Aaron Sorkin's *The West Wing*.

Objecting to a Pentagon arms sale to a Saudi-like country fictionalized as "Qumari," Allison Janney's C.J. ranted: "They beat women! They hate women! The only reason they keep Qumari women alive is to make more Qumari men. . . . The point is that apartheid was an East Hampton clambake compared to what we laughingly refer to as the life these women lead and if we'd sold M1-A1s to South Africa fifteen years ago you'd have set the building on fire. Thank God we never needed to refuel in Johannesburg."

President Bush and his team seem oblivious to the dangerous paradox involved in their scattershot pursuit of rights for Muslim women, even though Iraqi women are in danger of losing their rights and returning to the burka. Since the American occupation, Iraq has become much more fundamentalist.

The more Western a Muslim country becomes, the more urgently it needs to show it has retained its Islamic identity and the most painless way for men to do that is to tighten the burka on women. So the more those countries ape the West, or do what the West wants them to, the more women have to pay.

In a 2005 PBS reshowing of *Death of a Princess*—a 1980 documentary about the execution of a Saudi princess in an arranged marriage who committed adultery—Mona Eltahawy, an Arab journalist, explained why women have made little progress in Saudi Arabia, despite some Saudis' embrace of Western practices.

She explained that in Saudi society, the emancipation of women has been seen as the dark side of Westernization, a perversion and abandonment of Arab culture and tradition.

"So it's this paradox," Ms. Eltahawy says. "The more open and modernized you become, the tighter you must hold on to women in particular, and children, to show what a good Saudi you are and what a good Muslim you are."

Pierre Rehov, the producer of a documentary about suicide bombers called *Suicide Killers*, believes that sex is a central theme of their motivation. "There is complete separation of men and women in the Islamic Muslim society. . . . And the only hope to have a normal life for them in this situation where we have this deep anxiety of life, with deep anxiety of sexuality, with deep anxiety of everything which would appear normal in the rest of the world. The only solution for them is to experiment with delusions of absolute power, in which they are becoming beyond all kinds of punishment, beyond the civilization, beyond humankind. . . . So you end up having no other door to really enjoy life than destroying your own, by doing what you think is the right thing, which is destroying impurity. Islam is the only religion which is describing heaven, paradise, in such concrete terms. In the other religions, you know, it's kind of vague. But in Islam, you have this precise description of the women that you're going to have. They will all be virgins, seventy-two of them. Lakes of honey. You can drink wine. Everything which is forbidden on Earth during this temporary existence. According to some Imams, it's completely allowed in the afterlife. So you end up having no other door to really enjoy life, than destroying your own, by doing what you think is the right thing, which is destroying impurity. For these kids, everything which is not Islam is impure. And they have to give their life in the name of Allah to be in Allah's world. In other words, this is for them the only way to experience an orgasm."

The world's cloistered, arrogant fraternities can no longer justify themselves. Their indulgences have hurt the welfare of their most vulnerable—and valuable—charges.

* * *

Barbie may have started out based on a prostitute, but in the end she just could not be slutty enough to keep up with our sex-drenched culture.

It's funny, after all the old controversy over Barbie, that she was finally dislodged from her throne not by feminists but by her edgier punk rivals, Bratz.

Bratz dolls, "the girls with a passion for fashion," wear halters and midriff-baring tops and leather and stiletto boots. They have huge lips and eyes and names like Jade and Chloe and Jasmine and Meygen.

Barbie still generated $3.6 billion in global retail sales in 2005, but the forty-five-year-old doll's attempts to update—she dumped fey Ken for hunky surfer Blaine in 2005 and began aping Bratz—were not so successful.

For the first time, Barbie lost a top spot, when Bratz won a 41.5 share of the British fashion doll market, and Barbie has been sliding in other markets as Bratz soared. Mattel has tried to market Barbie to toddlers, as hipper, MTV-watching kids are defecting to Bratz.

Barbie's efforts to be cooler were not helped when Maureen Orth revealed in *Vanity Fair* that Michael Jackson's "fetish Barbies," a collection of bare-breasted dolls dressed in S & M gear, had been entered into evidence during his trial.

I never gave up on Barbie in the '70s, when she was considered un-P.C., even though Mattel watered down her original sloe-eyed look so dramatically she looked like a bland cheerleader. But I really began to feel protective of her when Saudi Arabia's religious police bullies began harassing her.

In 2003, the Saudi Commission for the Promotion of Virtue and Prevention of Vice put a warning on its official Web site that the "Jewish" dolls—banned in Saudi Arabia for a decade—were a threat to Islam.

The message chided: "Jewish Barbie dolls, with their revealing clothes and shameful postures, accessories and tools, are a symbol of decadence of the perverted West. Let us beware of her dangers and be careful."

This, from a hypocritical desert kingdom with more lingerie stores in its malls than Victoria has secrets, where the religious police let fifteen little girls die in a school blaze in Mecca rather than let them be rescued without their head scarves and abayas, so that there was no exposure of females to male strangers.

It's probably useless to start correcting the inbred Saudis on facts, but, just for the record, Barbie was a knockoff of a German doll named Lilly, marketed as a gag pornographic gift to adult men in bars and tobacco shops. Lilly was based on a prostitute in a comic strip, and the floozy blonde was transformed into the all-American brunet Barbie in 1959 by the late Ruth Handler, an American daughter of Polish Jewish immigrants.

(God help Betty Boop if the Saudis discover her true Jewish origins.)

Saudi Arabia, the breeding ground of the 9/11 hijackers and suicide bombers in Iraq, the place that is so eager to protect itself from "Jewish" toys and "the perverted West," remains our ally.

As they did with Barbie, the Saudi religious police came after me and tried to throw me in a dungeon. Peeking out from veils, I was stunned at all the racy clothing stores in the Saudi malls—cascading with so much lingerie, designer stilettos, bondage boots, transparent blouses and glittering gowns with plunging necklines that Las Vegas would blush. They even had lingerie apartheid. Only women could shop in the part of the mall with sheer zebra and leopard Dolce & Gabbana nighties and lacy Donna Karan items (presumably all for use only in the conjugal bedroom), and there was an abaya check-in, so women could shed their robes.

I was wandering around an upscale mall connected to my hotel one night, taking notes for a column on the Saudis' schizophrenia, a society engaged in a momentous struggle for its future, torn between secret police and secret undergarments, when four men bore down on me, two in white robes, one in a brown policeman's uniform and one in a floor-length brown

A-line skirt (not a good look). They pointed to my neck and hips, and the embarrassed Saudi diplomat I was with explained that I was being busted by the vice squad.

"They say they can see the outline of your body," he translated. "They say they welcome you to the mall, which is a sign of our modernity, but that we are also proud of our tradition and faith, and you must respect that." The police pointed at an inch of flesh they could see on my neck. Then they took my passport and began making notes about the crime, oblivious to the irony of detaining me in front of the window of a lingerie shop displaying a short lacy red teddy.

Eventually, when I told them I was leaving the country later that night, they released me, but being banned in Saudi Arabia left me with a lot of empathy for poor Barbie. Sometime later, I even bought one—Lingerie Barbie No. 6—who would surely be beheaded or stoned to death by the wacko Saudis. I first heard about No. 6 Barbie from an alarmed dad and *Times* reader in L.A.; I immediately sent for this "contraband" Barbie, and she still stands sultry sentry in my bedroom bookcase.

In 2003, FAO Schwarz was selling Lingerie Barbie No. 6 behind the counter, but only if you asked for her. The children's store continued to display other Lingerie Barbies out front, the ones wearing merry widow bustiers, peekaboo peignoirs, black satin bras and panties with pale blue bows, stockings and garters.

But not Lingerie Barbie No. 6. There were so many protests from parents about "Porn Barbie," as the L.A. dad dubbed her, with her waist-length red hair, silver satin teddy with black lace trim, textured stockings with black seams, black bondage stilettos and black "soft ribbons to gently hold your Barbie doll," as an ownership manual put it, that many of the toy store branches decided to hide her behind the counter and admit her existence only if a customer requested her by number.

"I really don't want the experience of looking at a *Maxim* cover and shopping with my two-year-old for a Wiggly Worm to be the same," said another creeped-out Hollywood dad.

It's tough to know where to draw the line against racy anymore.

Every once in a while Mattel goes P.C., which always seems ludicrous. First the company banned Barbie's mink stoles, and then, in 1989, the *Barbie* magazine thirtieth-anniversary edition published a résumé that gave her current occupation as "animal rights volunteer."

One of Barbie's early career incarnations was as an astronaut. But the 1965 baggy gray spacesuit didn't fly, so by 1986 Mattel had given Astronaut Barbie a hot pink miniskirt and silver space lingerie.

In '92, Mattel—then headed by a woman—got into it with women's groups when they introduced Teen Talk Barbie, who whined "Math class is tough." (Did Larry Summers program her?) She also chirped "I love shopping!" and "Will we ever have enough clothes?"

A group of feminists and parents calling themselves "the Barbie Liberation Organization" bought a bunch of Teen Talk Barbies and G.I. Joes and traded their audio circuitry. Their newly engineered G.I. Jane Barbie growled "Eat lead, Cobra!" and "Dead men tell no lies."

As penance, Mattel introduced new brainy Barbies to mark

the nubile one's thirty-eighth birthday. Making Barbie smart was like making G.I. Joe a conscientious objector. But they pressed forward with University Barbie, who shook her pom-poms in the cheerleader outfits of nineteen (mostly Southern state) colleges.

And, most depressingly, Dentist Barbie. "Dressed in a white dentist's coatdress, Dentist Barbie gives positive feedback to her patient with two different phrases, 'Let's brush,' and 'Great checkup!' " the press release said. Barbie's role in life is not to muck around with gingivitis, receding gums and whitening trays.

M. G. Lord, the author of *Forever Barbie*, commiserated with me. "Dentist Barbie is such a letdown from the early days when Barbie actually represented something," she said. "She was a sixties revolutionary, a highly sexual, unmarried woman with little career outfits in her wardrobe. She was the antithesis of the 1950s mother, a radical role model wobbling in on her steep stiletto mules."

She said Barbie was the precursor to the *Cosmo* girl, who has proved so durable that she lives on to this day as an inspiration for the plastic surgery boom.

Let's just hope we never get to Urologist Barbie.

· Seven ·

WHENCE THE
WINCE?

I t seems unfathomable now, in an era when women obsess on wiping out winces and removing wrinkles in their earlobes. But there was a time, long ago and far away, when women didn't only talk about skin. They talked about books, plays and politics.

We knew there were a couple different drugstore potions to slather on skin: Noxzema or Pond's. And we knew there were a couple different kinds—skin that tanned or didn't, skin that crinkled easily or didn't.

But the only way you could mortify your flesh in the old days was the way my sister, Peggy, did it: Sit up on our old tin roof with some aluminum foil and a bottle of baby oil and io-dine and bake until you gleamed copper.

In those days, you burned the skin to look healthy, not

knowing it was unhealthy. Now you burn the skin to get rid of sun damage, pouring acid on it or frying it with laser blasts to blot out your face and start over with fresh skin.

Americans are addicts of appearances, tightening, whitening and plumping every nook and cranny. We don't mind perishing by the image as long as we get to live by the image.

First besieged by boomers determined not to age, and now beset by a younger clientele, dermatologists are the demiurges of the millennium. Fat flows through their offices every day in a great circular, cannibalizing glob, a gelatinous Narcissus pool, suctioned out, injected in.

Have you ever noticed, Dave Barry asked suspiciously, that Kentucky Fried Chicken outlets often seem to be located right next door to liposuction clinics?

Skin savants have ways beyond number to mortify aging flesh: cutaneous laser resurfacing, ultrasound liposuction, acid and chemical peels, $90 30-milliliter vials of Cellex-C High Potency serum (less imposingly known as vitamin C); $250-a-session Velasmooth treatments, combining suction and laser, to reduce cellulite (about as much fun as a hot iron pressing on your thighs for an hour); hair-removal lasers, and the latest laser craze, Fraxeling, a machine that emits beams of light to vaporize lines and brown spots on the neck, chest and hands, for a mere three grand a session.

(When men think of lasers coming near their bodies, they think of *Star Wars* light sabers or that classic scene in *Goldfinger* when that lethal ray inches closer to emasculating James Bond.)

So now before a date, a modern girl isn't only gargling, flossing and glossing; she's Googling, Fraxeling and Paxiling. (Some young women pop a Paxil, marketed as a cure for shyness, before going out.)

We are molting like snakes and hydrating the dickens out of ourselves. In Hollywood, hydration is not only one of the most worthwhile ways to spend your time, it is the highest uxorious tribute.

Reading the reams written about the Brad-and-Jen breakup, I found the most illuminating part to be about their hydration habits. Jennifer Aniston declared that her idea of a great evening was to stay at home with a book and a big bottle of water, while someone on the production team of one of her movies declared that Brad Pitt had been a good husband because he kept Jen "well hydrated" on the set.

I never thought much about skin until I was given a column at the *Times*. In the first few years, trying to be a scold with good puns, as Jon Stewart describes the role of tweaking pols on both sides of the aisle, I found my job so stressful that my skin began behaving like a teenager's. My hair was a mess, too.

One Friday night at home, after I'd finished my Sunday column, I was applying various tonics while checking my phone messages. There was one that made my blood run cold.

"Hi, Maureen, Don Hewitt here from *60 Minutes*," a gravelly voice boomed. "We'd like to do a profile of you."

I happened to be passing a mirror in the front hall and, as I looked at my reflection, my horror grew. I had mayonnaise slathered on my hair, Clearasil on my face and a drumstick from Popeye's Fried Chicken clenched in my mouth. Hewitt was still rumbling on: "We could send Steve Kroft and a camera crew over to your house . . ."

Gasping, I dropped the chicken leg. I wrote Hewitt a note the next morning: "I would rather have my body tied to a stake in the desert, covered in honey and devoured by a horde of red ants than be quizzed on *60 Minutes*."

I realized I needed to start thinking more about maintenance. It was time to join my fellow baby boomers in their delusional belief that they could control their desiccation and environment with antiaging and antibacterial products, from "age-defying" panty hose and anticellulite sneakers to antibacterial ballpoint pens, calculators and running shoes. (The nutty trend of antibacterial washes persisted even after microbiologists warned that the avid pursuit of germless homes was endangering the long-term health of children by contributing to the threat of antibiotic-resistant microbes.)

On my birthday, I swung into action, dragging my girlfriend Alessandra over to Saks Fifth Avenue to check out the cascade of euphemistically titled "age-defying" miracle creams.

We careered up to the Estée Lauder counter. The woman there suggested a shiny gook to smear on your face that allegedly created the illusion of a soft pink light dangling over your head.

We bought it.

Then we moved on to the Crème de la Mer counter. Standing before an aquarium, the saleswoman gave us the backstory. She said the seaweed concoction had been developed by a handsome rocket scientist who had had his face burned off in an accident while he was testing fuels for NASA. He worked for twelve years in his garage to come up with a cream that would get his face back. I said it sounded too *Phantom of the Opera*.

"It has healing powers," the saleswoman said portentously.

I hesitated. It was $195 for 2 ounces, or $1,200 for 16.5 ounces. "It's so expensive," I demurred. Sharon Stone uses it, she told us. So does Sarah Jessica Parker.

We bought it.

We stopped before we got to the new line of "whitening" face creams, designed to make you look like a Kabuki dancer, or SK-II, the Benedictine brandy of skin creams, discovered twenty-five years ago by a Japanese monk visiting a sake brewery who noticed that a nutrient called "pitera," used in the yeast-fermentation process, gave the brewery workers "ageless" hands.

Sales of "age-repairing" potions filled with weird ingredients like tanbark oak and Chardonnay grape-seed extract have exploded. At last count there were 1,700 different antiwrinkle creams vowing to release the luminescence trapped under those icky old dead skin cells, and American women were spending $12 billion a year on emollients designed to make them conformists with perfect complexions.

Alessandra and I both splurged and went for facials at Tracie Martyn, a New York skin sorceress who caters to supermodels and celebs like Renée Zellweger and Sandra Bullock. Martyn, an English waif whose business partner and boyfriend is a Transylvanian, is reputed to be able to change the shape of your face and tighten it, temporarily, with electrical currents that come through wired pads she puts on your face. She told me, after the $287 facial, that she had made my face more heart-shaped, which sounded cool. But I couldn't see any difference, even though I was excited to see Susan Sarandon's lovely oval face in the waiting room as I was leaving.

When I try to keep up on beauty news, I get frightened and confused. We are a nation in mass denial that, eventually, gravity and French fries will have their way. There are all those Death by Plastic Surgery stories, like the sad saga of Olivia Goldsmith, the author of *The First Wives Club*, who died on a New York operating table, and the terrifying story of the forty-two-year-old wife of a rural Irish plumber who died after pretending to her husband she was going to Dublin for a business conference, and their sneaking off to have surgery performed by a much-sued doctor on Central Park South she had found through an Internet ad.

The catalogues that clog my mail are filled with snake-oil promises, mysterious chemicals and odd devices. The Self-Care catalogue offers Brain Gum to improve "cognitive functions by restoring a healthy level of phosphatidylserine in the brain"; the "Lip Enhancer," which "through a gentle vacuum process . . . keeps lips full and plump to 12 hours between uses"; and the magnetic face mask, said to increase blood flow to tone facial muscles. Sagging skin will be gone anon, the blurb vows: "The mask's 19 gold-plated magnets have a powerful 1,500-gauss surface, and are strategically located at your facial acupressure points." (In a related development, an *Allure* magazine "news bulletin" announced: "Biomecanica's battery-powered suction bra builds a bigger breast.")

I read a bizarre story in *Harper's Bazaar* burbling that "programmed water and nuclear submarine materials are finding their way into your face cream." Smearing fissionable materials on blotchy cheeks gave the *Hunt for Red October* a whole new meaning.

The high-gloss *InStyle* can make you anxious about things you've never given a thought to: For overplucked eyebrows, or "invisi-brow," the magazine advises, "you may want to look into getting follicle transplants (starting at around two thousand dollars, depending on the number of follicles needed). 'Hairs are taken from the back of the scalp and inserted at the correct angle of growth,' " said Bernard Nussbaum, a Miami hair-loss expert, who added that eyebrow transplants grow long and need to be trimmed often (if you don't want to start looking like Andy Rooney).

Another *Bazaar* story recommended "precision liposuction" involving "multiple micro reductions of hard-to-tone areas." But before I got up my nerve to even consider it, I saw a story in *USA Today* about the alarming increase in Death by Liposuction. "We're on top of this problem," asserted a Sacramento doctor who was the chairman of the plastic surgeons' association liposuction task force.

Lipsuction task force? In the '50s, women vacuumed. Now women are vacuumed. Our Hoovers have turned on us!

*   *   *

Beauty, as E. M. Forster wrote, creates its own rules of conduct.

We've seen studies showing the fearful tyranny of symmetry, that aesthetics are hardwired in the brain—that even babies have an innate sense of beauty, choosing to gaze longer at lovelier faces. (Conversely, and perversely, men tend to find baby-faced women more attractive.)

I went out once with a guy who didn't care for his mother, partly because he felt she was not attractive enough. My brother Martin, on the other hand, often told our mom how proud he was when she picked him up from grade school because he thought she was the prettiest mother.

So it shouldn't be surprising to learn that parents have the same beauty bias. Still, a 2005 headline in *The New York Times* was jolting: "Ugly Children May Get Parental Short Shrift."

"Canadian researchers have made a startling assertion: Parents take better care of pretty children than they do ugly ones," Nicholas Bakalar wrote.

Researchers at the University of Alberta observed that at the supermarket, less adorable tykes were more often allowed to engage in potentially dangerous activities—like standing up in the shopping cart or wandering off. Good-looking children, especially boys, got more attention from their parents and were kept closer at hand.

"When it came to buckling up, pretty and ugly children were treated in starkly different ways, with seat belt use increasing in direct proportion to attractiveness," the article said. "When a woman was in charge, 4 percent of the homeliest children were strapped in, compared with 13.3 percent of the most attractive children." With fathers, it was even worse, "with none of the least attractive children secured with seat belts, while 12.5 percent of the prettiest children were."

Haven't these parents ever heard of the ugly duckling? Do they read to pretty kids only about pretty ducklings?

Even if you're skeptical about supermarket science, the story conjures up poignant images of Pugsley-looking rug rats toddling off, or flying through the air and crashing into the rotisserie chicken oven because they're not belted in.

Dr. Andrew Harrel, the research team's leader, put the findings in evolutionary terms: Pretty children represent a premium genetic legacy and so get extra pampering. "Like lots of animals," he said, "we tend to parcel out our resources on the basis of value."

As Marilyn Monroe's golden, gold-digging showgirl in *Gentlemen Prefer Blondes* so deftly explained it to a wealthy prospective father-in-law: "Don't you know that a man being rich is like a girl being pretty? You wouldn't marry a girl just because she's pretty, but, my goodness, doesn't it help?"

A beauty bias against children seems so startling because you grow up thinking parents are the only ones who will give you unconditional love, not measure it out in coffee spoons based on your genetic luck—which, after all, they're responsible for.

But the world can be harsh. Surface matters more and more, and Shakespeare's lesson from *The Merchant of Venice* is ignored, when Bassanio knows to choose the lead casket, rather than gold, in a courting challenge to win the delectable Portia: "Gilded tombs do worms infold."

A 2005 analysis published by the Federal Reserve Bank of

St. Louis confirms what we all suspect—that the pulchritudinous get more money and promotions than average-looking schmoes.

Quoting the economists Daniel Hamermesh and Jeff Biddle, the study notes that being tall, slender and attractive could be worth a "beauty premium"—an extra 5 percent an hour—while there is a "plainness penalty" of 9 percent in wages (after factoring out other issues).

Researchers report that taller men are more likely to win in business and—except for the hapless Al Gore and John Kerry, who really worked at losing—get elected president. Correlating sixteen-year-olds' height with their later salaries shows beanstalks grow up to earn about $789 more a year for each extra inch of height.

In his best seller *Blink*, Malcolm Gladwell did a survey of half the Fortune 500 CEOs and found that (Jack Welch notwithstanding—or notwithsitting) the average CEO, at six feet, is about three inches taller than the average American man.

Research also shows that obese women get 17 percent lower wages than women of average weight and that dishy professors get better evaluations from their students.

There can be too much of a good thing. As Dan Ondrack, a professor at the University of Toronto, told *The Toronto Star* about the "Boopsey" effect—if women are too gorgeous, people assume they are airheads.

(Also on occasion, if women are too gorgeous, men don't want to hire them because they fear it will be a temptation, or what the nuns used to call "an occasion of sin." A man I know specifically looked for a personal assistant who was not too attractive. Another man in my office told me not to hire a knock-out blonde as my assistant because it would be "too distracting" for him. Women, too, can sometimes decide that they don't want to hire younger women who are too beautiful because it would be, as a girlfriend warned me about the knockout, "debilitating to see that at work every day." I hired her anyway; it wasn't debilitating.)

No one seems sure whether bosses tend to discriminate against less attractive people because they're less attractive, or whether more attractive people develop more self-esteem and social finesse.

But one thing's for sure: it's hard to develop self-esteem as a child when your parents don't strap you in the supermarket cart and, at the first abrupt stop, you find yourself hurtling past the Pop-Tarts toward the rotisserie oven.

* * *

I am expecting that one day soon women will turn into chimeras—the top half human female, the bottom half cow. Or maybe, like the she-monsters of Greek mythology, a creature with a rooster head, a human torso and hooves, a Cow-Woman that crows cock-a-doodle-do.

My ruminant fears run rampant because of all the wrinkle fillers made of cow goo that women are pumping into their faces.

"Husbands have to start worrying now," New York dermatologist Patricia Wexler says mischievously. "If their wives are ranting and raving, is it menopause or is it mad cow disease?"

What if pouty young Gotham beauties, sipping raspberry mojitos at Koi, start running around in circles trying to bite their tails?

What if high-powered professional women in leather skirts and Holstein-patterned heels clickety-clack up to the pool at the Four Seasons restaurant and start slurping at it like a trough?

What if pillow-lipped actresses in New York and Hollywood drop their celery sticks and demand salt licks?

What if elegant Upper East Side socialites, sipping Bellinis at Cipriani's, suddenly start foaming at the mouth, going all John Bolton on us?

American women are putting on the cow—inside and out. They inject buckets of bovine collagen, drawn from the hides of cows, into their lips and faces. They consume huge infusions of red meat, cheese, butter and cream on the Zone and Atkins diets. They truss themselves up in leather. They decorate their homes with zebra-patterned cowhide rugs and plots of grass—perfect for grazing. They slather on antiaging creams featuring collagen. Not to mention the Häagen-Dazs Dulce de Leche and Ben & Jerry's Cookie Dough they devour when depressed.

"Elsie did not die in vain," says Dr. Wexler. "We're using every bit of her."

Women who get skittish reading stories about new cases of American mad cow outbreaks, where they cart off the demented squirting cow with the bell on its head, have their choice of several other "injectable fillers," as these goopy emollients are known, for "facial sculpting."

If you want to trade mad cow worries for bird flu worries, there's Hylaform, an avian hyaluronic acid made of ground-up rooster combs. Imagine putting Foghorn Leghorn in your face, having that windbag rooster sing "Camptown races . . . doo-dah, doo-dah" in the grooves between your nose and your mouth.

There's also Restylane and Captique, soothing brand names for hyaluronic acids made of bacteria, and Sculptra, a polylactic acid. Several years ago, INAMED Aesthetics in Santa Barbara took the foreskin of one infant boy—the son of the original manufacturer—and replicated it into a supply of CosmoPlast and CosmoDerm that plumps lips for women all over the world ad infinitum. A bris to remember. This represents some sort of strange symmetry: Women inject their lips with baby boy foreskin to titillate adult male foreskin.

Dr. Wexler, whose face is so smooth she looks like she's walking around all the time bathed in Barbara Walters's lighting, which makes even the ancient look embryonic, has injected herself and her patients with it for years. She says she's not worried because bovine collagen comes from "a closed herd, a very elite club of cows. My patients want reassurance that they can go on guilt-free and wrinkle-free. They're not looking for written testimonials."

In a perfect setting for a creepy Robin Cook medical thriller, the Medicis Pharmaceuticals Corporation, which makes Restylane, is merging with INAMED, which supplies much of the world's bovine collagen, human collagen, rooster comb filler, bacteria filler, breast implants and a gastric band for obesity surgery that works like a noose to create a smaller stomach.

INAMED has had an FDA-monitored "closed herd" for over two decades—2,000 cows on 2,000 acres in Fremont, California, that eat grain, breed only with each other and are slaughtered on-site. (And a backup herd of 1,700 to 1,800 head.)

It's so exclusive, you picture the herd behind a velvet rope with beefy bouncers, or the cows having membership cards in their cowhide wallets, like some sort of bovine Soho House.

One patient of Beverly Hills dermatologist Arnold Klein pleaded with him in vain to visit the herd, to reassure herself that it looked healthy.

Once the collagen is sucked out, the meat is sold. A company executive brags that, because of fears of mad cow and foot-and-mouth disease, steaks and hamburgers from the closed herd, sold under the label "Prather Ranch," are in great demand in West Coast specialty meat stores and online.

Vanity nearly always beats out health fears.

"Most women would find the prospect of dying wrinkled a lot worse than the prospect of dying of dementia from collagen," says Richard Glogau, a San Francisco dermatologist. "As long as they don't drop dead thirty seconds later, they'll do it."

Tina Alster, a forty-five-year-old Washington dermatologist who injects herself with cow juice, agrees that the prospect of wrinkling is worse than the prospect of drooling and frothing: "I would rather be among the quarantined than on the outside of the ring. Let everyone else look horrible."

Vanity also trumps morality. "I've never had a religious patient ask about a kosher cow," Dr. Wexler says. "I've never had a vegetarian model object to bovine collagen. I've never had an animal rights activist object to cows getting killed for collagen. When it comes to cosmetic matters, women have a 'Don't ask, don't tell me, please!' policy."

*   *   *

In the 1985 movie *Brazil,* the director Terry Gilliam envisioned a nightmare future of shrink-wrapped visages and in-house plastic surgeons. A doctor assures a rubbery socialite that he can make her look twenty years younger, even twenty-five, "if we just drain the excess fluids from the pouches."

We may not have the flying cars and floating cities promised by *The Jetsons,* but we have Gilliam's shrink-wrapped faces. We now even have face transplants. Scientists had been practicing half-face transplants on rats, making rats with half brown/half white faces. These drastic transplants are supposedly for patients who have been severely disfigured by trauma, burns or tumors, but who knows where it will spread in a society psychotically obsessed with appearance-altering procedures?

As Dr. Nancy Etcoff, a Harvard psychologist who wrote *Survival of the Prettiest,* told *The New York Times* when Botox won FDA approval for cosmetic use in 2002: "We will look at wrinkles the way we look at cracked or discolored teeth— remnants of the past."

"It is as though," she continued, "we have given up on authenticity."

Actually, women have trusted artifice more than authenticity for ages.

Shakespeare wrote in his sonnets about women fighting " 'gainst Time's scythe" and "Time's thievish progress" by primping and painting—"Fairing the foul with art's false borrow'd face."

In his essay "In Praise of Cosmetics," Baudelaire urged women to "surpass Nature" and disparaged those whose "owlish gravity prevents them from seeking Beauty in its most minute manifestations." He called external finery "one of the signs of the primitive nobility of the human soul."

"Woman is quite within her rights, indeed she is even accomplishing a kind of duty, when she devotes herself to appearing magical and supernatural," he wrote. "She has to astonish and charm us; as an idol, she is obliged to adorn herself in order to be adorned. Thus she has to lay all the arts under contribution for the means of lifting herself above Nature, the better to conquer hearts and rivet attention. It matters but little that the artifice and trickery are known to all, so long as their success is assured and their effect always irresistible."

And as Yeats wrote in his poem "Adam's Curse," "And thereupon/That beautiful mild woman for whose sake/There's many a one shall find out all heartache/On finding that her voice is sweet and low/Replied, 'To be born woman is to know/Although they do not talk of it at school/That we must labor to be beautiful.'"

From Victorian corsets to Victoria's Secret buoyant water bras, from hennaed hair and pupil-dilating belladonna drops to French manicures and cinnamon and peppermint-stinging lip plumpers, women have always sought to look younger, prettier, healthier and more supple and fecund. It's all about faking better genes. According to Dr. Etcoff, men simply gravitate like zombies toward a "maximally fertile woman, or at least one who looks that way."

I came of age in the late '60s and early '70s, when kids of both sexes dressed in Indian cotton shirts and bell-bottom jeans and were more consumed with politics and dreams of equality than with fashion and cosmetics. I never related to the unstyled, unisex, un-made-up look of the early feminists, and I tangled with boyfriends who did not want me to wear makeup or heels. "The girls at Yale never wore makeup," one beau who was a recent Yale graduate lectured me, before going out to buy me a pair of Top-Siders, which came with a questionnaire asking how long my yacht was.

I always subscribed to the Carole Lombard philosophy: "I live by a man's code, designed to fit a man's world, yet at the same time I never forget that a woman's first job is to choose the right shade of lipstick."

Still, I assumed that one of the positive results of the feminist movement would be a more flexible and capacious notion of female beauty, a release from the tyranny of the girdled, primped ideal of the '50s.

I was wrong. Forty years after the dawn of feminism, the ideal of feminine beauty is more rigid and unnatural than ever.

As my pal Craig Bierko says, "Entitled women of a certain age in this country are filled with cow ass fat, bioengineered botulism spores and various heavy machinery petroleums, Mary Todd Lincolns trying to look like the pink, gutted husk of an Olsen twin."

I often wonder, had Gloria Steinem known in 1968 what was coming in 2005, from the catfighting on *The Bachelor* to women's obsession with Botox and breast implants, would she have ever have bothered climbing out of that *Playboy* bunny suit?

What would Gloria, who declared that "a woman reading *Playboy* feels a little like a Jew reading a Nazi manual," have thought of the millennial craze for *Playboy* bunny T-shirts among women?

When she wrote in 1966 that "all women are Bunnies," she did not mean it as a compliment; it was a feminist call to arms. Forty years later, it's just an aesthetic fact, as hordes of women go under the knife and needle to get those inflatable bunny proportions.

Instead of broadening the choices of how to look good, we have only broadened the ways we try to look alike. Women are headed toward one face, one body and one expression.

As Dr. Etcoff said in the *Times*: "We are in danger of doing something unthinkable, which is making beauty boring. When it is all so overtly about appearance, personal identity becomes almost trivial. It's as if people would rather choose a mask than look like themselves or their mother or daughter."

In a world of swollen implants and fattening fillers, exaggerated Barbie figures rule. "The incongruity of two bowling balls on an ironing board never seems to bother anyone," Steve Martin writes about Beverly Hills in *Shopgirl*.

The hardwired and underwired paragon of feminine beauty for American men has been a straight—or rather curvy—trajectory from Vargas girls to '50s pinup Betty Page to Jayne Mansfield to Pamela Anderson to Jessica Simpson (whose father, the former-youth-minister-turned-Jessica-manager, bragged to *GQ* that his daughter looked equally sexy in a T-shirt or bustier: "She's got Double Ds! You can't cover those suckers up!").

More and more women are willing to stretch and protrude to whatever extreme proportions satisfy male desires. Now that technology is biology, all women can look like inflatable dolls.

They're going for Barbie fem-bot breasts and that low Barbie waist-hip ratio—a waist that is at least 30 percent narrower than hips—that is so alluring to men.

Dr. Alster, a slender, glamorous blonde who wears Chanel suits and Manolo stilettos, tries all her own products. "In D.C., everybody wants to be a natural beauty," she says. "I say natural shmaturel. People always ask me, 'Have you had anything done?' I say, 'Of course I have! Who do you think we try out these lasers on?' I've had peels. I've Fraxeled. I do the bikini hair-removal laser. I use Botox and bovine collagen."

She does not, however, approve of the nation's mammary flummery. "Women do breast implants for men, not themselves, and it has to do with nearly all the plastic surgeons' being men," she says. "I would love perky breasts, but I'm not going to do major surgery to get them. I'm going to wear a push-up bra."

As *The New York Times*'s Alex Kuczynski observed: "What man would sew a sack of plastic into his leg, would put a foreign body into his own body?"

But maybe women are morphing because of their own deep-seated desires as well. The early feminists' tendentious attempts to demonize Barbie and to treat such innate female proclivities as shopping and makeup as trivial pursuits, and to prognosticate a world where men and women dressed alike in navy suits and ties and were equal in every way, were naïve and misguided.

"I think when it comes down to it, women are doing all this stuff not just for men, but for themselves," Dr. Wexler muses. "We're fulfilling our fantasies of the Barbie dolls we played with when we were young. And it's all about our self-esteem. Mothers are accepting of their sons unconditionally, but girls are never good enough. Now that your looks are something you can control, like eating, why not control them? Why do bulimics buleme?"

But everyone knows that "all that glisters is not gold," I protest, that what's on the inside is more important than what's on the outside. It's the lesson hammered home in great literature and sappy J.Lo movies. How can we get women to relax and believe it?

"Eliminate the male race," Dr. Wexler shoots back.

Professional strides have not made women less concerned about their looks, or curbed their compulsion to try to improve and improve and improve on Mother Nature, ad infinitum and ad nauseam.

A local Washington TV newscast reported in May 2005 that the number of eating disorders among women over thirty-five had gone up 33 percent in three years. Dubbing it a desire for "Wisteria waistlines," the segment suggested that middle-aged women were starving themselves to look like actresses such as the lithe suburban nymphs of *Desperate Housewives*.

Once the domain of stories about budget deficits and guerrilla wars, now TV news dwells on diets, dermatology and plastic surgery. It's hard to figure out what's happening in Iraq from TV news, but in April, the *CBS Evening News* and *Early Show* did a weeklong series called "Beautiful World," about plastic surgery trends from Ipanema to Iran. ("Iran, where the morality police used to confiscate eyeliner and lip gloss," reporter Elizabeth Palmer intoned, "is now the nose job capital of the world.")

• • •

The three stages of women, as Anna Quindlen defined them—pre-Babe, Babe and post-Babe—have now been expanded to four: pre-Babe, Babe, Botox Babe and Cher.

A few years back, some Hollywood TV producers I know were thinking about making a sitcom with Cher. Before they committed, they wanted to be sure that, after all the work she'd had done on her face, Cher could still actually move it.

They went to her house and secretly tested her ability to react, asking questions to elicit various emotions. They ended up not doing the show.

American women are evolving backward—becoming more focused on their looks than ever. Feminism has been defeated by narcissism.

No one wants to read *Ms.*, even when it desperately panders with a spring cover on "*Desperate Housewives*: Do We Hate It

233

or Secretly Love it?" Everyone wants to look at the size 0 bodies and age-ambiguous faces in *InStyle*, a magazine that blithely celebrates the trendy surface.

"Looks are the new feminism," says Alex Kuczynski, a reporter for the *Times* Styles section who has a new book on the volcanic "rejuvenation" industry called *Beauty Junkies.* "In order to have power, you've got to look as if you care about yourself. It's a banner way of advertising your competency. Look at Oprah—she's awesome, totally styled every day. I talked to high-powered women in New York like Peggy Siegal, the publicist, who told me 'Who has the time to have kids?' Just taking care of her looks is a full-time job. Our looks now take up a huge space in our lives."

Materialism has defeated feminism as well. In a sign of the times, Gloria Steinem was on the picket line when the first American De Beers store opened on Fifth Avenue in June 2005, protesting the evictions of Bushmen in Botswana to make room for diamond miners and the charges that the company dealt in "blood diamonds" used to finance civil wars in Africa.

Her presence meant nothing to young Hollywood beauties who are pleased to shill for the diamond industry in magazine layouts and personal appearances.

As Steinem stood outside, Lindsay Lohan was inside the party, gushing over the possibility that she could get to wear one of the big rocks.

Asked by reporters about the Bushmen controversy, she shrugged it off: "I don't get involved in any drama."

Once the poets connected beauty to truth and goodness; now beauty is linked to time and money. The new symbols of social status in America are visits to plastic surgeons and dermatologists.

There's nothing wrong with self-improvement, of course, except when it literally becomes self-effacement.

Millions of American women from their twenties to their eighties are erasing their faces, and freezing their features, some to the point of freakish death masks, by shooting up with the pretty poison Botox, a botulism neurotoxin that paralyzes muscles—the same strain of neurotoxin that is classified as a WMD. (Pretty much all the American weapons hunters found in Iraq after the invasion was a bit of botulism neurotoxin, meaning we went to war, basically, over a vial of Botox. Wrinkles of Mass Destruction.)

The nasty name of the poison has not stopped it from being wildly popular. INAMED has a similar product awaiting FDA approval called Reloxin. That brand name, test marketed and focus-grouped to a fare-thee-well, is meant to convey a sort of relaxing toxin, which is hilariously oxymoronic.

As weird as it seems, women are happy to sacrifice a range of expression to get rid of those little forehead and mouth furrows. "In a variation on *The Stepford Wives,* it is now rare in certain social enclaves to see a woman over the age of 35 with the ability to look angry," Kuczynski wrote in the *Times,* adding: "The wisdom that a person's character can be etched on his face, or Coco Chanel's observation that at 20 you have the face nature gave you, and at 50 you have the face you merit, may no longer apply."

A face with character is passé. A face without expression is chic.

"A scowl is a totally unnecessary expression," the always placid-looking Dr. Wexler likes to say. "A squint has no social value." (Darwin begged to differ, writing about the importance of expressions in *The Expressions of Emotions in Man and Animals.*)

New York doctors envision princess-to-frog (or dog) scenarios in which men marry smooth-faced women and, four months and no Botox injections later, wake up next to a shar-pei.

Maintenance is tricky, and if you get the wrong doctor you could find yourself trapped in Picasso's Blue Period, looking Cubist and body-snatched. Doctors advise patients after a Botox shot not to go shoe shopping or get their hair washed or lie down for four hours, so that the toxin doesn't seep down and inadvertently paralyze the wrong muscles.

The explosive success of Botox is an irony wrapped in a paradox for women. After all these years of trying to train men to respond better to emotional cues, women are making it even harder by erasing the emotion from their faces.

Men long carped that women were not suited for the workplace or the White House because they were too transparently emotional. So now will men, confronted with blank-faced brigades of Botox babes, carp that women are too opaque and blasé?

Actresses are ensnared in a cosmetic catch-22. They must look young to get juicy roles, so they do Botox, which makes it impossible to express themselves in juicy roles. They must look good to get cast in period movies, but then they look too sandblasted for period movies. The advent of high-definition TV has sent even more actresses and anchorettes racing to the pretty poison. Is Vanessa Redgrave the last famous woman on earth with wrinkles?

"Their faces can't really move properly," complained Baz Lurmann, the *Moulin Rouge* director, who pines for the frowns of yesterface.

Because many women don't know when to check themselves before they get into "trout pout" territory, they seem to be lemming toward one face. Sometimes in affluent settings, like the Oscars or the shoe department at Bergdorf's, you see a bunch of eerily similar women with oddly off-track features—Botox-smoothed Formica foreheads, collagen-protruding lips, surgically narrowed noses, taut jaws—who look like sisters from another planet.

Or you'll see a celebrity from behind and when she turns around, her face will have a creepy melting quality, like a Salvador Dalí painting.

"I had a new patient come in yesterday who said, 'Tell me you didn't do Goldie Hawn,' " said one top dermatologist. "It's a shame when people of great beauty do these age-inappropriate things."

In the future, Big Eyes–Little Nose–Big Mouth will be the sole survivor of the Face Wars, just as in the futuristic Sylvester Stallone movie *Demolition Man*, set in 2032 with President Arnold Schwarzenegger, there was only one restaurant, Taco Bell—the sole survivor of the Franchise Wars.

In decades past, each top glamour girl aimed for a signature face and measurements, a trademark voice, a unique walk. Jean Arthur was totally different from Jean Harlow. You never saw

Katharine Hepburn and Ava Gardner showing up in the same dress, or Audrey Hepburn and Marilyn Monroe looking like a pair of matching candles.

As actor Alec Baldwin told me, the originality and va-va-voom of Hollywood's classic glamour girls have been replaced with a more banal and nihilistic beauty ethos. "Fitness is the new stardom," he says. "The fittest people are the biggest stars. Used to be acute intelligence, humanity and/or beauty formed a star. Now it's the ability to eat less." (In Hollywood, an Altoid can constitute a three-course meal.)

In some wacky, self-defeating conspiracy, stylists have joined forces with surgeons to homogenize today's actresses, so it's hard to tell one from another, infusing awards shows with a safe, boring, generic look.

Once they glue on blond extensions and starve themselves into skeletons—who can tell Lindsay Lohan from Nicole Ritchie? Once they put too much goo in their faces, who can tell Meg Ryan from Melanie Griffith or Courtney Love?

At awards shows, the women seem to have the same seamless face, the same big chest/skinny torso body, the same Creamsicle fake orange spray tan and blindingly bleached and veneered white teeth, and, sometimes, even the same dress. In 2004, actress after actress paraded out at the Oscars in the identical mermaid silhouette, making me long for the good old wardrobe malfunctions of Cher, Barbra and Demi.

Chris Rock was right. Star power is in short supply in a town where women would rather be conventional than individual. It's the same problem Hollywood has making movies, a problem that has caused an extended box office slump: too much cloning, not enough originality.

Shakespeare wrote of the ultimate glamour girl, Cleopatra, a woman of superior intellect, bewitching conversation and many incandescent colors: "Age cannot wither her, nor custom stale her infinite variety."

No one is sure whether she was radiant or, like Scarlett O'Hara, just made men think she was beautiful. Cleopatra might have had rotten teeth, bad makeup and a hook nose—"Marc Antony in a wig," as historian Mary Hamer put it—but the queen of the Nile was the ultimate seducer, perfuming the sails of her boat so men would know she was coming from miles away.

She had no problem combining power and sultriness, being a kohl-eyed minx and a steel-eyed monarch. In 2001, the British Museum had a show on Cleopatra that included the only sample of her handwriting in existence. The "Royal Ordinance on Papyrus of Cleopatra VII," awarding tax privileges to Publius Canidus, Marc Antony's aide-de-camp, ended with the Greek word *Genesthoi*, or "Make it happen."

American women pay little attention to the art of beguiling conversation. As a guy I know says, "Women don't do droll anymore." They are mesmerized by surfaces, reinventing and reshaping themselves at a speed that would make Gatsby dizzy. The latest trend is about resurfacing and pumping fillers into the hands, and one Manhattan spa even offers a hand treatment, a soak in red wine and grape-seed oil, aptly named "the Grape Gatsby."

In 2001, I met Robert Wright, the NBC chairman and CEO, at a brunch at his home in Nantucket. I joked that the new genre of reality shows was getting so wacky that the next one would be a Fay Weldon–style makeover program where a bunch of women who had been dumped would go off to an island with a team of plastic surgeons, dermatologists, stylists and cabana boys, totally change themselves and come back to wreak havoc on their exes.

He shook his head, as though it were preposterous, while his wife, Suzanne, nodded, a gleam in her eye. In the next few years, *Extreme Makeover* and *The Swan* were hits (for other networks)—and women on the shows were getting cookie-cutter chin implants, brow lifts, nose jobs, breast jobs, liposuction and swarm-of-bees-stung lips.

The American Society of Plastic Surgeons tallied up the number of cosmetic surgeries and other procedures performed in the U.S. at 9.2 million in 2004, up 24 percent from 2000, with a price tag of $8.4 billion. The entire "antiaging" market is a financial bonfire of the vanities, going from a billion a year in 1990 to $15 billion in 2005.

"Plastic surgery is twenty-first-century haute couture," says Karl Lagerfeld. Like actresses, average American women are far more interested in plasticity than variety.

As Eric Wilson wrote in *The New York Times* in May 2004, so many women have had breast augmentation—especially in places like Southern California, Texas and Florida, that the fashion industry is being transformed: "The wave of implants is skewing the selection of designer clothes sold at some stores, favoring sizes and styles more ample on top and creating a new market for alterations."

Doctors say they're having a hard time stopping women from going beyond a C-cup. Wilson interviewed one marketing executive who had breast implants that increased her cup size to 34F. F? I didn't even know breasts went up that high. Wouldn't that require a forklift bra?

"They don't stop at F, they go to G and H!" said Maryam Kalantari, a saleswoman at the chic Sylene's lingerie store in Chevy Chase, Maryland, pulling out some of the humongous lacy apparatuses to show me. "Sometimes I fall forward just trying to fit them."

As comedian Tom Poppa observes, "A D is sexy. An F is scary." An F, he fears, might want to slop over onto his side of the bed after its owner goes to sleep and watch TV with him.

The *Times* story noted that with surgeons performing about 1.3 million augmentations and lifts in the last decade, a 257 percent increase since 1997, according to the American Society for Aesthetic Plastic Surgery, "The high-fashion industry is struggling to catch up to the new plastic silhouette." Even store mannequins are reflecting the change, getting plastic breast implants to match the overblown curves of their customers.

The epitome of modern beauty and sex appeal is a ringer for Jessica Rabbit, Angelina Jolie, who seems to have naturally what all other women are seeking unnaturally.

Everybody's getting in on every act. You have gastroenterologists doing liposuction, gynecologists doing laser surgery and dentists doing breast implants. (There are seven states where dentists are allowed to do cosmetic surgery.)

The aesthetics are very uneven. Some women, as Craig Bierko puts it, come out with faces that look "ripped, tugged and hot-glued into a permanent expression that most people would associate with falling from the top of a very tall building into fire." And he thinks for men, it's even worse. "I have yet to see a man come out of cosmetic surgery without looking transformed into some permanently astonished lesbian version of himself," he said. "It's terrifying. My friend's father just had his eyes done by the best, most highly sought-after cosmetic surgeon in New York City. And he doesn't look refreshed or well rested. He looks like he's being stabbed to death by invisible people."

Disturbingly, the fastest growing segment for plastic surgery is teens. The number of cosmetic surgeries performed on people eighteen and under reached 74,233 in 2003, a 14 percent increase from 2000. The April 2005 *Elle Girl*, a magazine whose copyrighted motto is "Dare to be different!," featured Paris Hilton on the cover with a headline: "Should teens get plastic surgery? We investigate the new trend."

Cosmetic enhancements have become so common that you can get "frequent-flier" cards for wrinkles—racking up rewards every time a dermatologist or a plastic surgeon sticks a needle in your face.

The Wall Street Journal reported that, following up on Pfizer's success with Viagra "value cards," which give repeat customers discounts, Medicis Pharmaceuticals, the maker of the filler Restylane, is offering a rewards program "to encourage injections every six months by offering gifts that escalate in value with each subsequent appointment—adding up to $375 after the fourth follow-up visit." A Restylane treatment is about $500 to $750 and lasts about six months. So Medicis says it aims to keep customers on track to maintain their "corrected look."

You just get the Restylane syringe box top from your doctor and send it in, as you used to do with cereal boxes to get toys. Allergan, the maker of Botox, which costs $250 to $750 a treatment, also gives doctors "VIP cards" to attract repeat customers with discounts on follow-ups.

Thus bribed by drug dealers who want to lure you into Restylane and Botox addiction, you can keep your "corrected look" going until you hit that "Alas, poor Yorick!" phase.

Women have become so obsessed with not withering, they've forgotten that there are infinite ways to be beautiful.

•   •   •

A friend of mine called after a holiday dinner.

She said the guests had been pondering a conundrum. No, not the six-party talks on North Korea's nuclear proliferation. They had been animated by animation. The earthshaking question they considered was: Why are men attracted to female cartoon characters, while women are not attracted to male cartoon characters?

It began when one woman at the table said her seventeen-year-old stepson found Disney's cartoon heroine Anastasia "hot." The grown-up men at the table all agreed, throwing

243

out names of other cartoon babes, such as Pocahontas and Jessica Rabbit.

The women scoffed that it was impossible to think of a single hot male cartoon figure.

"The superheroes, like Superman and Spider-Man, are all wearing leotards, so you've got a Marv Albert panty-hose thing going on there that's very unattractive," said my friend Tammy, recapping the conversation. "And the manly ones are thugs with no necks, like Fred Flintstone. And you couldn't go for George Jetson. It would seem so adulterous.

"The cartoon women, on the other hand, have these seductive voices and huge almond-shaped eyes. The animators create the ideal woman. But if a guy fantasizes about Jessica Rabbit, does he think about a cartoon body or a real one?"

I didn't puzzle over this at first. There was North Korea to worry about. But then my trainer, Aaron Sterling, told me he liked my hair longer and straighter.

"You look like Jessica Rabbit," he said, approvingly.

I wheeled on him, weights in hand. He conceded he loved cartoon babes, starting with a teenage crush on Ms. Pac-Man.

"She had really big lips and great makeup, in yellow and blue and red," he recalled in alarming detail. "It's not just the way they look. Their personality has to be good. I wasn't attracted to Belle in *Beauty and the Beast*. She acted like every guy in the village wanted her. But I loved Wonder Woman."

Why was he drawn to drawings?

"Real women don't have curves like that," Aaron explained. "And with real women, you can like the way they look at first, but then when they talk and move it's all over.

There's no charm. Animated girls never make ugly faces the way people do in real life. You never catch a cartoon figure at a bad moment."

He said he loved the hot girls in the movie *Sin City* because they were based on cartoon figures in Frank Miller's graphic novels.

I began to see the sick logic of it. Guys always asked, Veronica or Betty? (The quintessential pigtailed virgin/predatory whore, Mary Ann/Ginger, Jen/Angelina, sweet blonde/voluptuous brunette dichotomy has gained new life on hip cashmere hoodies and scarves at the L.A. boutique Kitson's that ask ARE YOU A VERONICA? or ARE YOU A BETTY?)

But you never hear girls musing, Archie or Reggie? Bart or Homer? And those dudes are not pictured on hip T-shirts at Kitson's.

While women are imbued with the concept of Prince Charming, they are not drawn to him in animated form. The golden boys who come to the rescue in toonland are sexless, despite square jaws and rippling pecs. Prince Charming is as lame a consort for Cinderella as Ken was for Barbie.

There have been cartoon babes since Betty Boop, who is still big as a design feature on everything from soaps to handbags, but the only animated rogue is a wascally wabbit, and his charm is pansexual.

With those long fluttering eyelashes and his cross-dressing, Bugs is too presexual (the antirabbit) to make a girl swoon. And certainly, the idea of being taken up in a UFO by Marvin the Martian or lassoed by Yosemite Sam holds no allure.

Disney heroines are often ridiculously nubile, and the male-dominated animation industry has put a lot of subliminal effort into titillating the male audience. Even the goldfish in *Pinocchio* was seductive, with long lashes and luscious lips. The makers of *Pocahontas* said they used Christy Turlington as a model for the lithe Indian princess, described by the *Times* as "an animated Playboy Playmate."

Teenage boys in America have not only embraced their own curvy cyberbabes, like Lara Croft of the video game *Tomb Raider*. They have also snapped up the sexy Japanese animated thrillers called "anime," about "the adventures of giant mechanized inter-dimensional sword-swinging ninja babes," as the Web says. A gorgeous scarlet-haired anime babe with protruding nipples was featured in Benihana ads.

Checking out Web sites featuring a strapless Belle and a topless Jessica Rabbit with a garter belt, I began to see this gender gap as inevitable.

Some really weird guy has a Web site called "Cartoon Girls That I Wanna Nail!!" He confesses: "I realize that a grown man like myself should be way past his fetish for animated beauty, but I swear, the older I get, the more beautiful the cartoons get. I can't wait 'til I have kids so that I can have an excuse for watching cartoons. As it is now, I am a twenty-one-year-old 'boy' who watches Batman and the X-Men 'cause they draw the breasts better in those cartoons than in others."

This guy links to his erotic fantasies about a gaggle of cartoon girls, from *Josie and the Pussycats* to Scooby's Daphne, and even has links to Peppermint Patty and Velma, conceding he's hot for them even though their sexuality is ambiguous.

For most guys, the more cartoonish the better. Perfect features, placid expressions, perfect bodies, no demands. (Maybe this yen is tied to men's attraction to childish female faces.)

While women find a wide array of men attractive for a wide array of reasons, men tend to be more predictable and visual in their responses. What men find sexy has hardly changed, despite a feminist revolution, except to grow more plastic and cartoonish.

From Betty Page pinups to Vargas girls to *Playboy* centerfolds, men are more easily aroused by iconography, while women hunger for that third dimension.

Three dimensions isn't too much to ask, is it?

* * *

We no longer have natural selection. We have unnatural selection. Survival of the fittest has been replaced by survival of the fakest.

Biology used to be destiny. Now biology's a masquerade party.

"What happens genetically when a man who has his nose done, chin augmented and ears pinned back is attracted to a woman who's had her eyes done and her lips plumped up and her face lifted?" Alex Kuczynski wonders. "And they have a baby and look at each other and moan 'My God, where did this ugly baby come from?' or 'Honey, that's not your nose' or

'Baby, whose ears are these?' I've talked to doctors who have already seen this happening."

Next up, no doubt, joining baby yoga and baby massage: plastic surgery and injectables for infants, so that metamorphosed parents won't have to be embarrassed when there's no family resemblance.

And since men often date women who look like them, in a literal interpretation of the Narcissus pool, women might begin getting surgery to look more like the men they want to snag.

Pat Wexler says some of her patients are genuinely startled to learn they're infertile because they're in denial about their real age. "These women don't look their age and they've been lying about their age for so long," she says, "they only remember their real age when they have to have a fertility workup. We look good on the outside but on the inside, we're rotting at the same pace we used to."

She said she has women in their eighties who have survived cancer, heart disease and strokes come in wanting to be pumped up. "I try to talk them out of it," she says. "I tell them, 'Look at all you've accomplished in life. Why do you care if you have a few wrinkles? You should just care if your shoes are comfortable.' "

One eighty-three-year-old she refused to shoot up with Botox died a week later of a stroke. "Thank God I didn't do it," Dr. Wexler shudders. "I would have been the 007 of dermatology—'Licensed to kill.' "

Tina Alster also tries to guard against overkill—women demanding what she calls "Daffy Duck lips" or fixating on earlobe wrinkles.

"Some people have hideously wrinkled faces," she says, "and they're worried about these creases in their earlobes because, God forbid, their diamonds should be next to their wrinkles." (Or, God forbid, the diamond should drop into a wrinkle.)

Dr. Wexler, who tends to faces from Calvin Klein's to Diddy's, tells patients who've lost perspective: "Some things you have to live with, even if you need Lexapro to deal with it."

A petite redhead, she wears Manolo Blahnik heels and clothes designed by famous people who are her patients and friends now. "I grew up on the Grand Concourse in the Bronx," the fifty-four-year-old said with an impish smile. "Who knew?"

She injects herself with Botox and says her great tragedy in life is that she can't do auto-liposuction.

"Lipo's my love," she says, dreamily, as though she were talking about George Clooney.

For her best friend's fortieth birthday, Dr. Wexler liposuctioned out two liters, shrinking the woman from a size 10 to a 6. The friend kept calling from boutiques to report how great she looked in everything.

But when the friend wanted collagen shots, Dr. Wexler balked. "I was deaf, like Thomas Edison. I said, 'When I catch up, we'll do you again.' I'd like to be a size two. I get angry, frustrated."

I joke that next she'll be called on to rush to Madison Avenue with her little black bag of needles, to give emergency treatment to patients who want to squeeze into that too-tight Roberto Cavalli.

"Don't kid yourself," she replies. "Of course I have to do that. How much fun is emergency lipo?"

She recalls the time a designer phoned from her showroom. An actress going to the Golden Globes had a fleshy back and her backless dress wasn't fitting property. She refused to change gowns, so Dr. Wexler had to pare down her back.

She said another emergency lipo job involved a middle-aged actress doing a period movie from the '50s which called for a lot of short-sleeved dresses. "Very unflattering," Dr. Wexler said sympathetically, "cutting at everyone's worst part of the arm." She vacuumed some of the flesh out of the actress's arms three weeks before shooting started.

The dermatologist is known as "the Queen of Fat" because she has the most elite collection of celebrity fat, stored in little freezers in vials kept in alphabetical order. It is extracted out of hips and buttocks so it can be reinjected into facial lines, depressions and lips.

"The ultimate recycling," she calls it. (Here's a concept for a zany comedy: Somebody sneaks into the Fat Queen's freezer and switches the labels!)

The freezers have an alarm system to make sure the temperature does not rise above minus eight degrees centigrade, making the fat flat.

"During the blackout two years ago, I was the only one in the city with backup generators for my fat," she reports proudly. "I know other doctors who had to throw their fat out. Do you think if a hundred women lost their fat, I'm going to survive?"

She says the "rejuvenation" industry has exploded because of women on the run. "They say, 'Tonight I'm going to a party with Anna Wintour or dinner tomorrow with Martha Stewart, what can we do today?'"

More men are coming in, often dragged by younger wives and girlfriends, or spurred by competition with younger guys breathing down their necks at the office. They want to get rid of lines, age spots, love handles and gaunt cheeks.

Vogue hailed the new vanity honesty: men and women, especially in Los Angeles and New York, who are willing to walk the streets and go out to dinner, black and blue, Fraxel-red, swollen and pinpricked. "You don't want to look like you did ten rounds with Mike Tyson," said a thirty-eight-year-old television reporter. "But a few pinpricks are as normal on the Upper East Side as a Maltese."

"It's more acceptable now," Dr. Wexler agreed. "People are going straight from my office to the boardroom and not caring or hiding as much."

My friend Frank Bruni told this story: "I was recently at a party where a man who I presumed was in his early forties said he had to leave and get home at a decent hour because he wanted to be rested for his Botox shots the next day. I asked him who his doctor was. He pointed across the room to a younger, even better-looking man, and it was then that I noticed that that man was surrounded by more people than any other at the party, and I realized why. He had the pretty-making poison in his pocket, so to speak. And, might I add, not a single wrinkle—not even a tiny fissure—on his face."

Hollywood agents use Botox to keep a poker face during negotiations. Vegas gamblers use it to keep a poker face during poker. (Kuczynski talked to the developer renovating Planet Hollywood resort and casino in Las Vegas, who was thinking of putting a little Botox salon in the middle of the casino.) Interior decorators use it to prevent wincing at their clients' bad taste. Older actors at the Oscars are starting to get those weird Botox bat foreheads. And since Botox can also freeze the sweat glands under the arms and on the forehead, Fortune 500 executives use it not to sweat in big meetings. Lawyers use it to cut down on soaked shirts and clammy handshakes at presentations and dry-cleaning bills at home.

For the first time in 2004, we had a presidential candidate who appeared to be a Botox user. When John Kerry's newly unlined, serene visage sparked rampant speculation that his attractive sixty-five-year-old wife, Teresa, a Botox aficionada, had turned him on to the wrinkle diffuser, I felt compelled to track down the sixty-year-old candidate and ask him about it for my *Times* column.

How could we elect a president who couldn't show his emotions? After all, the leader of the free world has lots of reasons to frown and wince and look startled.

I got an interview with Kerry after a rally in a high school gym in Evanston, Illinois. First I tried to give him the Cher test, asking questions that I thought might elicit a glower or a raised eyebrow. No luck. So, even though I was deeply embarrassed to do it, I took a deep breath and popped the question. I asked him about a joke Dick Cheney had just made at a big Washington dinner: that since Botox is related to botulism toxin, maybe U.S. weapons hunter David Kay should have searched for the missing Iraq biowarfare agents in Senator Kerry's forehead. Was this a way of mocking the Democrat for an effeminate vanity?

"No, I don't have it," he replied.

"Vanity or Botox?" I pressed, feeling chagrined.

"I don't have Botox," he said, "but whatever their game is, I don't care. That sort of thing is so childish. In the end, people will care about real choices that affect their lives."

Mmmmm. Seemed like a non-denial denial.

I gave up, deciding that maybe a poker face could be an advantage in the Oval Office. Liposuction might have benefited 335-pound William Howard Taft, who was always nodding off on speaking platforms. Certainly, Richard Nixon could have used Botox to stop his sweating in the debate with the cool, coppery JFK. And think how Al Gore would have benefited from freezing those condescending eyebrows and patronizing frowns during his 2000 debate with W.

The Holy Grail, or the Holy Groin, of cosmetic blandishments is, of course, penis size.

"Everyone's looking for that magic thing that will make the penis bigger," Kuczynski says. "That would open up a whole other universe of customers."

Dr. Alster says when men come in wanting her to use fillers to puff up their penis—"Mostly, it's an Asian thing"—she tells them "it's not my area of expertise."

She said that, once in the late '90s, she was speaking at an American Dermatological Association conference. The speaker before her was a Japanese dermatologist who gave the results of a study in Japan where one thousand men had had their penises injected with collagen. Only one hundred came back for a second go-round of pricks in their pricks.

"It makes it a little plumper," she says, "but it doesn't last that long, and it's incredibly painful."

It's not quite as bad as Egyptian vultures, who eat cow and horse feces to get the carotenoid pigments that will turn their pasty faces a vivid shade of yellow to entice mates. But younger women are being sold on the notion that they need prophylactic work done.

In her new book, Kuczynski, now thirty-seven, confesses that her own surgeries and Botox addiction began when she was twenty-eight. The beautiful five-foot-eleven, blue-eyed blonde already looked exactly like what many women were trying to become. Yet she still felt she needed to "ward off the evil pressures of time. I was brainwashed. Here I was a reporter and serious person, well educated, my parents did not believe in fripperies, and yet I was acting crazy."

She thought her upper eyelids were too fat, even though no one else noticed the problem, so she had surgery. She got fillers for five years until the awful day in January 2004, when her lips exploded. Her great friend Jerry Nachman, the fun and brash former *New York Post* editor and MSNBC editor in chief, had died. Alex decided to squeeze in a visit to her dermatologist on the Upper West Side to get a Restylane shot in her lips between the funeral and the wake at Elaine's restaurant on the Upper East Side, at which she was expected to give a toast. She had a Town Car waiting downstairs, but she never made it. She had an allergic reaction.

"Twenty minutes later, my upper lip was swollen to the size of a yam," she recalls. "I can't speak because my upper lip doesn't meet my lower lip. So instead of going to Jerry's wake, I'm lying on a gurney with a steroid drip. I went home and cried and cried and rocketed around my apartment, drinking vodka and thinking, 'I'm just like a character out of *First Wives Club*.' And Jerry is looking down at me saying, 'You are an asshole.' "

When London's *Harpers & Queen* magazine put out its list of the one hundred most beautiful people for 2005, the editors were surprised to see a shift away from Barbie and toward brunettes, larger noses and more unusual features and intelligent expressions.

Sofia Coppola and Nigella Lawson made the top five, and leading plastic surgeons told British reporters they were—mirabile dictu!—seeing a trend toward tolerating imperfections.

In London and in the U.S., there has been a move toward using "real" women in ads. Dove made a splash with its campaign showing six young women in underwear, some with plump thighs, to sell anticellulite cream (even though studies have refuted any efficacy in creams to fight cellulite). Nike offered a wry ad campaign for exercise gear with ads featuring hefty babes with copy reading "My butt is big" and "I have thunder thighs."

Who knows? If women all end up with the same face and body, men may gravitate toward the quirky. Then the chicks with the laugh lines and love handles will be the lucky ones.

· Eight ·

HOW GREEN IS MY VALLEY OF THE DOLLS

I t's a little what Anna Wintour would call "matchy matchy."

But to go with their plastic veneers, many women now get plastic emotions. They are lulled by Prozac, Zoloft, Xanax, Wellbutrin, Paxil, Klonopin, Vicodin, Ativan, Valium, Effexor, Celexa and Lexapro—all of which sound like planets where superheroes were born.

In April 2005, *New York* magazine did a story about the city's rampant pill-popping and infatuation with cosmetic psychopharmacology. "Using prescription drugs to work a little harder, sleep a little better, relax a little faster, has become a given in the city's meanstream," Ariel Levy wrote.

One mother of two living on Central Park West confided her love affair with Paxil: "People say 'I'm anxious' and I think, how quaint."

The New York Observer wrote in 2005 about the Ambien Generation, "where being turned on takes a back seat to being able to turn off."

The story began with an anecdote about a young man who ended up at the home of an attractive senior editor at a well-known fashion magazine. She was in her early thirties and "angling for some action."

"She was laying there and had taken her clothes off," he recounted. "Then, in completely slurred speech, she said: 'I just took two Ambien, so anything you're going to do, you better do it before I pass out.' She said she hadn't slept a night in seven years without her Ambien."

He called her attempt at pass-out sex "the most disgusting thing I've ever heard."

Boys don't make passes at girls who pass out.

In *The Stepford Wives,* husbands turn their mates into glazed fem-bots. Now women do it to themselves, with drugs or domesticity.

Martha Stewart (a haywire robot if there ever was one) led women—and culture—back to the wifely arts of cooking, gardening, decorating and flower arranging. (Stewart started her business in Westport, Connecticut, the model for the fictional town of Stepford.)

Hillary Clinton, once so angry about tea and cookies, went to Congress and acted like the senator from Stepford, eerily good-natured, fetching coffee for male colleagues.

If '70s feminism produced the squat and blunt Betty Friedan, this era has produced the sensual and zaftig Nigella Lawson, who wryly calls herself a "domestic goddess," and dishes up what fans call "gastro porn." More of a male fantasy than Stepford husbands could ever conjure up, the British cooking show hostess is always in the kitchen purring hot home economics advice, such as mangoes are "best eaten in their natural state, and preferably in the bath." Her recipes run along the lines of "Slut-Red Raspberries in Chardonnay Jelly." I've seen her book, *Nigella Bites*—featuring the author on the cover, openmouthed, downing a crustacean—for sale in lingerie stores.

There's even a retro trend of yummy mommies, women deserting the fast track for a pleasant life of sitting around Starbucks gabbing with their girlfriends, baby strollers beside them, logging time at the gym to firm up for the he-man CEO at home.

As Paul Rudnick, who wrote the screenplay for the *Stepford Wives* remake, slyly points out: "Men and women are working in tandem to create the Stepford wife of tomorrow. Once the technology advances, there'll be a Botox babe who runs on solar power."

Sometimes I worry that all American women have gone nuts. Okay, maybe not all. But certainly most.

Not to go all Tom Cruise on you here. I agree with Brooke Shields that women with postpartum depression—or any serious depression—may benefit from drugs. But a lot of women are popping pills for far less serious blue periods. And it's a bit chilling watching a lot of women I know sand down their faces and emotions.

A report from Columbia University in July 2005 found that the abuse of painkillers, stimulants and tranquilizers is more prevalent now than the abuse of illegal drugs such as heroin and cocaine. Fifteen million Americans—6 percent of the population—are abusing prescription drugs, the report contends, adding that two million of the abusers are mere adolescents.

The National Institute of Mental Health sponsored a study around the same time showing that more than half of all Americans will develop a mental illness at some point in their lives, often starting in childhood or adolescence.

"The key point to remember," said Dr. Thomas Insel, the director of the Institute, "is that mental disorders are highly prevalent and chronic."

Whenever you use the word "crazy" in print, you get hit with a blast of e-mails from Web sites funded by the pharmaceutical industry, which wants to continue to be our dealer, without any impediments to fake joy.

The diagnostic manual for the American Psychiatric Association expands like Topsy each time the drug companies put out more little colored pills with cherubic names.

"Pretty soon," Dr. Paul McHugh, a professor of psychiatry at Johns Hopkins University, told the *Times*, "we'll have a syndrome for short, fat Irish guys with a Boston accent, and I'll be mentally ill."

I have some anecdotal evidence to back up my claim.

First of all, I noticed some of my friends acting sort of Stepford-y, losing edge and empathy.

Then a doctor pal confided that she's surprised at how many of her female patients act loony even though they're on mood-smoothing pills—sometimes multiple meds.

Another friend told me she goes to a compounding pharmacy in L.A., where she gets testosterone to jump her libido, or "sensurround," a cocktail with ingredients like estrogen, progesterone, DHEA, pregnenolone and tryptophan.

Finally, yet another girlfriend who took a bunch of high school seniors on a spring vacation mentioned that all the girls were on antianxiety and antidepression drugs, some to get an extra edge as they aimed for Ivy League colleges.

And let's not even start on the hordes of kiddies—and mommies and career women—on Ritalin. One friend of mine had to fight an elite Manhattan school to keep her well-adjusted tween off Ritalin.

A middle-aged male journalist I know went on Ritalin after his wife sent him to a doctor. She complained that he had attention deficit disorder because he wasn't paying enough attention to her; after his Ritalin kicked in, he focused on the marriage and decided it was over.

It turns out that Jacqueline Susann, author of *Valley of the Dolls,* was the Delphic Oracle in Pucci. It isn't only neurotic Hollywood beauties any more who take hypnotics and narcotics. Now America *is* the Valley of the Dolls.

In Susann's 1966 book, Neely, Jennifer and Anne had to go to third-rate hotels on New York's West Side, to medical offices with dirty windows, and sweet-talk doctors into giving them little red, yellow or blue "dolls." Now doctors and pharmaceutical companies sweet-talk patients into feel-good pills.

When I admitted to my gynecologist a while ago that I was not in a serious relationship, he asked brightly, "Would you like antidepressants?"

Young professional women in Washington tell girlfriends in a tizzy, "Take a Paxil."

It isn't just women, of course. A young guy I know went in for a checkup and told his internist he was on edge because he was getting married and moving out of the country for a big new job. The doctor proposed an antidepressant called Serzone. My friend refused, pointing out that you're supposed to be nervous before you get married and start a new job.

In Zombie Nation, doctors now want to medicate you for living your life. Women have always popped mood-altering pills more than men. Studies show that women in most cultures have twice the rates of depression that men do. And now they feel entitled to speak up about their suffering.

A top psychiatrist told me women take more dolls because they're "hormonally more complicated and biologically more vulnerable. Depression is the downside of attachment, and women are programmed to attach more strongly and be punished more when they lose attachments."

There's even an antidepressant for women who compulsively shop called Celexa.

Nobody seems concerned with all those weird side effects they list, like your spleen going *SPLAT!* with a blind date at a swanky restaurant.

In a humor piece in *The New Yorker*, Steve Martin hilariously chronicled possible side effects: "WARNING: This drug may shorten your intestines by twenty-one feet. Has been known to cause birth defects in the user retroactively. . . . Women often feel a loss of libido, including a two-octave lowering of the voice, an increase in ankle hair, and perhaps the lowering of a testicle."

The Washington Post reported that Eli Lilly repackaged Prozac as the angelic Sarafem, in a pink-and-lavender capsule, and launched a multimillion-dollar ad campaign, with a woman irritably yanking a grocery cart, suffering from a new malady ominously called PMDD, premenstrual dysphoric disorder, an über-PMS that psychiatrists say may not be real.

Sales soared for "Prozac in drag," as Dr. Peter Kramer, the author of *Listening to Prozac,* called it, adding: "The liltingly soft name Sarafem sounds like Esperanto for a beleaguered husband's fantasy—a serene wife."

He finds it ironic that Prozac, the drug that was supposed to help career women assert themselves, has morphed into Sarafem, a mother's little helper to soothe anxious housewives, as Miltown and Valium did in the Stepford Wife era.

So women began taking mood dolls because they felt bored and dissatisfied, home with the kids. And now that women can have a family and a career, they need mood dolls to give them the confidence and energy to juggle all that stress. Progress. Don't ya love it?

As their libidos fade with age, women may opt to perk them up with testosterone patches—hailed by some doctors as the female Viagra.

A study sponsored by Procter & Gamble, which is marketing the testosterone patch Intrinsa—shouldn't it be called Extrinsa?—ascertained that women using the patch made whoopee four times more than usual in two months. The women may develop excessive facial hair, which might put a damper on things.

For women, the answer was not in expanding our blood vessels; it is the decline in female testosterone that causes languid libidos.

In the 1980s, the term "bed death" was used to refer to the often observed phenomenon that sex disappears in ongoing lesbian relationships because you need a guy and his testosterone level to provide the kind of excitement and tension that leads to sex. Some people suggested that the type of fusion of kindred souls that bonds lesbians and promotes affection diminishes lust. The Lipstick Lesbians of the '90s disputed this lesbian physics theory, insisting they were as sex-driven as anyone else.

Doctors have been trying to develop a female Viagra for years, preparing to bring it out just as health concerns developed about male Viagra in the spring of 2005.

I was watching the news with my mom, who lost her sight several years ago, when they reported the big story that Viagra and other impotence pills were suspected in causing blindness in a small number of users.

"Oh, no!" said Mom, who thought not being able to see was the worst thing that could happen to anyone. "Men should stop using that."

But how, I asked, would men keep it up?

She thought for a moment before replying, "Safety pins."

The blindness scare has not had much of an impact in keeping men from thronging to turn "a relaxing moment into the right moment," as the Cialis jingle goes.

I wouldn't expect a drug that warns its side effect might be a four-hour erection, as Cialis does, to lose popularity easily.

After all, when Propecia, the hair-growth drug, was found to cause impotence, that was not what sent sales lower. You could just get on a drug cocktail of Propecia and Viagra. It was the fact that Propecia didn't grow hair very well that sent sales lower.

Men are much more interested in erection and hair pills than in birth-control pills. Four decades after the Pill became available to women, researchers at the University of Kansas say their prototype for a male pill will take at least five more years to get to clinical trials.

Only 27 percent of women who practice contraception rely on men to use condoms or have vasectomies, according to the Alan Guttmacher Institute, a nonprofit organization focused on reproductive health issues. And it's not clear if women would trust men to take the Pill every day, even when it is perfected.

The sexual revolution that began with the Pill in the '60s revived with another kind of pill in the '90s. The generation of sex, drugs and rock and roll devolved into the generation of Viagra, antidepressants and lip-synching. (The rock and roll that once stoked our idealism now serves as background music for the commercials that stoke our materialism.)

Women, who already thought men were led too much by their anatomy, were more ambivalent than men about the arrival of Viagra. For each woman who celebrated Viagra, there was another who had nightmares about her leering sixty-two-year-old husband undergoing a satyric transformation and chasing twenty-one-year-old interns, his desk littered with empty Viagra bottles. Few wives wanted to worry about counting their husbands' pills.

Women are still dreaming of dolls that would increase male self-awareness instead of self-indulgence.

An unscientific poll of my girlfriends found that they would rather have a pill that could change a man's personality an hour after sex. A pill that ensures that he always calls the next day and never gets spooked.

A morning-after pill for men.

· Nine ·

HOW HILLARY SMUSHED CUPCAKES AND FILLETED FEMINISM

I f you want to know about the capital, look at its most prominent symbol, the Washington Monument. The Freudian
obelisk jutting up from the low city skyline reminds us that
history is shaped by sex.

"LBJ was probably right when he said that the two things
that make politicians more stupid than anything else are sex
and envy," historian Michael Beschloss told me.

Just consider how altered the contemporary landscape
would be if some of our most famous donnybrooks over sex had
played out differently.

Without Monica Lewinsky, we might well have had President Gore but no Senator Clinton.

If Bill Clinton hadn't been so consumed by the Monica

scandal and impeachment proceedings—and later Hillary's Senate campaign, because he owed her big-time—he might have finished off Osama bin Laden when he had the chance, years before 9/11.

If Clinton had not needed to pay back Hillary because she put up with a marriage full of dalliances, he might not have turned over a huge chunk of domestic policy to her without also giving her the benefit of his clever strategic advice on how to get her health care plan passed. (Don't make it too unwieldy or secretive.)

A guy in my office is certain that Bill Clinton's problems with Paula Jones, and therefore Monica and impeachment, could have been avoided if he had simply called room service at the Excelsior Hotel in Little Rock and ordered up a bottle of cold duck for Paula before he abruptly pulled down his pants. "She needed to be treated nicer," my friend said. "She needed some amenities."

Senator Joe Biden was nervous about persecuting a black man on national TV and still disgusted by belligerent Democratic interest groups from the Bork hearings four years earlier, so he caved to Republican demands to keep two additional female accusers of Clarence Thomas from testifying that Anita Hill was not an isolated example but part of a larger pattern of sexual misbehavior at the office. If Biden hadn't folded, and if Teddy Kennedy had not been so hamstrung by his own past sexual misdeeds and his nephew's Palm Beach rape trial that he was practically mute, Judge Thomas would likely not have been confirmed.

If Justice Thomas had not been on the Supreme Court in

the case of *Bush* v. *Gore* in the 2000 election stalemate, the decision might not have been 5 to 4 in favor of stopping the vote and handing over the White House to the son of the president who appointed Thomas.

If Al Gore had not been so intent on giving the perception that he was disgusted with Bill Clinton's sexual hijinks—remember that endless liplock with Tipper at his convention?—he would have let the Big Dog run in the 2000 campaign and probably won both the electoral and popular vote.

If W. hadn't gotten in on a platform of restoring "honor and dignity" and keeping bimbos out of the Oval Office, half a century of American foreign policy would not have been upended. Gore's foreign policy would have followed in the multilateral path of Bush Sr.'s.

With no W. and Dick Cheney, there would have been no unilateral preemptive doctrine in place. Allied diplomatic pressure and U.N. weapons inspectors could have ascertained that Iraq had no WMD. American kids and Iraqi civilians would not have been getting blown up every day for years. And if our military was not stretched so thin in Iraq, it could have focused on catching Osama before Al Qaeda metastasized and blew up London and Egypt.

If W. hadn't been propelled into office partly because of sex, he wouldn't have been able to restrict sexual freedoms, such as gay marriage and women's rights.

Like the Cleopatra's nose theory of history, which posits that if Cleopatra's nose had been a millimeter longer, Caesar and Marc Antony would not have gone to war over her, sex has often been a trip wire in American history.

When I first started covering politics at the *Times* in 1984, I devised a beat called "gender," so I could look at how sexual politics influenced elections.

It was the first of several ballyhooed Years of the Woman. But it actually ended up being the Year of the Manly Man.

When I look back, every fizzy triumph of feminism I covered over the last twenty years—Geraldine Ferraro being picked as the first woman to run on a major national ticket; the incendiary Hill-Thomas hearings; the ascension of "Two for the Price of One" Hillary Rodham Clinton to First Lady—ended up triggering a horrible backlash that set back the course of feminism, until, in the end, it sputtered out as a force. All those "You've come a long way, baby" highs added up to some "Step away from the car, ma'am" lows.

The emotional high point for feminism was the 1984 Democratic convention in San Francisco, where women popped champagne, cried and hugged when Ferraro was chosen.

But two decades later, there's still trepidation about putting another woman on a ticket—except in Hollywood, which is bringing us *Commander in Chief* with Geena Davis on ABC. Creator Rod Lurie said he patterned his Madame President on Martha Stewart Inc.'s elegant CEO, Susan Lyne, because he couldn't think of a woman pol who would fit the model "of rather unimpeachable integrity, very kind, very calm under pressure."

As Ruth Mandel, the director of the Center for Women and Politics at the Eagleton Institute at Rutgers, once told me, "When it comes to women, people are not ready to take more than a teaspoonful of change at a time."

With Hillary laying the groundwork for her presidential run, it's instructive to look back at that first historic race by another pragmatic blond pol. The junior senator from New York will face the same problems the junior congresswoman from New York did: How to come across as tough enough but not too tough. ("Nothing makes men more anxious," Gloria Steinem warned about Ferraro, "than for a woman to be masculine.") And how to appeal to the South and Southwest. Hillary got one Bubba, but can she get millions more?

One Southern blue-dog Democrat morosely watched what he considered a doomed Hillary juggernaut in the summer of 2005, noting that his constituents couldn't stand her.

"If I spent five minutes in public with Hillary Clinton," he said, "I'd lose my seat in the House."

Women's groups spent a year laying the groundwork for a Ferraro, assuming that first woman would be the vanguard of great things. But the Queens congresswoman who started out with so much metallic moxie ended up, as one reporter put it, "Cinderella with ashes in her mouth."

The issues and imagery of the campaign of "America's bride," as one magazine called her, reached deep into the collective consciousness of Americans.

When Harry Met Sally raised the question: Can a man and a woman be friends? *When Fritz Met Gerry* raised the question: Can a man and a woman be running mates?

At the San Francisco convention, the feminists were so giddy they were punchy; they thought of a slogan for the new ticket echoing the question Walter Mondale asked about rival Gary Hart: "Where's the beef?"

"The beef is a heifer," the women sang out joyously, crowing that Ferraro would shine up Fritz's "Norwegian Wood" persona.

Walter Mondale and Geraldine Ferraro were on a blind date with each other and history, with the women's movement playing yenta, and every move was minutely analyzed: Who should stand where? Who should walk first? Whether to touch? How to address each other?

Their debut was as awkward as prom night. They tried to present themselves as a briskly successful TV anchor team, but every time they did the traditional *abrazo*—one arm around the other's waist and one arm waving—they looked like a nice, middle-aged suburban couple hugging.

Could we trust them with the nuclear football when they looked like parents at their kids' high school football game?

The feminists were annoyed when Johnny Carson, the most influential political commentator of his day, joked about how angry Joan Mondale would be when her husband kept coming home late, saying he'd had private sessions with the vice president.

From the first, there had to be a policy on kissing.

"Mondale cannot, whatever he does, kiss her," Pat Caddell, the Democratic strategist, said ominously.

The late Bob Squier, another consultant, agreed: "He can't call her 'honey' or 'dear.' " He joked that phrases like a ticket with "broad appeal" and a candidate with "clean skirts" would now be verboten.

What were the odds that a little-known, five-foot-two woman with a New York accent whose favorite expression was

"Gimme a break!" could be taken seriously? Not good, especially after her campaign got mired in questions about her real
estate developer husband's sketchy finances and shady con-
nections.

The blue sky of the pink forces clouded quickly when the
Mondale camp's "smart-ass white boys," as the furious feminists dubbed them, got jittery about a backlash from white
male voters and froze the women out of the campaign.

With Ronald Reagan, a candidate who was, as Peggy Noo-
nan put it, like a great cowboy balloon in Macy's Thanksgiv-
ing Day parade, the Republicans quickly painted Mondale as
a pussy-whipped captive of special interests, especially the
pushy women's groups. The Democrat obliged by wearing an
apron in the *Mondale Family Cookbook*, even as Reagan
pumped iron on the cover of *Parade* magazine and Vice President Bush climbed into the cockpit of a World War II torpedo
bomber and talked about his war record.

The young male voters the Democrats needed were drawn
to the old stud, Reagan, and many women, too, wanted a
daddy figure.

The Ferraro campaign was the first I covered, an opportunity created by a climate where many editors parochially assumed women should cover the woman, and blacks should
cover Jesse Jackson's 1984 presidential campaign. It was like
falling through the looking glass to chronicle a presidential
bid with a female candidate and girls on the bus.

Oddly, the *Times* decreed that the candidate should inac-
curately be called "Mrs. Ferraro," even though her professional
name was her maiden one and her husband was named Zac-

caro. It wasn't until two years after this political breakthrough that Abe Rosenthal, then the executive editor, agreed to use the title "Ms." if women specifically requested it. (On the day of the announcement, Gloria Steinem sent Abe flowers.)

Matched against the current president's father, Ferraro confused the terms "first strike" and "first use," evoking a wacky picture of the redheaded Lucy yakking into the red phone, desperately trying to recall missiles launched because of a misplaced word. Dr. Strangelucy.

Wearing pearls and silk dresses, rejecting some male Mondale aides' entreaties to get into dark, man-tailored suits, she bounced amiably to her introductory music, even when it was "Five foot two, eyes of blue."

For the first time, a candidate running for the White House handed her pocketbook to a male aide as she began a news conference, and talked about abortion with the phrase "If I were pregnant" and foreign policy with the line "As the mother of a draft-age son."

Ferraro was patient when Jim Buck Ross, Mississippi's seventy-year-old commissioner of agriculture, called her "young lady," and asked her if she could bake blueberry muffins. But when another Democratic official presented her with a wrist corsage before a fund-raising meeting in New York, she drew the line and refused to wear it.

Ferraro had a hard time with that requisite totem of male campaigns: baby kissing. "As a mother, my instinctive reaction is how do you give your baby to someone who's a total stranger to kiss, especially with so many colds going around?" she told me. "And especially when the woman is wearing lipstick?"

When Ferraro cracked wise about her husband's refusal to release his tax returns—"You women married to Italian men know how it is"—she got in trouble for acting subservient. When she stopped male politicians from being protective and taking the microphone when she was heckled, she seemed self-consciously assertive.

Vice President Bush also had to walk a fine line running against a woman, between being courtly and being too macho. He stumbled after their debate when he bragged that he had "tried to kick a little ass" and then attempted to pass it off as "an old Texas football" expression.

The feminists said that Ferraro had become a lightning rod for what Steinem called "free-floating hostility to women in power that couldn't be overtly stated"—a claim Hillary would later make about herself, explaining her failed health care plan and dropping poll numbers as First Lady to Hillary Stout of *The Wall Street Journal* this way: "A friend told me I've turned into a gender Rorschach test. If somebody has a female boss for the first time, and they've never experienced that—well, maybe they can't take out their hostility against her, so they turn it on me."

In her memoir, Ferraro bitterly complained of sexism by the Catholic Church, Italian Americans, Rupert Murdoch and *The New York Post*, antiabortion demonstrators, Ronald Reagan and the Republicans, and the Mondale male staffers.

On the trail, she developed a persecution complex, bit her nails and gained thirteen pounds from eating junk food. When she felt patronized by Mondale's staff, she suggested that his aides "should pretend every time they talk to me or even look at me that I'm a gray-haired Southern gentleman, a senator from Texas."

But just as two other strong, outspoken women, Hillary Rodham Clinton and Teresa Heinz Kerry, would later try to sweep their own mistakes under the rug of sexism, so Ferraro did not acknowledge that she had accepted Mondale's offer to be on the ticket under false pretenses. During the overly trusting preselection interview, she was asked by Mondale vetters if there was anything in her background that could blow up and embarrass the campaign and she said no.

But as a former prosecutor, public official and savvy woman who was listed as an officer in her husband's real estate company, she either knew enough—or should have known enough—about her husband's tangled business and legal problems that she was obliged to acknowledge that they could erupt during the campaign. Which they did. (John Zaccaro ultimately pleaded guilty to an indictment charging him with conspiring to fraudulently obtain financing for a real estate deal.)

Instead, she pleaded ditziness about family business during the campaign, making Lucy-and-Desi cracks about Latin men.

Everyone thought the '84 campaign would forever change the public perception about men and women in politics, but it didn't. Ferraro never cried, but she looks small in retrospect. (She's now a vice president with a global consulting group, in remission from multiple myeloma, a rare blood cancer.)

When the Reagan-Bush ticket swept forty-nine states—losing only Mondale's home state of Minnesota—it simply underscored the fact that Americans like two-fisted, swashbuckling, wood-chopping, brush-clearing candidates.

And voters, male and female, can be put off by pols who surround themselves with the kind of people George Orwell once described as "that dreary tribe of high-minded women and sandal-wearers and bearded fruit-juice drinkers who come flocking toward the smell of 'progress' like bluebottles to a dead cat."

The Ferraro candidacy proved that women do not vote for women just because they are women.

One top Republican strategist told me bluntly: "It's been a longtime secret among political consultants that women hate women candidates. Women are bred to compete. It's the old thing: you get eleven guys, you've got a football team. You get eleven women, you've got a riot."

In the six presidential races I've covered—occasionally in high dudgeon, always in high heels—voters seemed drawn to the candidates who conveyed the most manliness, the ones who could win with a quip or a more studly presence in *High Noon* debates; convey the impression that they'd be tougher, first against the Russians and now against Islamic terrorists.

On the surface, presidential campaigns are a din of competing issues and a display of contrasting styles. But there is also a subliminal battle, played out in rituals like debates and photo opportunities, in which the candidates strive to show that they are superior in the knightly virtues of temperance, loyalty and courage.

"We act modern, cool and sophisticated," Robin Lakeoff, a Berkeley professor of linguistics, told me. "But underneath, we want a daddy, a king, a god, a hero. We'll take the heel if we can get Achilles, a champion who will carry that lance and that sword into the field and fight for us. We're not as rational as we think. It's sort of scary."

Western culture is rooted in millennia of hero legends, from Prometheus stealing fire from the gods for mankind's benefit to Jason getting past the dragon to bring back the Golden Fleece, to young Arthur pulling the sword from the stone to be king. On top of ancient myths, American culture has overlaid legends of frontier life, cowboy justice and cops and robbers.

Indeed, America began in the manner of a classic hero legend: A young hero (George Washington) led a rebellion against the cruel old king and parent (England) and became the father of the country himself.

One important campaign ritual comes when the candidate assures the voters that he has completed the "hero-task," as it is called by Joseph Campbell, that he has slain the dragon or the giant.

For George Bush Sr. and Bob Dole, the dragons were the Nazis and Japanese in World War II. For John Kerry, Bob Kerrey and John McCain, the dragon was the North Vietnamese.

For Bill Clinton, Dan Quayle and W., who managed to avoid going to Vietnam, there had to be more psychological Gorgons or Hydras from their past.

Clinton dramatized his account of the moment when, as a teenager, he stood up to an alcoholic stepfather, telling him not to hit his mother again. Dan Quayle contended that his character was tested when he survived the wild beast of politics—the traveling press corps—in the 1988 campaign. And W. offered the dramatic narrative of finding Jesus and fending off Jack Daniel's when he was still drifting at forty.

Having nothing else to offer, Ferraro tried to use her tense, live, two-hour televised news conference defending her family finances as her "heroine-task."

John Mihalec, a speechwriter in the Ford White House, wrote that a Democrat who wants to be president has to balance a consensus style and female-friendly ideology with a masculine personal style, as JFK did. "Above all," he said, "he must look, feel and smell as if he would not be taken to the cleaners in a poker game."

It shouldn't make you a sissy to care about women, the poor and the downtrodden, but Democrats have long been called the Mommy Party and Republicans the Daddy Party.

Walter Mondale, Michael Dukakis, Al Gore and John Kerry did not have that alpha oomph; Bill Clinton—perhaps because of his lusty appetites for everything from burgers to babes—did.

*   *   *

It was the worst culture quake that ever rocked Washington. It had everything combustible all rolled up into one story—race, sex, lies, power, pornography, hypocrisy.

The ferocious "he said, she said" 1991 hearings into Anita Hill's charges against Clarence Thomas were supposed to serve as a seminar on sexual harassment for the Senate men's club. The incendiary words of the prim professor and the defiant judge kept sinking, like some kind of psychic dentist's drill, into the most sensitive, least explored parts of the national consciousness.

I barely slept that week. I would sit bolt upright in the middle of the night, trying to fathom who was telling the truth and who was lying, as though I were watching a Hitchcock mystery.

Never before, and probably never again, will there be such blue language ricocheting across the green felt witness tables in the Senate Judiciary hearing room.

I bonded with my friend Jill Abramson, a *Wall Street Journal* reporter who has since become the managing editor of the *Times*, when we looked at each other across a long table in the packed hearing room, our mouths literally agape at the sworn testimony in that august chamber about pubic hairs on Coke cans, bestiality and a black pornography star nicknamed Long Dong Silver.

Before the hearings began, Hill's secret adviser, the late Lloyd Cutler, a wise and respected Washington lawyer, begged the feminists to keep Anita from uttering the word "penis" during her testimony. Cutler thought the Capitol dome would come tumbling down in shame.

The feminists ignored him. They wanted to let it all hang out.

Again and again, they yelped that grating and condescending phrase: The Senate old boys' network just didn't "get it."

"The times they are a-changin', and the boys here don't get it on this issue," said Pat Schroeder, the Colorado Democratic congresswoman. "They don't really understand what sexual harassment is, and it's not important to them."

Not important to them? The nation's capital had been built on a proud tradition of sexual misbehavior.

As Senate pages in the '40s and '50s, my brothers Michael

and Martin saw the rakish side of Capitol Hill life, like guards who checked offices after hours only to find senators engaged in "batrachian grapplings," as Aldous Huxley called it, with their secretaries; and like the famous Democratic senator who tipped the pages ten cents extra a day to fend off calls from his wife, who would scream: "I know he's with that woman! I'm coming down there!"

Whenever people complimented me on my coverage of that searing week in October, they observed that I had been able to appreciate the dramatic dimensions of the story because I was a woman. But it was a man, my boss Howell Raines, then the *Times*'s Washington bureau chief, who pressed me to pursue the story.

"Just because all the members of the Judiciary Committee are white men," I protested, "doesn't mean they're sexist."

"Why don't you make a few calls," Howell replied, in his deep, Chuck Yeager drawl.

The calls tapped into an electric current of anger among women about Republican attempts to attack the character of the victim.

"There is no understanding of the victim syndrome, of the fact that many victims of rape, incest, date rape and sexual humiliation are reluctant and ambivalent to go forth because of all kinds of feelings," Maryland lawmaker Barbara Mikulski hooted.

But like other champagne dreams of feminism, this cheesy melodrama also fell flat. Anita Hill disappeared back into academia. Clarence Thomas ascended to the Supreme Court. And pols went back to fiddling with young female aides.

Just as there was something opportunistic at the heart of the Ferraro campaign—her failure to be forthcoming with the Mondale vetters—so there was something opportunistic at the heart of the Hill matter.

Nan Aron and the feminists were genuinely concerned about Thomas's character—how he lied and how he treated people. The women's rights advocates had first been opposed to him on ideology, but could not win on that score. So they hunted down Hill and persuaded her to privately level a ten-year-old allegation at the eleventh hour—and then they leaked it.

Anita Hill was just a pawn. The feminists tried to turn her into the Rosa Parks of sexual harassment because, at all costs, they wanted to prevent Thurgood Marshall from being succeeded by a conservative black justice.

The feminists forced public hearings but they could not force men to truly evolve. (As Dorothy Parker so memorably put it, "You can lead a whore to culture, but you can't make her think.")

Only seven years later, leaders of the women's movement would be doing loop-de-loops trying to defend the feminist president Bill Clinton against cascading sexual harassment charges, as feminist icon Hillary and other White House henchmen plotted the attack on "bimbos" and "stalkers" who told on Bill, including sliming Monica Lewinsky as an eroto-maniac, a little nutty and a little slutty, just as Republicans had slimed Anita Hill.

As Jill Abramson noted later, "I covered both the Anita Hill and Monica Lewinsky stories. What I found most chilling in both cases was seeing powerful men marshal the resources of the government to undermine the credibility of two women who were private citizens who both, initially, had little desire to be in the center of the political arena."

Only a decade after the men of Washington were pronouncing themselves sensitized, we would be overrun with the swaggering Goths of the empire-building administration of George W. Bush. And President Bush would declare Justice Thomas one of his two favorite Supreme Court justices.

The men on the Judiciary Committee did not see Anita Hill as a victim because, even if her story about Clarence Thomas talking dirty was true, they felt she could have handled it with more aplomb and humor, not like some prudish schoolmarm. So what if he was the proverbial fox in the henhouse, harassing an employee when it was his job to make sure Americans did not harass their employees? Everybody knows how crazy men get after a divorce.

Senators were uncomfortable at the way Hill "came out of the night like a missile," as then Republican senator Alan Simpson of Wyoming put it.

It's a primal fear of men, women coming out of the shadows to call them on their bad behavior (and a valid fear, since many prominent whistle-blowers are women).

The Republicans painted Hill as crazy, even while keeping out all the evidence that Clarence Thomas certainly would have known the language of porn movies. Ever since Holy Cross College and Yale Law School, he had enjoyed watching freaky porn films—including the Mama Jama series, about a three-hundred-pound black woman, too large to move, who is serviced by various studs—and then chatting about them afterward. He kept his collection of *Playboy*s carefully catalogued.

The Democrats caved and the Republicans ruthlessly played to win—a dynamic that would continue to shape many political battles.

Onstage, the pols said they had learned important lessons about harassment. Offstage, one of Hill's main Democratic defenders told a Republican colleague on the committee that he assumed the pair had had a torrid affair that ended badly—even though there was no evidence of that.

Thomas escaped his "high-tech lynching" because he was able to come across as more of a victim than Hill. After he got confirmed, the feminists threatened payback. Some liberal Hollywood women said they would stop going skiing in Utah, the home of Hill's tormentor, Senator Orrin Hatch. And Betty Friedan announced that the first President Bush was "Public Enemy No. 1."

But Senator Hatch and the Bush dynasty flourished, as did skiing in Utah.

In retrospect, many people think Hill was prissy and humorless, probably not realizing that this is what drew Thomas to her. (She was so confused by his weird attentions, she asked a friend if her perfume could be the problem.)

"People forget that Thomas was essentially bullying her for his enjoyment—and it was about power, not sex," says the *New Yorker* writer Jane Mayer, who did a compelling book about the case with Abramson called *Strange Justice.* "In the years since

Hill's accusations, the whole American culture has become increasingly pornographic, so, her complaints are drowned out in a sea of Madonna-wannabes wearing underwear as outerwear, not to mention porn videos from pop culture idols and magazine cover girls Pamela Anderson and Paris Hilton—who have mainstream TV careers now despite the kinds of skin flicks that hurt Rob Lowe for years. Sex as a marketing tool is completely rampant, so Anita's complaints seem silly. And the pornographization of pop culture is another sign that the feminists lost."

The sight of the all-white-male Judiciary Committee, stunned into mute silence and bowed like a tree in a storm as Thomas bristled at them, did inspire more women to jump into politics.

In 1992, historic numbers of women were propelled into the cloistered world long dominated by white middle-aged men. They were known as "the Anita Hill class." Splotches of gold and pink and red began brightening the monochromatic landscape of Capitol Hill, as the number of women jumped by 200 percent, or four seats, in the Senate, and by 68 percent, or nineteen seats, in the House.

They began powwowing with the influential new First Lady, to make sure the budget reflected their concerns on women's health issues.

"It's almost certainly the first time that these guys on the budget committee heard words like 'cervix,' 'ovaries' and 'breasts' spoken out loud," New York congresswoman Louise Slaughter said.

"At least in that context," Hillary Clinton quipped.

For the first time, women demanded to use the gym and were regularly seen in the members-only elevators—and raffish old senators like Strom Thurmond had to learn to stop pouncing on them as though they were staff or elevator operators.

In the aftermath of the furor sparked by the Hill-Thomas hearings, male lawmakers—and men in offices across the land—trod more carefully.

"Anita Hill redefined the battle zone between men and women and created a new way of looking at an age-old problem," Jane Mayer said. "She put powerful men—and women—on notice in both the public and private sectors that unwelcome sexual pursuit could put them at risk of legal liability."

Only Charlie Wilson, the ebullient Texas congressman who loved Vegas hot tubs and had his own personal belly dancer on call, refused to succumb to the sedate and cautious new P.C. mood.

"I still try to irritate Pat Schroeder by calling her 'Babycakes,' " he told me, adding that he loved having more women around because "a couple of 'em are pretty cute."

Mostly, the hearings left men so befuddled that, for the next decade, men confused harassment with friendly palaver. Many stopped casual flirting or complimenting the way women dressed, which was not a net plus for women, because most women like to flirt and be complimented on their dresses.

"Now men are back to talking about women's racks in the office," drily noted one of my friends.

A bitter Thomas stopped reading newspapers, which is not

a good thing for a Supreme Court justice. (Or a president, in the case of W.)

In 1998, when Hill supporter Bill Clinton was dragged by Congress through another harrowing and historic "he said, she said" saga, the feminists were on the side of he, not she.

The feminists were not interested in the sordid truth of the affair, which seemed to indicate, at the least, a seamy abuse of power and a lack of concern for the feelings of his wife and daughter, and, at the most, a betrayal of the supporters who had brought him to the fair.

"You just don't get it" shifted to "Everybody does it." It's not sexual harassment, it turns out, if the harasser is a champion of women's issues. Or if the harassee are NOCD (Not our class, dear).

Thomas, it turned out, just chose the wrong kind of girl— Yale, Baptist, Southern, sedately dressed—to talk dirty to.

And meanwhile, Thomas's conservative backers were on the warpath about any sexual behavior in high places—even though this time the sex involved was between mutually consenting, ostensible adults.

The feminists never went into full cry when Clinton strategist James Carville suggested that Paula Jones was trailer trash, when Clinton lawyer Robert Bennett compared Paula Jones to a dead dog, when Clinton aide and Hillary confidante Sidney Blumenthal ran an oppo-campaign from within the White House to discredit Kathleen Willey and slime Monica Lewinsky as an unbalanced stalker.

"I can see my obituary now," the Ragin' Cajun once told me. " 'James Carville, Clinton Sex Defender, Dead.' "

The feminists saw Anita as a victim, but Monica as a predator. Anita merely followed Clarence from job to job; Monica pursued Bill from rope line to rope line.

Feminism was supposed to root out all those "he's a stud, she's a slut" double standards. But after all the decades spent trying to change the climate so that men could not claim that a woman who was raped or sexually harassed had it coming if she flirted or wore a short skirt or liked sex, the feminists let the Clintonites get away with painting Lewinsky as a slutty stalker because she flirted, wore short skirts and liked sex. The Clinton bimbo patrol took over and tried to persuade the public that a twenty-one-year-old intern was able to overpower the will of the most powerful man on earth and vamp her way past Secret Service agents to force him to do her vixen bidding.

When a Fox TV News poll asking the loaded question about whether Monica was "a young tramp looking for thrills," a majority of Americans agreed.

At the Hill-Thomas hearings, the parties, as well as the lobbyists, spin doctors and interest groups, were all motivated less by truth than self-interest. But Bill Clinton and his enablers made obscuring truth such an art form—it all depends what the meaning of *is* is—that truth became unattainable.

Clarence Thomas was just ahead of his time.

• • •

When *The Washington Star* folded in 1981, it was hard for me to find another job. I got a little desperate.

Finally I was offered a fine job at a magazine. One of its editors made the offer over dinner at a Washington hotel where he was staying. At the end of dinner, as I got ready to leave, this nice, attractive and happily married editor looked at me and said: "Stay."

The room reeled. I stammered something about meeting my boyfriend to celebrate my new job.

"Call him," the editor instructed, pushing a quarter across the table.

Feeling dizzy, I explained that I couldn't reach him, thanked the editor and rushed out of the hotel. When I got out on the street, I screamed. I was furious. I didn't know if I still had the job. Or what the job really entailed. I had come to him out of need, and he responded with an altogether different need of his own. I wanted to throw the job back in his face, but I knew I would not get another one that good. After agonizing all weekend, I showed up on Monday. The editor was professional and encouraging. He later apologized, and we were friendly throughout my tenure there.

Relations between men and women at work will always be fraught, no matter how many regulations are passed. The uneasy circling between the sexes is rooted in this dynamic: Women always fear that men are going to keep them from getting some advantage because of their sex. And men fear that women are going to get some advantage because of their sex.

When Anita Hill and Kathleen Willey came forward to tell their stories about sexual harassment, their critics yelped that these women were clearly lying, since they didn't press charges and never would have stayed on pleasant terms with men who had acted so crudely. How could they have continued to work with, telephone, write nice notes to or ask favors of Clarence Thomas and Bill Clinton?

Easy. Just ask most working women.

In 1991, feminist Ann Lewis fought conservatives who said Hill's credibility was shot because she had followed Thomas from job to job, and continued calling him.

Lewis lectured Pat Buchanan about the mind-set of working girls: "You have this really prestigious and powerful boss and think you have to stay on the right side of him or for the rest of your working life he could nix another job."

But in 1998, in her subsequent incarnation as President Clinton's communications director and chief rationalizer, she attacked Willey's credibility by saying that in '96, three years after the groping incident in the Oval Office, the former White House volunteer said she admired Clinton and wanted to raise funds for his campaign.

"It is such a contradiction," Lewis asserted.

No, it's not. Bosses often inspire feelings of admiration and disgust, attraction and repulsion, depending on the moment.

Women cannot always stand on principle when their superiors lurch over the line. They usually behave in more layered and self-interested ways. These difficult nuances of emotion and calculation cannot be captured by the black-and-white of sexual harassment law—which can make women look hypocritical and manipulative.

Women are accustomed to putting up with immature and wormy behavior by men in their personal lives—and in their professional lives. They have learned, through long years of being subordinated to men in the workplace, to use their wiles and wits to maneuver past eruptions of male libido.

I remember, in the wake of the Hill-Thomas hearings, how scathingly some black women talked about Anita Hill, contemptuous that she could not have simply put Thomas in his place, or laughed off his fetish for talking about X-rated movies.

And there's the Chris Rock theory of sexual harassment: "If Clarence Thomas had looked like Denzel Washington, this would have never happened. She'd be all, 'Oh stop it, Clarence. You nasty! Your fine self!' So what's sexual harassment? When an ugly man wants some?"

If women took action every time a boss made an unwanted pass or an untoward remark, they would be twice injured: first when they are treated like chattel, and again when they lose their bridge to a good job, a good recommendation and a good contact.

The dirty little secret of gender politics is that women can be opportunistic; in learning to sidestep the importunings of men, they have also cynically learned to turn them to their advantage, as former Fox producer Andrea Mackris craftily did when she took Bill O'Reilly to the cleaners for millions after taping his sex fantasies about loofahs and outdoor showers in the Caribbean.

Women know that they will, on occasion, get some extra attention because of their gender, or because they're charming or clever or attractive. They are willing to accept the benefits that come when a boss is taken with them.

That is why Paula Jones went up to Bill Clinton's hotel suite, and that is why Hill followed Thomas to another department of government. Hill and Willey were prepared to extract the good from the bad, and make their bosses' libidos work for them. It's a way of getting ahead in a world dominated by powerful men.

But often the woman views that attraction as icing, while the man mistakes it for the cake. There is a school of thought that sexual harassment is merely bad manners. But women (and occasionally men) must be protected from behavior that is offensive or vengeful.

There's nothing wrong with flirting at the office, of course. It can be the route to lifelong happiness, or at least bring joy to a dreary day.

A cautionary tale on flirting was the crash of the attractive thirty-three-year-old Jamie Tarses from her perch as president of ABC Entertainment in 1997.

She reportedly got out of her NBC contract after Michael Ovitz, then at Walt Disney, leaked that she had been sexually harassed by NBC's West Coast president, Don Ohlmeyer. But it is wrong for a woman to use that charge opportunistically.

Once at ABC, Tarses dissolved into a stereotype, a helpless girl who curled up like a cat at meetings, treated male agents and bosses like boyfriends and dates, and wanted men to make her big decisions and her tough phone calls for her.

Another seeming contradiction is that office harassers are often devoted husbands and generous colleagues; I've been stunned over the years to learn, time and again, about male friends, respected professionals and often very attractive guys, who frightened young women in the office, powerless subordinates, with inappropriate sexual pressure. (Sometimes the young women were not so frightened and used the inappropriate e-mails from a boss as leverage with a different superior to get a career boost for themselves.)

But self-interest, too, has its limits. A woman who is willing to be teased may not be prepared to be degraded. She may tolerate a boss's gaze but not a boss's hands. She may put up with one crack about a Coke can, but not a daily soliloquy on porno flicks. For women, there is a steadily growing cost in personal dignity for playing the gender game at the office.

So bosses beware. It is all very muddled. Some prices are too much to pay. When the line is crossed, some women may not only collapse into tears. They may also collapse into television. Or onto the Internet.

. . .

After Democratic front-runner Gary Hart's dizzy fall in 1987, when his picture with Miami model Donna Rice on the *Monkey Business* was splashed on the front page of *The National Enquirer*, the feminists were angry.

"Here is this guy who we thought of as one of the new leaders," one told me, "and then it turns out that his private behavior is of the most old-fashioned and stereotypical kind—women as objects. The contradiction and cynicism was infuriating."

The women were disgusted that Hart, as an undergraduate at Bethany Nazarene College, had "married up," as one Hart friend put it, wooing and winning Oletha (Lee) Ludwig, the pretty, athletic daughter of a former president of the college who was several social rungs above Hart, and then got caught "doing what all women fear all men want to do— dating down."

Washington Post columnist Mary McGrory referred to Hart as "the philosopher-philanderer."

Ann Lewis, then the national director of Americans for Democratic Action, predicted that the Hart debacle would have a lasting effect on the way voters, particularly women, viewed candidates: "In the wreckage of this campaign, it is clear that the old double standard is irrevocably dead. And in those aspiring to leadership, it is fatal."

A decade later, when Lewis was in the White House and defending President Clinton's reckless behavior, she did her very best to see that the double standard was alive and well.

When Hart defiantly returned to the '88 race for a pathetic ghostly encore, I was one of the few reporters covering "the Return of the Living Dead," as one of my colleagues called it. His campaign mostly consisted of walking around New Hampshire malls, shaking hands with curious shoppers. Occasionally, young men would push their giggling blond girlfriends next to the candidate, so they could get a picture of a little monkey business. Hart mordantly suggested he'd become "a nonperson."

There were many who thought Hart was disqualified on judgment rather than character. He grimaced when I asked why, after aides warned him that his Capitol Hill town house could be under surveillance by news organizations, he spent the weekend there with party girl Rice, taking her to his own wife's bed.

"I wasn't going to change my life because of reporters," he said, defensively. "I have the same rights as any other American citizen, and I can have whoever I want in my house. It was a matter of principle with me. I dug in my heels."

Well done.

"I never planned to be in Washington that weekend," he finished, wistfully. "It was a last-minute thing."

The nadir of this nadir came late one night at Boston's Logan airport. Without a cocoon of Secret Service agents and protective aides, Hart found himself in the unenviable position of being just another exhausted middle-aged guy looking for his luggage. He searched in vain for the right carousel, trailed by his irritated wife and a trio of reporters acting like difficult children.

"Ga-a-a-ry, you're not showing your leadership," Lee Hart called out loudly to her stonefaced husband. "Ga-a-a-ry, what about your leadership?"

My late friend Michael Kelly, who was covering the spectral campaign with me, found this scene from a political marriage so hilarious that, after the Harts left, he literally rolled around the floor of the airport, laughing.

A woman scorned is not fun to campaign with.

Gary Hart, like Clarence Thomas, was just ahead of his time. It turned out a philanderer could be elected president— twice.

● ● ●

Perhaps the absurdist P.C. low point came in 1993, when the Navy, embarrassed by the Tailhook scandal, issued a folder to Navy and Marine officers, using traffic-light colors to group acceptable and unacceptable forms of behavior between the sexes.

A black-and-white institution was struggling to deal with the grays of sexual interaction with a color chart.

The green zone (Go) included "placing a hand on a person's elbow" and "everyday social interaction such as saying, 'Hello, how are you?' or 'Did you have a good weekend?' " The yellow zone (Slow down to stop) included "whistling," "unwanted poems," violating "personal space" and "questions about personal life." And the red zone (Stop) included "sexual favors in return for employment rewards and threats if sexual favors are not provided" and "sexual assault and rape."

As one Army officer based at the Pentagon told me sarcastically: "Oh, gosh, I didn't know saying 'Good morning' to someone is a green zone, and I'm really glad to know that rape is a red zone."

The color-coded sex alerts are still in effect, even more confusing in an era of color-coded terror alerts.

Political correctness backfired on the feminists. To their dismay, Bob Packwood was the first big fish caught in their D.C./P.C. net.

In the late '80s, working in the *Times*'s Washington bureau, I had the same conversation with Packwood three days in a row.

I had never met the man. But each morning, the powerful senator from Oregon would call and tell me he'd seen my picture, posing in front of Air Force Two at sunset, in *Esquire*'s annual "Women We Love" feature.

"Come over to my office at six," he'd ooze, "and we can have a glass of wine. I've been wanting to discuss your work for a long time."

Each time, I'd fend him off by noting that I worked for a daily newspaper and was on deadline at 6 p.m. But the next night, he'd call with the same request—not even bothering to make the time later so that I'd have to come up with another excuse.

Finally, the calls stopped.

I know there are many women that Senator Packwood offended during his long career as a letch. But, maybe because he had no power over me, I just found him sad.

He was known around town as "The Tongue." His awkward kamikaze kissing technique, requiring an almost impossible balancing act, was described in the 1995 report of the Senate Select Committee on Ethics: "In his Senate office in Portland, Oregon, Senator Packwood grabbed a staff worker, stood on her feet, grabbed her hair, forcibly pulled her head back, and kissed her on the mouth, forcing his tongue into her mouth. Senator Packwood also reached under her skirt and grabbed at her undergarments."

It took some time for the story of his sexcapades to come out. The women's groups loved him, because he was a leading supporter of abortion rights and other women's causes, and he gave women the top jobs in his office. So they wanted to believe him when he claimed that his accusers had come on to him. (It's that old erotomania thing—the irresistible urge to get your hands on an unappetizing man.)

The feminists tried to protect him at first, supporting his re-election bid in 1992, even though he had had the hilarious gall to jump on an abortion lobbyist who visited his Oregon office.

The lobbyist, Mary Heffernan, a feminist leader in Oregon, said she didn't disclose the incident for a decade because "I was a lobbyist on an issue I cared very deeply about and he had a great deal of power."

It was the first time a Washington politician got thrown out for bad behavior with women. That had always been a perk in the capital, not a blot on the copybook.

It was not even his pouncing that made his colleagues in the Club squirm. It was his inept pouncing. The Bad Boys of Capitol Hill have always misbehaved grandly—be it a wasted Wilbur Mills going onstage with the stripper Fanne Foxe, "the Argentine Firecracker," and jumping into the Tidal Basin with her. Or Wayne Hays hiring blond Elizabeth Ray as a typist when she didn't know how to type. Or Teddy Kennedy and Chris Dodd making a waitress sandwich in 1985 at a Capitol Hill boîte.

Bob Packwood reduced this French farce to a cartoon. He was like Mr. Magoo, groping indiscriminately, not knowing if he was going for a girl or a tree. Once, after a big Washington dinner, he gave The Tongue to a journalist he had just met while she was trying to hail a cab. Another time, in the *Times* Washington bureau, he tried to pick up a reporter who was covering his downfall.

And as Senator Kennedy and Senator Dodd did their liberal duty and voted in favor of public hearings on Packwood's behavior, which never occurred because he resigned, what might they have been thinking? A fine institution sullied by such a pathetic record of incomplete passes?

A decade later, an attractive Senate intern named Jessica Cutler boasted in a blog from her Capitol Hill computer that she and her girlfriends regularly took money for sex from big shots on the Hill.

The Tongue and Jessica could have bartered and groped the night away with impunity. Bob Packwood, it turned out, was just ahead of Jessica's time.

●   ●   ●

The whole episode with Bill, Monica and Ken Starr was so strange and farcical, it was as though the nation's capital were bewitched, caught up in a sexual fantastical fever that would break, as in *A Midsummer Night's Dream*.

For months, Washington was drenched in sex.

The man simply could not stop thinking about the thong underwear. He couldn't believe Monica had pulled up her jacket to show it off. It so inflamed his imagination. At meetings, at briefings, at the most unlikely times, his mind suddenly reverted to the image of those straps, quickening his pulse, making him catch his breath.

But it was the cigar that undid him. He was driven by the thought of what had been done with it. Suddenly the capital became a city of cigars. He saw them wherever he went. They ignited his desire. When he was alone or talking to other people, he took secret pleasure in letting smoke rings drift through his mind.

There were times when he worried that he might be a sex addict. He couldn't stop thinking of Monica: what she wore, when she wore it, where she wore it, or didn't wear it. Her little letters were so brazen, promising such wild pleasure. Everything she scribbled, every gift she gave, mesmerized him.

And then there was the power of her voice over him. He knew that he was entering the dangerous territory of obsession. No matter how much he heard Monica talk about sex, it was never enough.

He was a busy man. A powerful man. A serious man. But there were times when all he could remember were the sizzling phone conversations. They filled his head like a drug. People warned him that he was endangering his legacy. Friends and strangers tried to pull him back from the brink of his single-mindedness. But it was too late.

He had become the helpless victim of his cravings for ecstasy.

The big picture was lost. He hungered only for the details, all the stirring and seamy particulars. Nothing was too small or insignificant for him to consider, to turn over and over in his unappeasable mind.

He wanted to think about her eating cherry chocolates. He imagined her wrapped up like Cleopatra in the Rockettes blanket or panting in that Black Dog T-shirt. He kept seeing her in that blue Gap dress. It was too tight, and he was glad. Again and again he was visited by images of a man's roving lips. He knew it was wrong. But he liked to dip into sin. He needed a release from all the pressure, from the extraordinary responsibilities of being a very public man.

When he went to church on Sundays, he wrestled with his conscience. He wondered if he needed professional help.

He worried at times that he was abusing his power and hurting the country. He even fretted that the Constitution itself might be damaged by his obsession.

And sometimes it wasn't easy to behold all the human damage that he had already caused: ruining a young woman's life, dragging all sorts of people through the muck, wounding reputations and bankrupting those who came near him. Would the presidency survive his lust? It didn't matter.

Every time he heard the legal definition of those words, "inappropriate intimate contact"—sex of any kind, in any manner, shape or form, arousing or gratifying—he felt a fire burn.

He had his own definition of sex. Still, he was drawn to the endless discussion of the existential meaning of sex—its forms, its uses. He was a lawyer, but this was not just tortured legalism. This was tortured eroticism. He liked to parse the lurid definition over and over and over again, gaining pleasure from repetition: "breasts," "genitalia," "inserted," "stain."

His acolytes and subordinates became agents of shamelessness. It seemed that everyone around him, everyone in the city, everyone in the country, was talking about what he wanted to hear. All of them had become his collaborators in perversity. He was spending millions and millions of dollars to drag an entire nation down to his twisted level.

He knew how strong he was. He was the most powerful man in the land. He could reach into every recess of the government to satisfy himself. And the prospect of impeachment didn't frighten him.

In fact, the more he fixated on the strap of that thong, the more certain he was that he could hang Bill Clinton with it. And of all those naughty words he loved to hear, none filled him with more pleasure than "impeachment."

After all, nobody could impeach him. He was Ken Starr.

*   *   *

When women finally came into power in Washington, they were in the mood to collect some scalps.

They skewered Clarence Thomas.

They cooked Bob Packwood.

But by the time they got to Bill Clinton, women had lost their appetite to search out and destroy all chauvinistic and harassing behavior. It wasn't in their interest this time, and they were confused. Were these men dangerous predators? Or were they merely loony lechers?

There was a disturbing pattern developing. The powerful men getting in the most trouble over women seemed to be getting the least satisfaction from women. The guys being crucified for sexual misconduct appeared, on closer inspection, to be acting more strange than swaggering, more dysfunctional than macho.

"Who put a pubic hair on my Coke can?" Now there's a crafty come-hither line. Clarence Thomas's insistence on jabbering about creepy X-rated movies seemed more bizarre than brutish. Packwood's habit of grabbing hair and forcing his tongue down the throats of women was yucky, to be sure, but also pathetic. They seemed like such losers to have caused so much angst.

Reading Ken Starr's dirty best seller, it was apparent that the Republicans were huffing and puffing, trying to impeach a president for the first time on the grounds of illicit sex, even though the illicit so outweighed the sex.

First a feminist liberal lynch mob tried to kill off a conservative Supreme Court nominee over sex when the real reason they wanted to get rid of him was politics. Then a reactionary lynch mob tried to kill off a Democratic president over sex when the real reason they wanted to get rid of him was politics.

Starr's prissy and salacious documentation proved that the president had been wrongfully accused. We had assumed that Bill Clinton was a lusty, carefree Lothario with his young intern, when he was actually a timid, tortured Lothario. When he was found out, he ungallantly dismissed his dalliance as a mere mechanism for relieving Oval Office tension. The adolescent Bill trysts, with Monica in a navy Gap dress, had none of the glamour of JFK's rendezvous at the Carlyle Hotel with Marilyn in a white-sequined Jean-Louis gown.

Rather than joining the capital's proud pantheon of droit du seigneur, Bill Clinton joined Messrs. Thomas and Packwood in the embarrassing pantheon of maladroit du seigneur. It was Monica who came across as the red-blooded predator, wailing to her girlfriends that the president wouldn't go all the way. It was Clinton who behaved more like a teenage girl trying to protect her virginity, insisting on holding back, reluctant to remove any clothes, even pushing away Monica at times and pulling up her slipping bra strap, according to her testimony, and once even finishing off lovemaking in the sink.

"I'm trying to not do this and I'm trying to be good," the president told her primly.

Monica was the one who bristled with testosterone. She told investigators about her inept inamorato: "He just seemed to get so emotionally upset about it. It seemed a little strange to me. There was sort of foreplay to the foreplay."

While she was not a stalker, since Clinton encouraged her interest for quite some time, she was certainly aggressive. (Far more ballsy than Marilyn Monroe, who described her affair with JFK to her shrink this way: "Marilyn Monroe is a soldier. . . . The first duty of a soldier is to obey her Commander in Chief.")

Monica pretended she was carrying papers to get into the Oval Office and brazenly gave her man thirty-eight presents—including a frog figurine, a letter opener decorated with a frog and a copy of *Oy Vey! The Things They Say: A Guide to Jewish Wit*.

As the Oval Office affair wilted, Monica got bolder. "I asked him why he doesn't ask me any questions about myself, and . . . is this just about sex . . . or do you have some interest in trying to get to know me as a person?" she told investigators.

By way of riposte, she said, the president laughed, said he cherished their time together and then "unzipped his pants and sort of exposed himself."

She sensed he was "putting up walls." When she complained to the president that she had not had any hugs for months, he quipped, "Every day can't be sunshine."

Of their last encounter, she said: "This was another one of those occasions when I was babbling on about something, and he just kissed me, kind of to shut me up, I think."

He didn't call. He didn't write. She began to suspect she was being "strung along." Trapped in a stereotype, Monica became the raging, vengeful Glenn Close character in *Fatal Attraction*.

"PLEASE DO NOT DO THIS TO ME," she wrote in a draft of a note to the president. "I feel disposable, used and insignificant."

She demanded a big job at the United Nations or in the business world in New York, as compensation for his ruining her life.

"I don't want to have to work for this position," she said. "I just want it to be given to me." She sent the president a "wish list" of jobs ("I am NOT someone's administrative/executive assistant") and enclosed an erotic postcard and her thoughts on education reform.

Now if President Clinton had taken Monica's advice on education reform, that might have been an impeachable offense.

She sent him a note that read: "I am not a moron. I know that what is going on in the world takes precedence."

I remember reading an interview with Judith Exner, where she talked about how lonely it was dating JFK. Whenever she wanted him to focus on her, he was focusing on Castro. Cuba, Cuba, Cuba! That's all he cared about.

Just so, when Monica wanted Bill to focus on her, Sudan, Sudan, Sudan! That's all he cared about. She was getting impatient. "I need you right now not as president, but as a man," she wrote him. "PLEASE be my friend."

Getting nervous over her fits, Clinton reminded her, "It's illegal to threaten the president."

Bill could not be punished as a brazen brute when he was just a sad philanderer. Ken Starr's bodice ripper was not grounds for impeachment, only divorce.

Except that Hillary didn't want one, of course.

⁕　⁕　⁕

There was a time when I would get furious and fire off an angry note if someone cast me in a catfight with a woman colleague. I assumed that catfights would fade as women progressed. They seemed so retro.

But now I've resigned myself to the fact that the fur will never stop flying. From professional women's tennis spats, to Lindsay-vs.-Jessica feuds in celebrity mags, to Katie-vs.-Diane and Katie-vs.-Kelly duels in the morning, to the Hillary-vs.-Jeanine smackdown in New York, to scraps among the *Desperate Housewives* actresses, catfights are great for the publishing business and for show business. And for men, catfights will always be considered good wholesome fun. (As Jerry Seinfeld said when Elaine asked him why men loved catfights so much: "Because men think if women are grabbing and clawing at each other, there's a chance they might somehow kiss.")

So, as long as everybody's baring "jungle red" nails, as in

Clare Boothe Luce's *The Women*, I may as well tell you about my catfight with Monica Lewinsky.

I was sitting at my desk one night, trying to decompress during the impeachment mess and do three months' worth of expense reports so that American Express would stop using those tiresome words "declined," "denied" and "not a prayer."

The phone rang. It was my friend Michael Duffy, an editor at *Time*. He offered to whisk me off to the Bombay Club across the street, where I could revive my spirits with a little vindaloo.

I was coming back from the ladies' room when I saw her. She looked demure. Oval wire-rimmed glasses. A sky blue jacket buttoned over a long black-and-white flowered skirt. The strong jawline and wide smile turning down at the edges were familiar.

I am, after all, a trained observer.

"That girl looks a little like Monica," I told Duffy.

"It is Monica, stupid," he replied. "See, she's with her father and stepmother and her mother and her mother's fiancé."

What cheek! Monica Lewinsky had come to Chelsea Clinton's favorite restaurant, right across the park from the White House, the one where Chelsea celebrated her seventeenth birthday with her parents.

Monica's presence at the Bombay Club suggested the former intern was still trying to grab the president's attention, like some love-struck adolescent loitering outside Billy Clinton's biology class.

In person, she did not come across as a vulnerable victim or dizzy Valley Girl. She was sipping a Cosmopolitan and striding around with blazing confidence. You could see how, with a pizza or Starbucks latte as a prop, she could easily talk her way into any office, even an oval one.

At one point, she bounded over to the piano player to request a song. On the way back, she stopped to say hello to Duffy, whom she had previously met. She said she had taken "the magic carpet" out of the Watergate, where she lived next door to Bob Dole, to have an evening out.

Mike introduced us. Her smile went cold. She leaned over, bracing her hands on her knees, so that our eyes were level. She was In My Face.

"Do you mind if I ask you something?" she said, poised and icy. "Why do you write such scathing articles about me?"

Now, in the years I'd had my column, which occasionally requires me to be a teensy-weensy bit critical, I'd always been afraid someone I'd written about would upbraid me in public, or, worse, throw a drink in my face, as Julian English did to an Irish pol at the Gibbsville country club in *Appointment in Samarra*.

But so far, nobody had. Suddenly, I experienced deep impact, and it's Monica! I didn't reply at first. My brain was fogged with chilling images of Monica and me wrestling on the floor, like that scene in *Dynasty* when Joan Collins and Linda Evans pulled each other's hair in the pool.

Besides, I was distracted by Monica's song request, which the piano man was now playing: "Send in the Clowns." It *was* rich. We *were* a pair.

I tried to pull myself together and come up with a trenchant answer. I hadn't written anything mean about her, really. I defended her against Democrats painting her as a stalker.

She was still crouched, waiting.

I might have told her that posing provocatively in *Vanity Fair* with fuchsia feathers and an American flag was not a smart move for a young woman in the middle of a plea bargain.

I might have told her that I felt sorry for her, that I knew it was not easy to be in love with a president, that I had reserved my most scathing commentary for Ken Starr. And, secondarily, for the president that Monica labeled "the Big Creep," who never should have fooled with an impressionable—and prolix—intern.

In the end, though, I wimped out. "I don't know," I told her, shrugging lamely. She sashayed away, looking triumphant.

Later, I learned that Monica had gone into the ladies' room after our encounter and had a cell phone meltdown with her publicist. So she was a volatile blend of brassy and deeply vulnerable—something Bill Clinton should have noticed a lot sooner.

I really wish I had passed on to Monica what my mom told me when I was about her age and moving to New York: Stay away from married men. They're long-tailed rats.

*   *   *

I don't think Hillary started out wanting to destroy feminism, or what was left of it. It was just collateral damage.

When the *Animal House* president messed up, he had to be dragged back from the precipice by the bimbo patrol.

Bill Clinton has always been surrounded by two kinds of women: the flashy ones who love the guy, and the serious ones who love what the guy stands for.

The serious policy types have always had to step in to try to save him from the flashy climbers.

"Saturday Night Bill" would mess around with women with big-cut hair and low-cut dresses and short skirts and then, if he got in trouble, "Sunday Morning Bill" would run hide behind the sedate skirts of high-toned feminists—including his wife and cabinet members.

Because Clinton married up and dated down like Gary Hart, it was easier for his lieutenants to slander ex-peccadilloes as "cash-for-trash," "trailer trash" or, every wife's worst nightmare, office cupcake seductresses.

Hillary had her choice of siding with her truth-telling, thong-wearing, husband-stealing sisters or her dissembling, thong-seeking, wife-betraying husband.

As part of their conjugal/political deal, or their "passionate codependence," as James Carville calls it, she always chose her husband and sold out her sisters.

It was a bold hat trick: She finished off what was left of feminism, yet remained a feminist icon. She rules over "Hillaryland," a cultlike universe of Ellen Jamesians who are determined to see their warrior queen take back the White House from the hypermasculine and domestically Dickensian reign of the Bushies.

That macho relentlessness may yet get her into the White House, where she can consign Bill to the East Wing to worry about matching the color of the roses to the rim of the china while she worries about China trying to buy up our oil companies.

During his political career, Bill Clinton enjoyed the services of a machine designed to do whatever was necessary to deflect stories about his erotic misadventures, including smearing women who dared to suggest that there had been trysts. In the 1992 campaign, Betsey Wright stopped what she called "gold diggers" or "bimbos" by hiring the San Francisco private investigator Jack Palladino and paying him more than a hundred thousand dollars in what were delicately termed "legal expenses." He would dig up dirt on the women and threaten to shred their reputations if they went public.

After Hillary vouched for her husband on *60 Minutes*, Bill owed her his presidency. Surely, Hillary knew or suspected that Gennifer Flowers was telling the truth, yet she led the campaign to defame the lounge singer. (Bill had to fess up to sleeping with Flowers during the Jones case deposition.)

The feminist role model didn't flinch at supervising the vivisection of her husband's girlfriends because she felt they were instruments of a conspiracy, pawns of the right wing. (Sort of the way Anita Hill was a pawn of the left-wing feminists.) It doesn't add luster to the image Hillary likes to promote of herself as someone who protects women and the vulnerable in society. It means she cares about women unless they get in the way of the Clintons' mission to help humanity, in which case they're expendable.

The Clintons always maintained that there should be a zone of privacy for their private lives, even though their private lives were fraught with public consequences.

They campaigned in '92 on a slogan of "Two for the Price of One," and their marital bargain played a critical role in determining public policy and in shaping the arc of their public difficulties.

The deal was this: She would endure infidelities if he gave her power. She proceeded to pretend that the power she was given was power she had earned. "They are holding large lead weights over each other's heads," said one Clinton friend.

Some White House officials said that Bill did not step in to help her with a health care plan that was clearly ballooning out of control because he did not dare to challenge her after news reports that Arkansas state troopers had fetched women for him. "She has a hundred-pound fishing wire around his scrotum," one of her deputies on health care told me with a little smile.

Bill Clinton never seemed to understand that it was way too late to be a JFK swinger in the Oval Office. He should have realized it watching the Hill-Thomas hearings.

For decades, the rules of politics were very simple. As the Democratic strategist Ray Strother summed it up: "If a politician stayed on his bar stool, he wasn't drunk. And if he didn't get caught, he wasn't cheating on his wife." But for several years before Clinton came to town, it was clear that a gallows had gone up along the Potomac. With journalists willing to report more, with women coming into power more, the old libertine rules were vitiated.

In 1989, John Tower's nomination for defense secretary went down amid opprobrium about his skirt chasing and hard drinking, even though Bush officials told me they could get him down to two glasses of wine a day, and even though some senators came to the floor to vote against him with liquor on their breath.

Everyone realized then, as one GOP consultant put it, that hypocrisy was going to be punished with more hypocrisy. The late John White, once a top Democratic official, lamented that "there used to be better ways to gut a guy besides putting his personal mores through the meat grinder."

Allen Drury, the author of *Advise and Consent*, mocked the new morality to me: "One must tell all and promise all and be a good, good boy and promise to be a good, good, good boy forever after."

Bill Clinton knew the rules had drastically changed. He promised to be a good, good boy. But he wasn't. It was a dangerous game.

As Big Jim Folsom, the governor of Alabama in the '50s, said, when an aide warned him that his opponent was sending out a beautiful woman to trap him into a compromising position, "Boys, if they use that bait, they'll catch ol' Jim every time."

In 1991, during the Hill-Thomas hearings, the curtain parted on the Senate to reveal a sight at once grotesque and hilarious: a bunch of out-of-touch old white guys trying to fathom truth in sex.

It had the quality Dickens called "the attraction of repulsion." America was riveted by the bawdy seminar on the perils of sex in the federal workplace. We thought those wrenching hearings would illuminate gender politics and modernize the Senate.

Wrong. Lo, many years later, the curtain parted again. And, like, Hel-*lo,* as Monica would say, what did we see but the grotesque and hilarious sight of a bunch of out-of-touch white guys trying to fathom truth in sex. That same old boys' club, once again slouching toward C-SPAN to instruct America on the perils of sex in the federal workplace.

And who could believe, all those years later, that Strom Thurmond, pushing a hundred, was still center stage and still Tang-colored?

The Supreme Court case about sexual harassment, *William Jefferson Clinton* v. *Paula Jones,* crystallized the tension between the sexes: Women fear that men will have their way and then slither away. Men fear that women will come back and boil their bunnies.

Feminists agonized over Paula, never sure if they offered her so little support because she was not their sort, or because they did not find her outrage credible.

When I first met Jones in 1994, she was racing around a Manhattan hotel room, thrilled to be in the big city and thrilled with her new contract to promote No Excuses jeans.

I asked why she was taking on the president.

She looked at me, her blue eyes growing large. "He 'sposed hisself and tha's not right," she said, in her soft Arkansas twang.

Paula showed that a woman need not wreck her life by bringing sexual harassment charges. Things really picked up when she went after the president, with a free teeth-to-toe makeover, an entourage eager to depose Clinton, a publicist who instructed her on the merits of semimatte sienna lipstick rather than fuchsia, the Paula Jones Legal Defense Fund, which paid to board her dog, Mitzie, and a new role writing breathless fund-raising letters about the president's anatomy to the mailing list of a conservative Christian right legal group, the Rutherford Institute. ("But then something happened that both shocked and humiliated me . . . Horrified, I stated that 'I'm not that kind of girl.' ")

The Clinton defense team gave feminism another body blow in June 1997, when the president's lawyer compared Jones to a dead dog.

"The president of the United States is not going to apologize," Robert Bennett said on the *ABC Sunday Morning Show*. "And if she insists on a trial, we'll have a trial. . . . I had a dog like that who just wanted to catch cars, and he successfully caught one one day, and I have a new dog." (Bennett was known in Washington as "the president's dick's lawyer," just as the private investigator he used was known as "the president's dick's dick.")

In response to Jones's charges, Team Clinton sent forth a legion of men to besmirch Jones as a jade who wore short skirts and flirted. And Bennett became the latest Clinton henchman to dirty himself trying to prettify the boss.

Feminists, who had been loath to support Jones, were shocked to hear Bennett on *Meet the Press* threaten to root around in the lingerie drawer of the president's accuser. The lawyer was full of blustery intimidation, making sure the press knew that he had installed one of her old lovers in a posh room at Washington's Willard Hotel and had taken a sworn statement about Jones's habits.

"Bennett is trying to revive the old argument, 'This is a

trashy woman,' for no other reason than to back her down," said Patricia Ireland, then the president of NOW.

Ireland conceded that the feminists were having a tough time. "It's harder for us to deal with the bad behavior and bad treatment of women by men who stand with us on policy," she said, sounding weary. "We've been getting a lot of e-mails and phone calls from women saying: 'How can you go after Clinton? He's appointed more women, blah-blah-blah.' Clinton made that comment about the Astroturf in the back of his truck. It showed his desire to be seen as a 'real man.' You can be a wom-anizer, and, yes, even women can find that attractive. . . . I keep wanting to turn to him and say, 'Grow up.' "

But Bill Clinton could not grow up when it came to sex. Susan McDougal said that Bill had told her he loved being governor because "women are throwing themselves at me. All the while I was growing up, I was the fat boy in the Big Boy jeans."

Writing about the case in *Slate*, Robert Wright, the author of *The Moral Animal*, pointed out the biological paradox: "From nature's point of view, a central purpose of pursuing sta-tus is to convert it into sex. Yet . . . the very point of being alpha male is considered evidence, in modern America, of unfitness for the job! Talk about defeating the purpose."

Hillary ended up shelling out $375,000 from her private trust to pay off Jones. Ouch.

Jones, now living in Little Rock with her husband and three kids and studying for her real estate license, continues to leech off her fifteen minutes of infamy. In July 2005, she visited the Clinton Presidential Library wearing a T-shirt bearing the logo of the paid sponsor that offered her the highest bid. (Vainly trying to show she has class, she rejected an offer from a brothel.)

When the story broke about Clinton's pizza girl, the feminists formed a cordon around the president, and Hillary was a party to the White House debate that raged about the best way to demonize That Woman.

But Clinton didn't throw himself on the mercy of the public. He threw himself on the mercy of his strategist Dick Morris—who had been embroiled in his own sex scandal in '96 when it came out that he was cavorting—and toe nibbling—with a call girl across the street from the White House at the Jefferson Hotel. (The funniest part was when Morris tried to impress the two-hundred-dollar-an-hour hooker by showing her a draft of an Al Gore speech.)

Clinton, who ran a White House where the truth was employed only to the extent it was useful, asked Morris to poll to find out if he should tell the truth or lie.

So the president ended up giving such a tortured definition of his tryst that Judge Susan Webber Wright wrote: "It appears the President is asserting that Ms. Lewinsky could be having sex with him while, at the same time, he was not having sex with her."

The only question was whether the White House should paint Monica as a friendly fantasist or a malicious stalker. Even some of the veteran Clinton defenders felt a little nauseated by the Monica campaign, after smearing so many other women who were probably telling the truth as trashy bimbos.

It was a tricky matter going after another young woman, one who sent mushy valentines to Bill in *The Washington Post* personal ads, and presents by messenger, and who paid $250 to get into a fund-raiser; a girl whose friends said she was "like, suicidal," a young woman who had already been traumatized by the creepy, sex-crazed Ken Starr and his marauding gang of FBI agents.

The Clinton dust busters fretted that the public might recoil at seeing, yet again, the tactic of hacking away at Bill's inamoratas, shifting reality to save the big guy from taking responsibility for his "dark side," as Leon Panetta called it.

But they forged ahead.

Hillary told Sidney Blumenthal, as he later testified, that "she was distressed that the president was being attacked, in her view, for political motives, for his ministry of a troubled person." Hillary's good friend Charlie Rangel told reporters about Monica: "That poor child has serious emotional problems. She's fantasizing. And I haven't heard that she played with a full deck in her other experiences."

Blumenthal testified to Starr's grand jury that after the intern story broke, Clinton told him: "Monica Lewinsky came at me and made a sexual demand on me" but he rebuffed her. Clinton also said that Monica had told him, "They call me 'The Stalker,' " importuning the president: "If I can say we had an affair, then they won't call me that."

Hillary knew she could count on the complicity of feminists and Democratic women in Congress. They accepted the trade-off: The Clintons would give women progressive public policies as long as they didn't mind Bill's regressive private behavior with women.

Lewinsky, after all, was fungible. What really mattered was

the fate of the Republic and the fate of the Clintons. (For them, it is the same.)

One top female Democratic lawmaker shared her fury with me privately: "Why couldn't he just keep it in his pants for eight years so he could get something done? It's the grossest kind of infidelity, just sheer constant physical relief and satisfaction, really using, in the crudest way, somebody who was obviously extraordinarily gullible and obviously madly in love with him, somebody who would have done anything for him, and doing this in the Oval Office. I'm having a very hard time with it. I don't want to be an enabler."

But in public, they supported him. Carol Moseley-Braun implied on *Meet the Press* that the Lewinsky story could be seen as a triumph of Democratic diversity efforts: "Not so many years ago, a woman couldn't be a White House intern."

Gloria Steinem wrote a defense of Clinton in the *New York Times*'s Op-Ed page, arguing that his "clumsy passes" at Willey and Jones were not wrong, since the president understood that "no means no."

"Welcome sexual behavior is about as relevant to sexual harassment as borrowing a car is to stealing one," she said, explaining that the feminists could not cut Clinton loose just because he had been boorish: "If the president had behaved with comparable insensitivity to environmentalists, and at the same time remained their most crucial champion and bulwark against an antienvironmental Congress, would they be expected to desert him? I don't think so."

Clinton could have just fessed up, admitted he was just ministering to Monica, that he threw her across the desk and ministered to her 'til dawn, as Michael Kinsley might put it. But instead he sent out his feminist spokeswoman, his wife and his female cabinet members to vouch for his fidelity (at a time when his military was court-martialing soldiers for adultery).

The first female secretary of state giving the Presidential Scamp cover over his affair with the Girl Who Delivered Mail was a low point in women's rights.

Madeleine Albright told Cokie Roberts: "As an American citizen and as a friend of the president's, I accept what he said. . . . I have no problems whatsoever assuring other leaders about the credibility of the United States and the president."

By the end of their tenure, the Clintons had turned the feminists who fought so hard against Thomas into hypocrites. And Bill had turned Hillary Clinton into a martyr, more popular with Americans once her husband had humiliated her and stripped her of her hauteur.

The Clintons made everyone around them succumb to Faustian deals. In the case of the feminists, they could have their feminist president named Clinton, and, perhaps in 2008, even a female president named Clinton.

The only thing they had to give up in return was the integrity of feminism.

* * *

After decades spent trying to dissuade powerful men from thinking they could have their way with less powerful women, feminists suddenly had a terrible confession to make: They panted for power—take me, take me!

First, Larissa McFarquar wrote in *The New Yorker* about Bill Clinton that "it would be a rare young woman who could resist . . . a chance to sleep with a man who is a) the president and b) a babe."

Then ten women, including some feminists, a fashion designer and a retired dominatrix, participated in a 1998 panel for *The New York Observer* that resulted in a story headlined "New York Supergals Love That Naughty Prez."

"I think that there's been a shift in the cultural climate since the time of the Anita Hill hearings," said Katie Roiphe, the novelist. "People are reacting against that sort of sexual policing, and we've turned in the other direction. Now this virile president is suddenly fulfilling this forbidden fantasy of this old-fashioned taboo aggressive male. I think women are finding that appealing."

Erica Jong, the author of *Fear of Flying* and inventor of "the zipless fuck," enthusiastically agreed. "Oh," she said, "imagine swallowing the presidential cum."

Elizabeth Benedict, author of *The Joy of Writing Sex,* chimed in: "And it's also, it's like every girl's dream. You can be the president, but you can fuck the president, too."

Finally, in *Mirabella* magazine, Nina Burleigh described the erotic fantasies she had about President Clinton while she was playing hearts with him on Air Force One during her stint as a *Time* White House correspondent.

"The president's foot, lightly and presumably accidentally, brushed mine under the table," Nina wrote. "His hand touched my wrist while he was dealing the cards. When I got up and shook his hand at the end of the game, his eyes wandered over my bike-wrecked naked legs and slowly it dawned on me as I walked away, he found me attractive. There was a time when the hormones of indignant feminism raged in my veins. An open gaze like that, at least from a man of lesser stature, would have annoyed me. But that evening, I felt incandescent. It was riveting to know that the president had appreciated my legs, scarred as they were. If he had asked me to continue the game of Hearts, back in the Jasper Holiday Inn, I would have been happy to go there and see what happened. At the time, it seemed quite possible. It took several hours and a few drinks in the steamy and now somehow romantic Arkansas night to shake the intoxicated state in which I had been quite willing to let myself be ravaged by the president, should he have but asked."

Defending her "Lust in Her Hearts" piece to *The Washington Post*, she noted that she would have happily given the president a blow job "just to thank him for keeping abortion legal."

Talking to Arianna Huffington, Nina added, very presciently, as it turned out, about the muscular, patriarchal theocracy that was coming in America: "I think American women should be lining up with their presidential kneepads on to show their gratitude for keeping the theocracy off our backs."

Hillary, too, had her salivating fans.

When she ran for Senate, Tom Junod wrote an overheated piece in *Esquire*: "She has a sexy mouth, I think. That slight palatal overbite gets to me. She seems expert at marshaling her mouth's resources, at inspiring its ingenuity. . . . When she is pouncing on the possibility of an idea, her lips extend their reach into her cheeks and carve out a wolfish, carnal line, as though nothing could please her more than her own hunger. . . . Her laugh is the sexiest thing about her, in fact; it packs a lewd wallop. . . . One could imagine her talking dirty . . ."

Ah, well. In a society where women seem very much more interested in being seen as bombshells than brains, why shouldn't someone see Hillary that way?

• • •

Unless the former First Lady and president become the future president and First Lad, Bill Clinton may be bookended in history by Monica's plea to him, "I need you right now not as president, but as a man," and Hillary's explanation of why she stayed with him: "He was not only my husband, he was also my president."

It makes you wonder whether Hillary would have forgiven Bill if he were merely her United States trade representative.

Remarkably, Bill and Hillary were able to turn her humiliation into a campaign asset. She became like the victimized wives, beloved by women, in those harrowing movies on the Lifetime channel.

Historians will long ponder how it was that the First Lady became wildly popular and capable of winning a Senate seat only when she played the doormat card. She became a heroine, as Jane Mayer wrote in *The New Yorker*, when she went from seeming too controlling to seeming unable to control her own husband. It was easier for many women to identify with that.

In his book, *The Survivor,* John Harris, who covered the Clinton White House for *The Washington Post,* recounts that when Hillary began running for the Senate in 2000, Bill was perusing the poll numbers, and noted: "Women want to know why you stayed with me."

There was an awkward pause among the strategists, but Hillary did not seem embarrassed. "A half smile crossed her face," Harris recounted. " 'Yes,' she responded. 'I've been wondering that myself.'

"The president gave his answer: 'Because you're a sticker! That's what people need to know—you are a sticker. You stick at the things you care about.' "

Harris concludes uncynically, after all his reporting, that Hillary stayed with Bill because "she loved him, and felt loved by him in return," and because "their sense of shared mission" and their love of politics gave their relationship heat.

Their current shared mission is their most daunting: The Clinton political dynasty wants to take back the White House from the Bush political dynasty that took back the White House from the Clintons after they snatched it from the Bushes.

Some of their old benefactors have turned on the Clintons, tired of their Tom and Daisy Buchanan selfishness and carelessness. "She can't win and she's an incredibly polarizing figure," DreamWorks mogul David Geffen said dismissively, speaking at the 92nd Street Y in October 2004, to hearty applause. "And ambition is just not a good enough reason."

And Republicans are thinking: If it was that easy to paint a Northeast liberal and decorated Vietnam war hero as a girl, think how easy it will be to paint a Northeast liberal girl as a girl.

Karl Rove started early to try and infuse 2008 with the same dynamic that worked in 2004: Republicans with big cojones versus whiny, sissy Democrats.

"Conservatives saw the savagery of 9/11 and prepared for war," he told the New York State Conservative Party in June 2005. "Liberals saw the savagery of the 9/11 attacks and wanted to prepare indictments and offer therapy and understanding for our attackers."

With War Room speed, Senator Clinton demanded that the Bush administration "repudiate" Rove's remarks. "I'm old enough to remember how deeply divided our country was in Vietnam," she said. "I never want to see that again."

She also chimed in that Rove should be fired when it was reported that he had leaked the identity of undercover CIA operative Valerie Plame to undermine her husband, Joe Wilson, a critic of the Bush administration's rush to war in Iraq. (Rove's lame excuse, that he leaked only her job and relation to Wilson and not her actual name, was a masterpiece of Bill Clinton–style parsing.) If Rove goes down, Hillary can stick tongue firmly in cheek and campaign on a platform of returning dignity and honor to the White House.

The senator has no intention of throwing like a girl. That's why she joined the Armed Services Committee, and that's why she voted to give W. the authorization to go to war in Iraq with a bogus rationale, and suggested that more troops might be needed.

Just as her husband was obsessed with maintaining his "political viability" during the Vietnam draft, Hillary had to keep her own political viability in mind during the debate over a preemptive invasion that W. had obviously already decided on.

If she has to run against a war hero like John McCain, Hillary may even revive her incredible story about how when she was twenty-seven, living in Arkansas with Bill, she went to the local Marine recruiting station to see about joining up with the active forces or the reserves. She said she was swiftly rebuffed by the recruiter, who took a dim view of her age and thick glasses.

"You're too old, you can't see and you're a woman," she said she was told, adding that the recruiter suggested she try the Army. "Maybe the dogs would take you," she recalled him saying.

For her "heroine task," she will have to use her strength in overcoming the Vast Right-Wing Conspiracy (and the raft of Hillary-hating books that conservatives drive to the top of the best-seller list).

If her Serial Canoodler husband gets caught in the middle of her campaign, it would be tempting, but tough, to play the victim card again. At that point, a lot of the country would say, enough already, and reject another round of forced hand-holding, scenes of Bill in quarantine at Martha's Vineyard, couples therapy and Tammy Wynette defenses on *60 Minutes*.

The onetime frizzy-haired hippie chick is now channeling her inner Midwest Goldwater Girl. She knows a female candidate could never get away with having love beads in her jewelry box. (Even a worn copy of Carole King's *Tapestry* might be too much.)

And certainly, a woman running for president could never confess—as W. did to me the day he announced his presidential bid at the Bush estate in Kennebunkport—that she's weak on foreign policy but knows who to turn to for help.

If a woman candidate said she would rely on the kindness of advisers to tell her what to do with the "East Timorians," or stumbled on the pronunciations of several global hot spots, as W. did, she would immediately be dismissed as a dizzy dame.

Laziness and lunkheaded answers didn't stop W. from becoming the president, just as laziness and chuckleheaded answers didn't stop Dan Quayle from getting anointed by Bush Sr. Men can still wing it and get to the Oval Office. Women can't.

It was assumed (falsely) that Junior had hung around his father's White House long enough to pick up some knowledge, even subliminally, on his dad's favorite topic of foreign affairs. And before 9/11 made him focus, W. shrugged off foreign policy with the bravado of the cool frat boy who isn't studying for his chemistry exam.

Hillary learned a lot from the health care debacle. She has a compelling speaking style, and the sort of driving ambition that may make politicians unpleasant but also makes them succeed. She blazed her own path in a new state, with a deep knowledge of complex public policy issues and a genuine passion for the political life. Out in the country, she could benefit from the same thing that helped her win New York: Expectations for her are so bad.

I have no doubt Hillary is smart, adaptive, has "a backbone of steel," as James Carville says, and could run a far tougher campaign than the other women I've covered running for president.

Elizabeth Dole was wound too tight, like Nurse Ratched trying to give us our meds, coordinating her shoes to the podium carpet, a girdled Southern deb with a clenched smile designed to show she could be trusted to tuck those nuclear codes into a pony-skin Fendi baguette. (Even her husband, Bob Dole, seemed dour about her prospects, suggesting he might write a check to the campaign of her rival John McCain—a move that sent him to the marital doghouse, especially embarrassing given that he was then a Viagra spokesman.)

Patricia Schroeder, on the other hand, was not wound tight enough. Famous for telling a male colleague on her first day on Capitol Hill, "I have a brain and a uterus and I use them both," Congresswoman Schroeder had an unfortunate tendency to call programs she did not like "icky," sign her congressional mail with a smiley face and punctuate thoughts with exclamations like "golly," "doggonit," and "yippy-skippy."

I also have no doubt that Hillary could run a tougher campaign than the Democratic men I've covered running for president—the henpecked Walter Mondale, the wishy-washy Michael Dukakis, the sighing and prissy Al Gore and the flipping "skipper" John Kerry.

As one of her oldest confidantes put it, when asked if Hillary would ever hire back her nemesis Dick Morris to help with a presidential run: "Hillary would hire Hitler if she thought it could get her elected."

The lady who hated the title Lady doesn't flinch and she doesn't stop coming.

"She's never going to get out of our faces," says Leon Wieseltier. "It's more than ambition. It's a mixture of covetousness and mulishness. She's like some hellish housewife who has seen something that she really, really wants and won't stop nagging you about it until finally you say, fine, take it, be the goddamn president, just leave me alone. Except of course that in this case you can't say be done with that, because what she craves is too important."

You see a graying Gary Hart around Washington and he still carries himself like a pariah—even after doing such good work warning in advance about terrorist attacks and even though he now lives in a society without shame.

The jangly Hillary Rodham Clinton rebranded herself into the more clubbable HILLARY!, collaborating on legislation and going to Senate prayer meetings with the Republicans who once tortured her and her husband, turning the other cheek to reporters who had razzed her as First Lady. She has a talent for morphing that puts Madonna to shame.

At her best, Hillary reminds me of the well-meaning Dorothea Brooke in *Middlemarch.* Or of Sarah Brown, the mission doll in *Guys and Dolls,* taken with a charming rake and trying to save the world, but fun if you'd get her out for a night of sweet rum drinks in Cuba.

(In her memoir, Hillary tells a funny story about the State Department warning her to hide from Castro, who wanted to meet her, at Nelson Mandela's inauguration: "I'd suddenly spot Castro moving toward me, and I'd hightail it to a far corner of the room.")

When I had dinner with Hillary once in a revolving

restaurant in Lexington, Kentucky, during her headbanded, "Call me Rodham" phase in '92—we presciently sipped a White House brand of white wine—she had a sly sense of humor that she has never been able to incorporate into her public persona.

At her worst, Hillary can be maddening. She resents the Saint Hillary image even as she stresses her religiosity. She always circles back to being in the right, never able to admit to having a materialistic side that has sometimes led her into inexplicably tacky choices, from her dealings with a dubious savings and loan operator in Arkansas to her hundred-thousand-dollar windfall in commodities; from her complicity in turning the White House into Motel 1600 for fat-cat donors to her backing up a truck to the White House to haul away $86,000 worth of loot belonging to the People's House to furnish her new house.

And how to explain the woman who earnestly preached '60s feminism and activism engaging in such low-rent attempts to avoid Senate ethics rules as negotiating an $8 million book advance before she took office and rushing at the end of her First Ladydom to accept largesse from wealthy benefactors in Hollywood so she could buy china and silver for her post– and pre?– White House life in an Embassy Row home?

The Bushes feel the entitlement of the aristocracy. The Clintons feel the entitlement of the meritocracy.

Over and over, we found ourselves grappling with the nettlesome issue: What is Hillary owed?

She clearly thought reparations had to be made for the time she spent as a "lady lawyer" in Little Rock, for what she had suffered in her marriage, and for what she had sacrificed by going into public service instead of having a high-powered law career.

She chafed at the material sacrifices, according to David Maraniss's Clinton biography, *First in His Class.* When Dick Morris, the governor's political consultant, told her that voters would be angry if she built a swimming pool at the governor's mansion, she blew up.

"Why can't we lead the lives of normal people?" she asked angrily.

Her sense of what was due her sometimes dulled her sensitivity to conflicts of interest.

"She didn't understand how, after all she'd given up for a life of public service, the media could question her ethics," wrote James Stewart in *Blood Sport.*

The best description of her "We want to do good so we can break the rules when we need to" ethos came from a top aide to President Clinton, who explained it this way: "Hillary, though a Methodist, thinks of herself like an Episcopal bishop who deserves to live at the level of her wealthy parishioners, in return for devoting her life to God and good works."

She used to bristle at what she called "derivative" power after seeking power derivatively. During her husband's first presidential campaign, the uneasy realization hit her when she got some stationery delivered with the "Rodham" dropped out of her name: "Now I was solely 'the wife of,' an odd experience for me." She sent the stationery back, stat.

But as First Lady, she was never willing to acknowledge the tensions and problems caused within the administration by the two-for-one deal. Everyone tiptoes around any president's wife. But when the boss's wife is also a boss, aides are even more afraid to say, "I don't think this works."

That's a side of her that "bugs" some people, as Ben Bradlee once put it to me. "Some might say that she destroyed feminism by going after her husband's inamoratas and not standing up to her husband," says Jane Mayer. "But you can also say that she advanced feminism by showing a shrewd, almost male self-control in devaluing emotion and sentiment in favor of ambition—her own."

Indeed, if she becomes Madam President, she will reinstate "Hillaryland" in the West Wing, bringing along Ann Lewis and all the other hard-core feminists who now orbit her. Then she would be responsible for both betraying feminism when it suited her needs and bolstering it when it suited her needs. And that would show a most manly kind of narcissistic survival skill.

Hillary's game plan to get back to the White House has been to bet that the Republicans go so far right, seems so insensitive to minorities, as they did during the Katrina disaster, and become so polarizing, that she will seem less polarizing. In some ways, her image problems haven't changed that much from the '92 campaign, when a *New Yorker* cartoon showed a woman asking a salesclerk for a jacket and saying, "Nothing too Hillary."

Once, when I was covering her during Bill's campaign to unseat Bush père—a time when the would-be First Lady kept lapsing into saying what "we" would do in the White House—a television reporter from Columbus, Ohio, stuck a microphone in Hillary's face and said: "You know, some people think of you as an inspiring female attorney mother, and other people think of you as the overbearing yuppie wife from hell. How would you describe yourself?"

A look of annoyance glittered through her blue eyes; later, on her campaign plane, she told me drily: "I'm too old to be a yuppie."

Mickey Kaus wrote long ago in *The New Republic* that Hillary was "a false feminist." "Nepotism," he said, "is not feminism."

Hillary seemed more in the tradition of all those widows and daughters on the subcontinent who step in, after their husband or father dies, to lead their nations. At best they are pseudofeminists. Feminism is supposed to be a form of self-reliance, not a free—or even costly—ride on the coattails of the career of powerful male kin.

(Of course, if Hillary, the know-it-all from Yale, clutched her husband's coattails, W., the know-nothing from Yale, clutched his father's.)

Absent her husband's strengths, Hillary never would have been First Lady. Absent her husband's weaknesses, she never would have been the senator from New York. She owes her election, in part, to Monica. She couldn't move up until she was pushed down.

Because of her air of sanctimony, entitlement and the sense that the rules do not apply to her because she is there to Do Good, people want to see her Put in Her Place before they can like her.

Maybe now that she has her own gig in the Senate, we can retire the question of what Hillary is owed. But something tells me she won't allow it to go away. Hillary, after all, has a genius for making her self-interest seem like idealism.

The junior senator from New York has been making a name for herself without exactly leading. She has been differentiating herself, trying to show complexity and maturity, reemphasizing her position that there should be fewer abortions to appeal to the center, moving away from the Teddy Kennedy–Michael Moore–John Kerry wing of the Democratic Party.

But she has not been putting herself forward too much; she has been playing the freshman worker bee rather than the pushy queen bee.

She was strangely silent on poor Terry Schiavo. Trying to curry favor with red staters and Lieberman Democrats, she meekly allowed Tom DeLay and Bill Frist to push for the shameful and hypocritical legislation that allowed the Schiavo case to be snatched from Florida state jurisdiction and moved to federal court.

But at the first news conference in which she announces her candidacy, she will have to explain what we ought to do with the intractable war in Iraq she voted to authorize. And if she is the least bit vague, she'll be asked if she has a "secret plan," like Nixon.

In order to triangulate politically, Hillary Clinton has to compartmentalize cognitively. But will triangulation work again?

Will the "I am woman, see me grow" senator ever be genuinely self-reliant from her husband?

Or are men necessary?